Escape From Ireland

Jennylynd James

Copyright © 2013 Jennylynd James

All rights reserved.

ISBN-13: 978-1495979095

ISBN-10: 1495979091

DEDICATION

This book is dedicated to my parents Gloria and Kenneth James for their years of nurturing and patience helping me to develop my talents.

FOREWORD

This book chronicles misadventures during a six and a half year stay in the Republic of Ireland. How did a person of Caribbean descent end up living and working in Ireland? It all began in 2004, when I left a lucrative food industry position in posh Westlake, California and travelled to Europe to get unique international experience in the food industry. I had interviewed for numerous positions in the United Kingdom, with no success. Then, by a stroke of luck, I managed to get an interview in Dublin. An Irish company recruiting for their UK office spotted my resumé and contacted me about a new Technical Manager's post in their Dublin office. They flew me to Dublin for the interview and I was hired.

After working with the company for a year and a half, I discovered the job was not what I expected. I then took off on another unique adventure starting my own food business. The Celtic Tiger was at its height. Irish were spending and travelling more than ever before. The sudden prosperity and affluence led people to expand their food tastes, well beyond the traditional meat and potatoes.

I took advantage of this newfound interest in food and started a business to promote Caribbean food in Ireland. Running my business led me off the beaten track to many farmers markets, agricultural shows and food fairs. I sold to delis and independent supermarkets throughout the country. Meeting numerous colourful characters in my travels helped to shape the way I view the world today. I also won and lost true love.

CONTENTS

Foreword ... v

1. A Bumpy Landing ... 11
2. Dating in Dublin ... 32
3. Bring in the New ... 43
4. Putting Down Roots ... 64
5. A New Dawn ... 90
6. Escapes and Escapades ... 122
7. Nationwide Coverage ... 137
8. Riding the Love Rollercoaster ... 156
9. Moving to Tramore ... 180
10. Taste of the Caribbean ... 198
11. Moving On ... 217
12. The Dragon's Den Experience ... 248
13. Goodbye Bad Boy ... 264
14. Escape from Eire ... 281

Farewell Recipe

Glossary of Current Irish Slang Words and Phrases

ACKNOWLEDGMENTS

Special thanks to my daughter Tiffany for encouraging me through the lengthy process of remembering and recording our many adventures in the Republic of Ireland. Many thanks to Derbhile Graham of www.writewordseditorial.ie for the countless hours spent editing the first draft. Your wisdom and experience were invaluable. Thanks also to Marguerite Orane of www.freeandlaughing.com for numerous words of wisdom, coaching, and encouragement from inception to promotion of this memoir. You provided great inspiration for me.

1
A BUMPY LANDING

Arrival

I fell on the conveyor belt, clutching a large suitcase nicknamed 'mini fridge'. I could not help but laugh hysterically as a kind lad helped me up before I went around the bend. That was my introduction to Dublin Fair City. I arrived on Thursday 1st July 2004, on a10 hour overnight flight from Los Angeles. We arrived at the crack of dawn. With an eight hour time difference between Greenwich Mean Time and Pacific Time, it was very hard to stay awake. The airport looked old and dated. Though it was 2004, I felt I had stepped back into the 1950's. Black and white photographs of hundreds of Irish emigrants arriving in America lined the walls. Floors were tiled with brown and beige coloured linoleum and buildings were painted in beige oil paint. It reminded me of an old Caribbean airport. We even had to walk to the terminal, which I found quaint. We walked down a staircase from the jet, and across an airport roadway, with attendants controlling the flow of passing vehicles and crossing passengers.

The immigration officer asked why I had come to Dublin. I showed him my job offer from the company and he said "Carry on". I would have to get a formal work permit and have my passport stamped in town. Well, that seemed straightforward enough. And then I was free to collect my luggage. Bleary-eyed, I wondered what I was doing here. With nothing to declare, I walked through the green gates, pushing a trolley laden with three mini fridges and two pieces of hand luggage. A 40 foot container from California would be following in a few weeks' time. The jet lag was catching up and I had to get some sleep.

I stepped outside. The air was chilly, damp and grey. I had

heard it rained frequently in Ireland, but did it have to rain on my arrival? The sky was overcast and the heavy clouds looked ready to pour rain. I joined the line or "queue" as Dubliners called it, at the taxi rank. When my turn came, a taxi minivan was summoned to take all my bags. They could not fit in a car. The driver loaded the van and asked what I had in all those bags. Had I come to live in Dublin?

'Yes, of course,' I replied. 'I've flown in from Los Angeles'.

The driver was small, with short limbs and a mop of prematurely grey hair. I was disappointed not to find a red haired driver. I had been programmed in America to see the stereotypical Irish red headed leprechaun. I could tell he wasn't old, yet he wasn't young. His round stomach was probably the clue. He had piercing green eyes and a thick accent that was not easy to understand.

I asked him to take me to the Harcourt Hotel on Harcourt Street. Since I had pre-booked and paid for this hotel online, I got a special deal. I was thrilled with my online purchase for a city centre hotel. Little did I know I was being taken on the scenic route from the airport to downtown, or Ân Lâr as the locals called it. I told the driver that I didn't know Dublin at all, so he must have decided to give me a tour. The area around the airport was grassy, but with hints of new construction to come. There was a new parking lot on the left. There were plans for a new terminal to replace the modest little building, and for hotels near the airport. One could see signs of modernisation and transformation taking place.

There was construction everywhere as we drove along. The driver showed me the new Tesco Extra construction on Malahide Road. New sports grounds were being erected along the way. I remarked that instead of high rises, the urban sprawl seemed to be quite flat. Many old houses were mixed in with shops, pubs and bookmakers.

'What is a bookmaker?' I asked my taxi tour guide.

It was quite puzzling to imagine so many places making books.

'That's where ya bet on da harses! Ladbrokes, Paddy Power, or Hacketts could make yah a farchun'.

'Well, I have never bet on a horse in my life. I wouldn't know what to do'.

Betting seemed to be a national pastime. The slew of pubs that lined the streets showed that drinking was also a national pastime.

Along the way, I also learned about the weather and the Celtic Tiger, a term used to describe Ireland's rise in financial fortune. I also learned about the best places to live in Dublin, the political parties, the government, and other gems from the taxi driver's store of knowledge.

We finally got to the Harcourt Hotel, former residence of George Bernard Shaw. I was charged €38 (euro) which I rounded off to €40, even though the meter actually showed a tip was included. I thought I got an excellent deal. This price, however, turned out to be a good rib tickler when I described my journey to colleagues at the office the following week.

Harcourt Hotel was smack in the middle of the city. I had a room facing the street. It was a Georgian style building with large rectangular windows, old wall paper, and dated carpets. I felt as if I were staying in a museum. I could hear the wooden floors creak when I walked around. There was a painting of George Bernard Shaw on the wall in the main foyer, to remind everyone that he once lived there. Adjoining the hotel was a pub and beer garden, and also the D2 night club. This pub had a dining room to serve hotel guests and business people in the city during the week. They sold breakfast, lunch and dinner.

I was very hungry after the long journey. Without delay, I deposited my luggage in the room and went promptly to the dining room for breakfast. The menu had a few selections, but the Full Irish Breakfast caught my eye. I ordered the Full Irish and was amazed when the large 'fry up' as the locals called it, arrived. The breakfast consisted of an egg, rashers (bacon), a piece of black pudding (blood sausage), and a piece of white pudding, baked beans, a hash brown, brown soda bread, and a steamed tomato. Why would anyone steam a tomato? It was my first steamed tomato. I thought they were supposed to be eaten sliced and fresh. I was so hungry I ate ravenously and washed it down with a cup of tea. Then I went back to the room for a well deserved nap.

The Big City

I took a nap for two hours and felt refreshed enough to explore the city. My tourist maps showed St. Stephen's Green, the beautiful Victorian park in the middle of Dublin, and St. Stephen's Green shopping centre. I decided to walk by the park and down the pedestrian shopping street, Grafton Street. The cobblestone streets, old buildings, quaint boutiques, and restaurants reminded me of books I had read on European cities. The sky was constantly grey and there was a little chill in the air. It was July and the middle of summer, but I still had to wear a light jacket. Luckily, I had packed two raincoats for the journey, one red and one lime green. One could never be over-prepared for cold and rain.

I walked with my shoulders back and my nose in the air, as if on a fashion runway. With my long, dark, chemically processed hair, lily white teeth and very dark brown skin, I must have been a curiosity to the other city dwellers. I walked with purpose, going absolutely nowhere but for a stroll. I did not see any other black women as I walked through the city that day. I had to smile at some of the staring faces.

Dublin was packed with business people in their suits and tourists from many countries. The sun never broke through the cloud cover. No wonder people had such pale skin, I thought. The most interesting tourists for me were the large throngs of Spanish and Italian students. They were easily identifiable by their brightly coloured knapsacks, dark hair, and darker skin compared to their Irish counterparts. They roamed around the city in groups of 20 or more and seemed to enjoy the adventure.

I walked around St. Stephen's Green shopping centre and observed modern shops and cafes. The mall had three or four floors and they were all full of shoppers that afternoon. I even saw an old American favourite store, T.J. Maxx, but it was called T.K. Maxx in Dublin. As I ventured down Grafton Street, I noticed the high prices of clothing and shoes compared to America. I wondered how people could possibly buy all these goods. Everyone had two or three shopping bags.

I went around a corner and sat in a chocolate shop which served coffee and hot chocolate. It was amazing how the shop owner could squeeze tables, chairs and high stools into such a small space. A very narrow counter top provided space for cups and plates. As I looked out at the fashionably dressed city people, it finally hit me how alone I was in this city. I would have to find ways to meet people very fast.

I wound my way back to St. Stephen's Green and saw that a big crowd had gathered. It was for the opening ceremony of the Luas, Dublin's new light-rail service. New trolley lines were being installed around Dublin to bring people from the outskirts of the city to An Lár. It was a big party with free rides on the new trains all day. I thought I heard the strains of steel pan, the national musical instrument of Trinidad and Tobago. I was right! A small steel band was playing jazz and other music along with guitars and drums. I stopped to enjoy the music and decided to say hello to the musicians when they were done. The musicians looked like older gentlemen in their 60s. The one I spoke to said they had moved over to Ireland from London many years before and lived north of Dublin in a town called Drogheda. He then proceeded to give me a wink, look me up and down, and ask if he could keep in touch. Imagine my shock. I thought I had met a kindred soul during my lonely day. The old geezer was trying to make a pass at me! I said goodbye and made a quick escape.

I got back to the Harcourt in time for the lunchtime carvery. This was a traditional roast luncheon served at some pubs: roast beef, roast turkey, or roast pork would be served with potatoes and mushy vegetables. The pub meal, at €9, was considered reasonably priced compared to meals at the typical Dublin restaurant. I asked for the roast turkey meal and ordered a glass of Guinness. I told the bartender I had to try Guinness since it was my first time in an Irish pub.

'Good on ya,' he said.

The first sip proved very difficult to swallow. The black stuff was bitter- sweet, thick, and vile, in my opinion. Why were people enjoying this drink? I was not a drinker. I never even drank beer. I could not understand the attraction. It must be an acquired taste which I had not yet acquired. One patron ordered mashed potato, potato wedges and chips (French fries) for her meal. This was all smothered in gravy. She must really like her potatoes. Meat and vegetables were not on her agenda. I had heard that Irish people loved potatoes with each meal and wondered if this woman was a fair representation of the population.

I returned to my room to study my tourist brochures and

plan the next step to settle into life in Dublin. That night I discovered the cult television program, Big Brother, which was being aired for hours. After midnight, the sensational TV cameras focused on sleeping house mates. I could not sleep because it was afternoon in California. So I flicked through TV channels, repeatedly coming back to Big Brother. One house mate turned, another yawned, and one snored. The next housemate turned in the bed, another stretched and yet another stared at the ceiling. It was hard to determine the point of the programme. But it was popular nonetheless. People must have been watching.

Every night that weekend, I realised my error in having a room with a street view. I had specifically asked for a front room so I would not be looking out onto a strange wall every day. However, since it was the weekend, many people were partying at the D2 nightclub every night. Revellers would drink, scream, sing, and call out to friends. Smokers stood outside the club and chat before going back in. The smoking ban in buildings had been introduced the year before and no smoking was allowed in the club. This made for loud conversations out in the street in front of the doors of the club. I wondered what sense it made to stand in front of the doors. All the smoke was blowing right back in. At any rate, it was a step in the right direction. The population as a whole seemed to smoke heavily. I was shocked to see how many women smoked. In Trinidad people would frown on a female smoker, but in Dublin it was well accepted.

From 2:30am, the slow, reluctant journey home began. Groups left drunk and ready to face the world, or so they thought. Intoxicated patrons could be seen rolling out onto Harcourt Street into taxis of all sizes, laughing hysterically. I spied on them from my bedroom window every night, envious of the fun they were having. I did not know anyone to go with me to the D2 night club. And I did not dare go alone. I shared in their drunken jokes as I observed from the window.

I watched in horror as male revellers urinated on the sides of buildings. They did not bother to hold back anything. What a mess it would have been to clean up store fronts the next morning. This was how the young Irish partied.

Orientation

On Monday morning, I eagerly awaited the arrival of one of my new work colleagues, Ray who was designated the role of orientation and welcome committee. I had my third full Irish breakfast in a row. By this stage, I was feeling completely bloated and in need of a serious detoxification and cleanse. I vowed never again to indulge in the 'fry-up'. Ray was to take me to view rental homes and show me where to find everything. I had done a review of several properties on the internet before coming to Ireland. The advantages of the internet were now coming to fruition. I had studied the location of the workplace in St Margaret's and the location of my daughter Tiffany's new school, and decided on rental homes half way between the two.

I was cautioned by a Dublin acquaintance in advance which areas to avoid and which were acceptable. She told me South Dublin was the best place to live. South Dublin meant south of the Liffey River. It was fascinating to me how different the population, the accent, the character, and the beliefs of city people could become, just by crossing the simple barrier of a narrow river. Since I had chosen to live on the Northside for the convenience of work and school, I needed expert advice on what was acceptable.

'You don't want to go anywhere near Ballymun, Finglas or Cabra. There are too many gangs and it has a bad reputation,' said my Dublin acquaintance. 'We never go anywhere near those areas. Focus on Glasnevin and Drumcondra. These areas are more suitable. Clontarf is lovely, near Dublin Bay. Malahide has a yacht club and rich people live in Howth'.

My acquaintance had an odd accent, half British and half American. I was to learn later that her accent was a posh South Dublin accent.

'Swords and Santry are cheap and cheerful,' she added. 'Hmm. All sorts live there! I wouldn't bother if I were you'.

Armed with this advice and warnings, I knew where to look and where not to look.

Ray was a cheerful, prematurely grey scientist with spectacles. He was from Belfast, Northern Ireland. He had lived in the UK for many years. He and his partner had moved back to Ireland and settled in Dublin. His happy disposition and knowledge of the city put me at ease right away. Our first stop was to a service station, or "Garige" as pronounced by the locals.

'You need a map of Dublin City and a Road Map of Ireland, so you'll know how to get around', he said.

His accent was musical and very different to those I had heard so far. The road maps were the wisest purchase I made in my first week in the Emerald Isle. Ray showed me how to look up the street name reference at the back and find the exact page and location on the map. Ray knew about all the tourist sights and restaurants off the beaten track. He was a walking encyclopaedia and knew things that were not in the tourist brochures.

Asking for directions was an amusing or frustrating exercise depending on one's disposition. I never took myself seriously, so I enjoyed this experience immensely. Directions were given in reference to the pubs.

'Turn left at the Bleeding Horse, then right at Gallagher's pub', I was told. Go straight past the Autobahn and turn at Murphy's'.

Our journey from the Harcourt Hotel on the South side of Dublin, across the Liffey River to the North side, was an adventure in city traffic. We drove through narrow streets, which were clogged with traffic. Roads were torn up and hundreds of cranes towered over demolished old warehouses on the Quays. These were being replaced with glass and concrete high rise buildings. Bus lanes appeared and disappeared. Drivers who were tempted to sneak onto them and bypass the tortuous lines of traffic were stopped by gardai (police, pronounced gardee) who looked as if they had just finished secondary school.

As we crossed the Liffey River, we ambled through the traffic, eventually coming to Drumcondra Road. I liked the red brick Victorian style homes along the way and imagined myself living in one of those homes. There were Georgian style mansions, with large rectangular windows and grey concrete bricks. Their real beauty lay in the doorways. They were painted in rich hues like navy blue, dark green, burgundy, and purple. The doors had brass knockers and white pillars on either side. I decided that the first home I bought in Dublin would have a Georgian doorway. It would be emerald green with a brass lion knocker and two white pillars.

Even though I had recently arrived, I was determined to buy a home within six months, so I was looking for a short term lease. My American dream of home ownership was still alive, thousands of miles across the Atlantic. Ray took me to see all the apartments on my list. Unlike most rentals in other countries, Dublin rentals came complete with not only furniture, but also pots and pans, cutlery and everything one needed. This was brilliant for me. I only had to open a suitcase and move in.

We saw an old house off Drumcondra Road. It was modestly furnished, but had a musty smell. The neighbourhood seemed quiet and neat but lacked character and I couldn't see myself living there. Next, we went to see an unfurnished place near Clontarf Castle. It was a rare find. The townhouse was very clean. Its proximity to the waterfront was good for long walks. But without furniture and not knowing when my 40-foot container of belongings would arrive, it made no sense to take that place. We carried on.

Next, we saw a small house in Finglas. Even though I had been forewarned about Finglas, its convenience to the work place caught my attention. I had to look. The place was sparsely furnished. It was laughable to see the one chair and small bed that passed for a furnished bedroom. The rent was not cheap.

We took a break and went to the lunch time carvery at Botanic House on Phibsborough Rd. The food was as good as pub grub could be. It had no flavour, but it was filling.

After lunch, I finally saw my dream rental home. It was a red brick Victorian house on Ballymun Road presented by the Property Partners Estate Agents. There were buses into the city centre at its doorstep. The home had two reception rooms, three bedrooms upstairs, a 100 ft back yard, a large kitchen and a whirlpool bathtub. It came fully furnished, to a very high standard. I had seen this home advertised on the internet even before arriving in Dublin. Being a chronic worrier and planner, I had called from California and made an appointment well in advance for viewing. I was sure I would like it. The rent at the time was €1,400. By Southern California standards, this was a good deal. I felt quite justified in signing a lease, even though Dubliners would have said it was pricey.

When we pulled into the driveway, I imagined that my little

daughter, Tiffany and I would be very happy there until I could buy my own home. Tiffany was still in the United States at my sister's and was to join me in a month. The doorway had a beautiful stained glass floral pattern. Above the door was a glass window arch. A bright atrium was attached to one reception room at the back of the house. The back garden was huge; a 100 foot lawn all the way to the back wall. As the tenant, I was going to be responsible for keeping the lawn tidy. It was a frightening prospect for me, since we always had a gardener at my home growing up in Trinidad. For the first time in my life, I would have to learn how to use a noisy lawn mower powered by kerosene. I embraced the idea as one of life's adventures. The kitchen had a little gas stove with a gas cylinder. It reminded me of one my granny used in Trinidad when I was a child. It was supposed to be faster than an electric range. How was I going to find replacement gas cylinders? Where would I get kerosene for the lawn mower? Who would show me how to pull the cable to use the monster? I would have to ask a taxi driver, I thought.

The home was being rented out on a short term basis by a lady who had recently divorced and needed some time away. This was absolutely perfect for me. I asked the agent for a six month lease, paid the deposit and rent, and was given the keys. Everything was falling into place, just as I had planned.

My rental home was on Ballymun Road. It was a wealthy looking house. However, I had no idea of the depth of fear the word Ballymun had to Dubliners. I was told nobody would live within a 20 mile radius of Ballymun in the past. What did I know? My house looked pretty on the internet. From what I could tell in daily news reports, the city was safer than any other place I had lived. And even if Ballymun had a bad reputation, the fear planted in the heads of the locals wouldn't affect me as a newcomer.

The Office

It was time to meet the people at the company. Ray again met me to show me how to get to the office using all the back roads around Dublin Airport. I tried to take note of landmarks like bill boards, open fields, and trees along the way before reaching the gates of the company. It all looked the same except for pockets of construction. It was very confusing and I wondered if I would ever be able to remember which road to take through the many fields when I got my car. We saw a group of cars parked off the roadway. People were relaxing and watching the runway. A food van was offering refreshments.

'What were they doing,' I asked.

'Oh, spotting planes. It's a favourite pastime".

This was really different for me. Why would people spend their time looking at planes landing and taking off? I would rather be flying. I guessed anything could be the subject of entertainment, especially with food and drinks readily available. The Irish were a funny lot.

Since it was summer, a lot of green bush had grown up on either side of the roadway. In some areas, trees formed green canopies, like the ones in the Caribbean. I could well have been on the Eastern Main Road driving to Sangre Grande in the East of Trinidad. It all looked so tropical and green. The vegetation was thick. The air was humid and it looked like it would rain at any minute.

As we reached the gate, Ray punched in a code and the barrier lifted. I was greeted at the main doors by Kathy.

'How was your trrrip from Califorrrnea?' she said in a thick Scottish accent, rolling every r. 'We were expecting you. Please wait a minute and I`ll call Lisa'.

Lisa was the Human Resources Manager and would take me through all the particulars of the job. She was prim and proper with hair pulled back in a bun. Her face was stern and her glasses gave her an air of intelligence. She must have been in her twenties but her outfit belied her youth. I could not read her emotions. Her accent was plain and easy to understand. This was good news, since I had had to focus really hard to understand everyone I had met since I arrived.

After being advised of the pension plan, deductions for tax purposes and other necessary documents to sign, Lisa gave me my contract. She advised me that I would have to wait for a work permit to be processed and she hoped it would be approved!

What did she mean she hoped it would be approved?

I had travelled thousands of miles from California, sold my home, and put my worldly possessions on a 40 foot container bound for Ireland. Her ease and casualness with this shocking situation baffled me.

'These things take time, but someone in the company knows someone in the immigration office,' she explained. 'He'll work on the application quickly and get back to us within a week'.

That situation reminded me of the 'buddy, buddy' system in Trinidad.

I would have to sit tight for a few days and await my fate. The company had given me a generous moving allowance to cover all expenses. I was to stretch this for the first few weeks as I settled in. The uncertainty was unnerving to say the least. The Irish were way too easy going for me. I had survived several years of living and working in American paranoia and found it hard to relax.

That day, I was introduced to many people in the main office: accounts, human resources, and marketing. It seemed each function was managed by just one or two people. That was puzzling in comparison to the relatively large size of the company. IT staff, I was told, were very important and I had to get to know them very well. They controlled my computer. I met the lunchroom lady and then we went downstairs to meet other staff. The office was a basic prefabricated unit. It was very simple compared to the ostentatious marble floored entryway at my corporate American office.

As I was shown through the small dark corridor, the ladies room was pointed out: three small cubicles with wooden doors. So 1950's, I thought. What about the granite counter tops I had seen in America? The lunchroom or canteen was exactly what I imagined a factory canteen would look like: basic tables and chairs, a sink for washing up, and some microwave ovens to reheat food. A novelty for me was the large conveyor belt toaster. Everyone toasted bread at tea break. The large glass windows looked out on the factory.

I was led down a narrow dark staircase to the office I would share with at least 20 other staff members. This office had bright fluorescent lights and glass walls that looked out to the factory. I would never know what was happening outside the factory once I entered. I felt a bit claustrophobic but had to fight off the feeling. I realised that this office would be my home away from home for while.

Everyone was friendly enough. The task of remembering so many names, and really strange names in my opinion, was daunting. I used funny images and the person's features as reminders. When in doubt, I asked for Patrick. Chances were that a Patrick would be there. Patrick, Padraig, Paraig and other variations of St Patrick, the patron saint of Ireland, were very common names for men. In the office, we had ginger Patrick from operations, and Patrick from transport, and Patrick from the warehouse. Declan was also a popular name in the office. If you shouted Declan, at least two heads would turn around.

I had to learn new names like Niamh (pronounced Neeve), and Siobhan (pronounced Shevon). Most people's names were abbreviated by co-workers if they were more than one syllable long. So Nathalie was Nat, Anthony was Ant, Christopher was Christy, and I became Jen, short for Jennylynd.

My 'office' was a cubicle next to the other technical managers, the quality assurance team and the logistics team. We were supposed to interact in this open structure, since our desks were connected. In my opinion, it was a cost saving measure, with as many desks piled into the space as possible.

I was invited to the morning meeting just to see what things would be like. Most people in the room participated: sales, production, quality assurance, and technical managers. I listened in disbelief as a representative from each group explained operational problems from the day before. The discourse was in English, but it may as well have been in Greek. I understood nothing and maintained a thoughtful face. I secretly wondered how I would survive and speak their language.

At 10:00 am, everyone stopped for tea and toast. This was a strange phenomenon for me. In America, the drug of choice was coffee. People sipped and worked at their desks. I followed my colleagues blindly to the little lunch room. The rolling toaster churned out slices of white and brown bread. There were cubes of butter and various jams to spread on the toast. The resident cleaner/canteen lady and her helper cleaned up after everyone. We were to all leave our dishes in the sink. I mused at the generosity of the company, providing tea and toast for everyone.

Learning the Lingo

Over the next few days, I got used to all the slangs and the culture on the job. The staff showed no mercy when it came to teasing, even though I was a newcomer. I was not sure if people were just insensitive or they were out to cause me trauma. I decided it was probably good natured fun. All I knew was that the workplace humour was very different to that of corporate America. Teasing and public ridicule on the job were widely accepted. I didn't realise this and got very offended when jeered a few times for not keeping up or even understanding the local parlance. Very unprofessional, I thought. How could they laugh at their colleagues?

How was I to know when John asked for a 'biro', he meant a pen? I asked if this was a word derived from Latin. The office laughter was uncontrollable. I rapidly began compiling and storing a mental dictionary of Irish slang to help me keep up with conversations. So many words. So little time.

Have Wheels, will Travel

My adventures in vocabulary were only the beginning. I had to get a car fast because there was no way to reach to work in St Margaret's using public transport. And I couldn't possibly ask anyone to collect me every day. As I was taking a taxi in to work, I asked how I might buy a car....

The driver shouted 'Dah Buoy and Sail, Dah Buoy and Sail'. I could not understand what this meant. A TV show? A store? A street? I had to ask for clarification. It turned out to be a weekly newspaper listing everything people wanted to buy or sell. I raced to the Supervalu store at the corner of Ballymun Road to get my copy of the Buy and Sell after work.

Sure enough, there were dozens of listings of cars. What I didn't realise was that old cars cost four to five times more that cars in California. I limited myself to purchasing a second hand car for a few thousand in cash, which would be no more than five years old. I identified where the various car dealers or garages were located around the city, then I had to plot the bus routes for each location. I ventured to a dealer on Prussia Street, just outside the downtown shopping district. A nice violet 'Love Bug' caught my eye, and it was in my price range too. But I couldn't jump at the first thing I saw. On the 19A bus passing through Phibsborough, I spotted a yard full of vehicles, so the following day I went there for a wander around.

The psychology of the folks running garages had me baffled. I walked around for a good 15 minutes without anyone noticing me. I had to actually go into the office to get someone to show me some cars. The economy was so good at the time that there was no rushing after customers. They would be doing me a favour to sell to me. I spoke to one of the lads to find out how I could get an Irish driver's license. I knew from previous experience that the license from another country may be valid for a very short time. I would have to get a local license as soon as possible. The good man told me to go around the corner and take 'Dah Teory Tess' first. I couldn't understand what he was speaking about. I must have asked about three times.

After some discussion, I was told to 'Buoy de booook at Eason's and stoody fa de Teory tes'. Finally, I understood. The good man was advising me that I had to do the theory or written test first in order to get the Irish driver's license. I got detailed directions as to where to buy the book, and also the nearest test centre and off I went. I was confident that I would pass the driving test. I had been driving for years.

In the meantime, I still needed to get a small car to go to work. The Buy and Sell took me to a garage way out on

Greenhills Road, Walkinstown, near the Red Cow Roundabout. The Red Cow Roundabout was being transformed into a major intersection for the M50 motorway and the M9 going west of Dublin. It was no longer a roundabout, but the locals still affectionately used the Red Cow name. This was a bit confusing. The route was full of industrial warehouses, which looked the same. Thank God I could read maps. I was glued to mine.

The bus from Dublin city centre dropped me off near the Walkinstown roundabout which had six exits. I walked around that roundabout twice, dodging traffic and wondering which exit was actually Greenhills Road. There were no street signs to give me a clue. Reluctantly, I asked a passer-by for directions to the Nissan Garage on Greenhills Road. I always liked to pretend that I knew where I was going and walk with a purpose. Finally, I showed up at the garage and was greeted by a young, friendly salesman, which was very refreshing. He was quite cute, with a tuft of red hair coiffed into place with gel. His colleague had the stereotypical dark hair, blue eyes, and pale skin. They were both well dressed in shirts and ties and were ready to serve.

I told them I had recently flown in from California and needed a car right away. I had to sit through stories of a lad who had worked in a bar in Boston for a few months and another who had hitch hiked around the United States before running out of money and having to move back. One of the salesmen took me around the yard. I gave him my upper limit of €4,000. We settled on a white Nissan Micra with minimal mileage. I said I was anxious to get the car, so he said it could be arranged that very day. I must have been the only person to walk into their office and put a car purchase on my credit card that day. They looked at me in amazement. My US credit card, with its enormous limits, was a handy tool in Dublin. I felt relieved to be able to wave the bus goodbye that day. After numerous calls to the credit card company, everything was arranged.

I had no insurance but promised to get it next day. It was on the To Do List. The lads were now on overtime. I asked them to give me directions out of the district before they left. They gave me a drawing of roundabouts, landmarks and assorted arrows to get from Walkinstown to Ballymun Road. There was no need to go through the city. Just get onto the M50 motorway and "Bob's yer uncle" (I would be ok).

Unfortunately, it was the peak traffic hour of 6pm. Every Bob and his uncle were on the road. I had to constantly remind myself to drive on the left side of the road, since I was used to driving on the right in the United States. The wheel was in the wrong place and my right hand kept reaching for the stick shift, which was now on the left. It took ages just to drive from Greenhills Road to the dreaded Walkinstown roundabout. Again, I went around twice. At least this time I was driving. The puzzle was to determine which of the six exits would bring me to the Red Cow roundabout and then to the M50 motorway. By the grace of God, I was able to get onto the M50. Traffic was at a crawl. Nothing moved in any direction. I was so tired and hungry. I tried flicking through the radio stations to find some distraction. There was no CD player in the Micra. That would have meant more money.

Paying at the toll booth on the M50 caused enormous traffic in both directions. I wondered what benefits the motorway could have if it had such a major stop along the way.

After what seemed like an eternity, I finally approached an exit that said Ballymun Road. Nobody was more overjoyed to see the apartment towers of Ballymun than I, after spending an hour and a half in traffic. I had the knack of being in the wrong lane when trying to exit from a roundabout. Why weren't there plain old traffic lights to take vehicles from one side of an intersection to the next?

Escape From Ireland

Again, I had to make my way all around the Ballymun roundabout twice to get into the correct lane and exit.

I finally passed my home on the opposite side of the street, in front of Albert College Park. I could not get to the driveway because there was a large traffic island was in the middle of the road. These little details hadn't been apparent when I was travelling by bus. I followed the road all the way down to where it joined Mobhi Road. Only there could I turn and go back to 119 Ballymun Road. What a challenge. It was already getting dark.

Next, I had to figure out how to open the gate of the driveway and get in. All the traffic would be at my heels. I had to approach this with care. I signalled long before the turn, at least three houses away. When I reached my driveway, I drove at two miles per hour. I had to be visible to the traffic behind. The convenience of that nice bus stop in front of my house was then a distant memory. I tried to manoeuvre around a bus dropping off passengers. This clearly upset the driver and the car behind me, as I turned ever so carefully onto the pavement in front of the house. The bus driver honked at me.

'Drive yer car!' he shouted.

With a five hour excursion under my belt, I deserved a warm bath in my whirlpool bathtub with jets.

2

DATING IN DUBLIN

Social Animal

I settled into a daytime routine at the job the next week when my work permit came, but I had nothing to do in the evenings. I was alone in a big house in the city. I bought the Sunday Independent, one of the popular newspapers. Sifting through the articles, I tried to find something worthy to do on evenings after work. I had so many interests and was sure the newspapers held the key to future friends and acquaintances. If only I could get out. I spotted an advertisement for lectures at the Dublin City Hall, sponsored by Perrier.

I decided to go to the lecture and stand around with a glass of sparkling water and chat with someone. No reservations were needed. I got dressed up after work on Tuesday evening in a fine little dress, pastel pink with splashes of violet, lovely short frilled sleeves and a V neck low enough to show cleavage. Would I look desperate? Was this outfit ok? Would I meet any nice guys? Would people be snobbish? Would they only be interested in the free wine? How many people were going to be there? All these questions raced through my mind as I got ready, putting on just the right amount of makeup. I had to wear my red raincoat. I hadn't expected it to be so cold in July and I had no cardigans or sweaters. They were all in the 40 foot container en-route to Ireland. My toes were freezing in my high heeled sandals, but I couldn't bear the thought of putting out money to buy boots in July. I was determined to hold out for a while.

According to my calculations from the online map, I only had to walk from the last bus stop on O'Connell Street for about 10 minutes to Dublin City Hall. As the bus drove along, I took in the sights and sounds along the way. The traffic was hectic at 6:30pm. The bus was full of people going this way and that. The noise, talk and chatter made the trip very interesting.

O'Connell Street was a massive construction site at the time. An island was being built and statues were being put in. The traffic had to be re-directed around everything. I was told by an Irish acquaintance that O'Connell Street had become very run down and I should never go down there. I never listened to anyone until I could see it for myself, so I was there in the flesh, taking in the scenery.

Right in the middle of O'Connell Street was the Dublin Spire. This large spike was a work of art stuck in the middle of the street to commemorate the new millennium. It was fondly called 'The Spire in the Mire', 'The Stick in the Sick', and other unflattering nicknames. I left the bus near the Spire and crossed the Liffey onto Dame Street. Everything was just as it appeared online. I continue my walk through the busy downtown area. Shops, restaurants and pubs all bustled with activity on a Tuesday evening.

As I went past the Dublin Castle gates, I came to the dome shaped building that was Dublin City Hall. It was a very impressive structure, a square building in Corinthian style, with three fronts of Portland stone. When I went in, I found that the lecture had already started. It seemed every seat was occupied, with standing room at the back. I tried to make my way to the back unnoticed and shrink into the crowd. If I was going to be late, I didn't want people staring at me.

I half listened to what was being said. Focusing on all the new faces was more interesting. Not everyone had red hair. I tried to count the number of red heads in the crowd. Most people seemed taller than the average leprechaun. Another myth was dispelled. I looked at the business suits and the city styles. The waiters ran to and fro, setting up glasses of wine and Perrier. Then it was back to the speech. I was so bored; I had to pinch myself to concentrate. After all, it was an evening out. Finally, the speaker said the magic words "And in conclusion…" By this time, I was fully awake and so was the audience.

Everyone was invited to take a glass of wine or Perrier. Was I the only one heading for the Perrier? People guzzled wine and chatted. I drank my water and circled the room, looking for a friendly face. I gave a few nervous smiles to one or two and then walked with purpose to the other side of the room. I saw a group of three and approached them.

'Hello, I'm Lindy,' I said. 'Just arrived in Dublin. What are your names?'

They were Spanish and Italian students who visited Dublin every summer. The visitors were happy to practice English with me. I latched on to them for idle chatter and to belong to a group. After half an hour, I looked around. The crowd were guzzling more free wine and getting steadily louder. I made a quick departure, promising to see my new acquaintances at the next lecture. So it was back on the 19A bus to Ballymun Rd., Glasnevin. I was happy to return to the comfort of my newly adopted home. I hoped the next adventure out would be a tad more interesting, or it would all be in vain.

Speed Dating

I went online to see what was happening in Dublin and my eyes caught an advertisement for a speed dating event on Thursday evening at a bar in town. Ah ha, I thought. That would certainly give me a thrill or a scare, as the case may be.

I filled in the application form, then hesitated for five minutes, walked to the kitchen, and drank some water. Then I came back and hit the send button. I waited with bated breath to get home from work on Thursday, so I could get ready for the event. How many guys would be there? Would they be cute or geeks, or jocks, or what? Would they have met foreign girls before? What would they think of me? What should I wear? I had to look cute but not tarty. My wardrobe was limited, because everything seemed to be in the bloody container en-route to Ireland. Should I put my hair up or should I leave it down? How much make up should I wear?

I settled on a blouse and jeans with high heeled sandals. My hair was straightened and left loose. I wore a reasonable amount of makeup. Knock them dead, I thought. Too bad if they don't notice.

The event was in a bar on St. Eustace Street in Temple Bar. This was the old cobble-stoned, touristy part of the city. Looking for the right bar took some time, but I was early. I must have been one of the first to get there! The organisers were at the door to welcome me, checked my name on the list and gave me a name tag. They said attendees could get drinks at the bar. There was dancing that night after the event. I promptly ran to the ladies' room to powder my nose. No guy would see me as an eager early bird sitting alone. Yikes. There were one or two other girls in the ladies room, so I was not alone. I chatted briefly with them. They were both there for the speed dating. One had done it before and the other girl was a first timer. I pretended to be a first timer. I had done this in Los Angeles but it proved useless. So as a first timer in Dublin, I waited with bated breath. I sized up the competition. Too fat, I thought. Mmm, looks a bit tarty. Some of them might like that.

What was I doing? I did not have to compete with these

girls. These lucky Irish lads would surely be happy to meet this newcomer who had arrived just two weeks before. A Caribbean woman who had come via Los Angeles: now that was a story!

When 7:00 pm came, it was time to start. There were 20 men and 20 women. We each had numbers and five minutes to get acquainted before the bell rang. The men moved on to the next table while the ladies stayed seated. My stomach was in knots as I nervously checked out the prospects. Some looked interesting from a distance, but only time would tell. The organisers gave us forms to take notes and a check sheet to hand back at the end of the night. Should we find a match, we were to put a check mark next to the person's name. If a girl selected a guy and he also selected her, then that would be a match. The organisers promised to forward an email by the following evening to each participant with the matches. This all seemed easy enough to follow, and so the game began with the first bell.

The noise of the discourse at each table was deafening. I had to shout over the din to be heard and make an impression. I had read a book which said to let the guy do most of the talking and act coy. I tried to practise during the short five minute meetings, but it was not easy. My first prospect was arrogant, telling me about the extreme wealth in Ireland at the time. He must have imagined I had dropped in from the bush in Africa.

I wanted to ask him if he even owned a property and if things were so great, what was he was doing at this event? I wanted to tell him I had just sold my California property, making a huge profit with which I bought a house in Florida. I even had money left over to bring to Ireland as a down payment for a property. However, I acted polite and coy and just smiled at his conversation.

The next guy was Dr. Who's Who. He probed relentlessly,

with one question after the next. He gave many names of people I could not possibly know, since I had recently arrived. He seemed two feet tall. If I went out with him, I could never wear heels. Even in flat shoes I could eat soup off the top of his bald head. No, No, No, I decided.

Then Eddie sat in front of me. This tall, lanky hunk with longish hair really had me hooked. He had the most wicked smile and teasing green eyes. I was mesmerised by the conversation. Maybe it was the piercing eyes that searched my cleavage, or his big hands. He looked like a bad boy in his jeans and shirt, which had a couple of buttons undone. I checked yes. Triple yes. My heart was aflutter. Then the bell rang. We both stared longingly at each other as we parted. I had to meet him again at all costs.

Next came the fireman; tall and drop dead gorgeous. I liked him, but he seemed pre-occupied. The conversation with him was light. I amazed myself at how stupid I could become around a good looking man. He probably knew the effect he had on women. I checked a big yes and the bell rang. Next was a red headed IT guy. We had a very lively discussion about Dell computers. He would be quite handy to date, I thought. If my computer were ever to crash, he could fix it for me.

As the night went on, I used various justifications for checking yes: an interesting face, a friendly smile, a worthy job. I must have checked at least ten possibilities from the lot. It took almost two hours to wrap up the session.

Everyone was fascinated at my move.

'Why would you leave the sunshine for rainy Ireland?' they asked.

'I had a keen sense of adventure', I told them.

They were further impressed that I had only been in Dublin two weeks and was already speed dating. I figured I could sit alone in the big house on Ballymun Road at night, or go out and meet people.

The organisers wrapped up the evening's proceedings, promising to send each person a list of matches and corresponding email addresses. They were leaving it up to us to get in touch. We were then invited to stay and enjoy drinks at the bar with late night dancing. Like Cinderella, I made a quick departure. I was all talked out for the night and could not concentrate for another minute. I put on my red raincoat, which by this time acted as a cardigan and coat. As I stood at the bus stop, out of the corner of my eye, I spied Dr. Who's Who. I pretended not to see him. I held my breath, looked indifferently in another direction, and he disappeared.

I went to the office the next day and worked with extra zeal, attacking each project. I could barely contain my excitement as I waited for the evening. After dinner, I turned on the computer and waited for the fateful email. At 6:30pm, there was nothing in my inbox. Nervous time was spent returning email messages to friends. I could barely contain myself. Finally, just after 7pm, as promised, an email showed up from the organisers. The suspense was killing me.

I opened the email… and…there were seven matches!

I screamed with excitement. Irish guys loved me! This was a huge boost for my ego. I had died and gone to heaven. I waited for my matches to contact me.

Seven Dating Nights

In the next week, I juggled seven dates into my calendar. My first date was with the red head Dell guy at General Mao's restaurant for Asian Fusion dinner in Dun Laoghaire. This was a smashing venue. In fact, everything was smashing, since I was new in town and on a date. I listened to his conversation, trying to appear as interested as possible, but I didn't hear a word. I just looked at the freckles on his nose. I was fascinated by his mop of shiny red hair. The food was tasty, but I realised right away that it would never work. No spark, no interest. We promised politely to keep in touch.

The next date was at Neary's pub off Dame Street. According to my notes, this man was very good looking. I dressed up and this time wore my green rain coat. Of course it was cold and it rained constantly. I found the pub easily with my trusty online map. Oh what a hunk, I thought when I saw him. I could get to like him easily. We managed to squeeze into a tiny slot at a table upstairs. It was a Wednesday night. What were Dubliners thinking? This was not a special holiday; just a week day! We could barely hear each other over the din. I told him a bit about Trinidad and some of our favourite foods, most of which were fried. He was not impressed with fried food. He was a healthy eater in a place where chippers ruled; a food snob. There were many periods of long silence. After a few attempts to entertain him with conversation, I decided it was time to go home. He was a gentleman and walked me back to my little car. We promised to keep in touch. What a looker. If he wanted to see me again he would call.

The next day, I had arranged to meet Dermot, a good looking divorced dad from Dalkey at O'Neill's pub, Suffolk Street. I was early as usual. Instead of embarrassing myself in looking desperate, I walked along the other side of the street. Then I walked back down the left side, taking in the neighbourhood. I finally entered the pub and looked around. I could not remember what this one looked like, just that he was pleasant. I stood with a nonchalant air, waiting to be recognised. A good looking lad approached me. He had brown hair, blue eyes and was only one inch shorter than me in heels. He would do, I thought. We sat and chatted for a while. After one drink (a juice in my case), he asked if I wanted to move on to the Odeon to see Aslan. They had a concert that night.

'Oh that would be fabulous', I said, wondering who was Aslan. The group was simply one of the biggest Irish rock bands with many well-known and popular songs. As we entered the crowded dance floor, people were screaming out the words to Hurt Sometimes. Since I didn't know any words, I just danced like a maniac and smiled. This was a great date; lots of fun. I imagined I could get used to that life. But, would I have energy for work the next day? If my date was on Friday night, of course I would.

I had the opportunity to learn about restaurants, pubs and clubs in Dublin all in one week. Not bad for a newcomer. There must be some reward for the nerves and preparation involved in meeting total strangers in a new city.

Friday night was my much-anticipated date with lanky Eddie. We were to meet at The Bank on Dame Street, a restaurant in a converted Victorian building, for dinner. Luckily, the bus took me straight to Dame Street. And there he was, tall, dark and handsome, still with that wicked look in the eye. We sat down for dinner and could barely look at the menu. The lust was evident. I calmed myself by studying the menu carefully. I had already eaten before leaving the house, just in case the date would not pay for dinner. You never know these days. One had to take precautions, and since I was always hungry anyway, I could always have a second dinner. I combed the menu which was short. Then I asked "What are bangers and mash?" He said they were very good, and I had to eat that. Since I had no clue, I said I would have it. I didn't realise Eddie had pulled wool over my eyes, encouraging me to choose the least expensive item on the menu: sausage with mashed potato.

Eddie was very attractive and he knew it. His goal must have been to bed every woman he came in contact with. He could undress a woman with his eyes. Eddie was from Tullamore, County Offaly. He had moved to Dublin to make his fortune in what was then a booming property development market. He did a great deal of name calling and location referencing, which was lost on me.

As it was getting late, I had to pull myself away, saying I had an early start in the morning. Eddie waited with me at the bus stop. He started fidgeting and a few items fell out of his pockets, including a condom.

'Oh. What is this I'm seeing?' I said, 'You came prepared!'

He nervously grabbed all the bits and pieces and placed them in his pockets.

Thankfully, my bus appeared. He gave a quick hug goodbye and I was off, totally mesmerised, with my head in the clouds.

On Saturday night, I met Cian at Sin É, a pub on the banks of the Liffey River. What seemed to be a dreary pub at the front turned out to be a huge venue with a dance floor a mile long at the back and a basement with another bar and dance floor. My date decided to teach me the basics of the Irish language. I had to use the ladies room so he told me to look out for the sign 'Fir" since the men's toilet was 'Mnâ'. Just look for the first letters as in English. To my shock, it was the opposite. A lad approached from the 'Fir' room wondering where I was going.

I had only had cranberry juice, so I didn't even have drink as an excuse. But with so many new words to learn, it was easy to fall prey. It was a good night out and we promised to keep in touch. I was still swooning over bad boy Eddie, so I could not focus on another soul. Needless to say, Eddie and I met again for another date downtown the next weekend. He asked me if I wanted a drink from his bottle of beer.

'No thanks. I don't drink beer. The back wash might kill me'.

He knew where the most traditional bars were located in the city. He showed me pubs like McDaid's, Davy Byrne's and the International Bar. Irish literary scholars and writers had once frequented these pubs to get inspiration for their work. The likes of James Joyce and George Bernard Shaw had drunk in these places. The old wooden stalls and smoke stained ceilings of the pubs harked back to their former glory. Then we went to a small rave in a basement club on William Street near Powerscourt Townhouse Centre. Everyone seemed intoxicated, or high on drugs, or getting there. We bobbed around to the electronic beats.

I gave Eddie a ride back to his home in Christchurch since I had my car. He had a neat little townhouse which he had refurbished. As, I looked through the window of the kitchen into the dark courtyard at the back, I asked if he had a swimming pool. What was I thinking? Eddie informed me if I looked really hard to the left I would probably see the pool. He fixed some cheese on toast and we snuggled on the sofa for a snack and a drink.

I complimented him on his culinary skills, especially the use of butter and onion… delicious. Then I got a little nervous, as his hands started a well thought out exploration of unknown territory. That was my cue to leave graciously. I had to inform Eddie I was not a loose woman. I had standards (which I was struggling to define in my own head in the heat of the moment). So he would have to wait. But could I?

3

BRING IN THE NEW

A Full House

More serious matters needed to be taken care of, since my girl, Tiffany, was coming to join me in August. I had to make arrangements for primary school and a nanny, clubs and activities. A host of details needed finalising before the big day. My aunt, Audrey, who was retired and living in Florida, was to travel with Tiffany from the United States. She was my mother's youngest sister; a woman with broad facial features, short cropped hair, dark skin and large round eyes. I was delighted she could stay with us for a month until I could get settled and hire an au pair to help full time. My new role at the company was very challenging and as with any private enterprise, I did not dare ask for time off or special privileges. I felt compelled to work all my hours from Monday to Friday, no matter what.

Tiffany was a happy, carefree child, with olive coloured skin, large round brown eyes, puckered lips, and long, thick hair, usually worn in one or two braids. Her father was Polish, so her features were as mixed as her heritage. Like any child, she was inquisitive and asked 'Why?' about everything and nothing. I tried to raise her to display the manners and social graces that were becoming of a young lady. Since I had only one child, I was able to expose her to many cultural activities. From the tender age of three, she had studied ballet and ice skating. Her favourite Christmas treat was to see the Nutcracker Ballet. I wanted to find equally interesting activities for her to enjoy in Dublin, so I had to ask many people for ideas. The best ballet schools and activities took place at 3:00 pm, just after school finished. It was not a city for working mothers.

I prepared the rooms for Tiffany and Audrey, and I went eagerly to meet them at the airport. I hoped that they would absolutely love the new house. They were not disappointed. They praised the red brick exterior and the high ceilings, the fireplaces, the conservatory, and the big back yard.

I had to plan activities for the house-bound Audrey and Tiffany every day. When I arrived home, dinner was always ready. I had a tasty, hot meal. The only snag was that after dinner, Tiffany and Audrey wanted to go out. Go out? I wanted to kick back, relax in my whirlpool bath tub with jets, and unwind after the day's activities. Work responsibilities had started piling up. I was at the end of the honeymoon period. The 'newcomer' was no longer treated with love and adoration. It was time for me to work hard.

Every weekend, we did a trip somewhere, driving along the Irish coast. It was summer, and in between the cold and rain, the city had festivals, so I had to keep up with events in the newspaper. We happened to be driving along the coast south of Dublin one Sunday when we ended up in Dalkey. My dear aunt Audrey was a church going woman, so of course we had to go to Sunday Mass, which I had skilfully avoided prior to her arrival. We took part in the Mass as if we lived in the neighbourhood. The congregation was very friendly and many children participated in the service. We calmly signed up Tiffany to read a passage at the next week's Mass. I then wondered if I could possibly find the same route I had taken quite by accident while driving along the coast.

But my keen sense of direction led us there again the next Sunday. Tiffany read very well and everyone praised her effort. As a kind gesture when we were leaving the church, my aunt flung holy water at me, shouting "The Lord Bless You and Keep You". I was on the verge of laughing at her for putting such faith in a bowl of murky water outside the building. However, I maintained a straight face and accepted my 'blessing'.

Grazyna arrived a week later. She was a Polish second cousin from my ex-husband's family. I had asked his family to help me find an au pair. I needed someone who could take Tiffany to school every day, collect her at the end of the day and help with homework and meals. During the Celtic Tiger, many Poles were flocking to Ireland to get jobs and flee unemployment in Poland. Grazyna came for an adventure and change. I had no idea what to pay her so I went online. One site said €100 for the week with room and board, so that was it. I imagined she could take English lessons during the day somewhere while Tiffany was at school. Grazyna was a plain, tall, stocky girl who did not smile much. She had limited conversational skills in English, but with my Polish/English dictionary, I was determined to make this work. I showed her how to make simple meals, which seemed to have been skipped in her former experiences. We all went around sight-seeing before Audrey had to go back to the United States.

Irish Summer

With a ready baby sitter, I was still able to go out on the town now and then. I happened to meet a kind government man called Cathal. He was straight laced and skinny, with a balding head over which a few thin strands of remaining greasy hair were stretched to create the illusion of coverage. He smelled of yesterday's perspiration and cologne. By all accounts, his shirt and pants had missed the efforts of an iron. However, he was very polite and very generous. He offered to take me to some of Dublin's most famous venues, especially when he got complimentary tickets from associates. I thought that if I could ignore his smell, the strange habit of sitting back and looking at me sideways and the piercing eyes that didn't blink, everything would be fine. I also had to ignore his attempt to impress me with the fact that he was well placed in his government office and made a salary of €90,000. He also owned a house in Tullamore, County Offaly and expected to get a promotion soon. This was too much information in the first ten minutes of a date.

Cathal took me to see a Chinese Opera at the National Concert Hall. I was delighted to dress up and finally sit in Dublin's famous concert hall. However, its glories were faded. The seats were made with hard lacquered wood and it needed a complete overhaul. The show was unique, with English subtitles and high pitched or low pitched songs, depending on who was singing. It was a bizarre state of affairs, since the story line was not evident to most in the audience. However, the event provided the opportunity to hob nob with Dublin's elite.

One Saturday night, Cathal and I went dancing at Break for the Border, one of Dublin's fun dance spots, with two floors and DJs. Cathal went to get my juice. While I swayed nonchalantly to the music, a burly, muscular lad approached.

'Where are you from?' he asked.

'Trinidad and Tobago.'

He seemed extra pleased.

'All the beauty queens come from Trinidad and Tobago. I'm Shane.'

It turned out just that week there was an advertisement on the radio which actually featured an announcement of Ms Trinidad and Tobago. So I was an instant favourite with Shane.

'I'm from Finglas', he said.

My radar went up immediately. Anne, my Dublin

acquaintance, had told me to be cautious of Ballymun, Finglas, and Cabra. No Shane, No. Go away! I thought, as he danced enthusiastically in front of me. Cathal returned with my juice. He flexed his skinny chest and limp arms at burly Shane.

'She's with me,' he said.

'I didn't know,' Shane bleated, and slowly moved away.

Don't fight over me, boys, I thought, as I chuckled at the pair.

Cathal also took me dancing at the Gaiety Theatre's late night dance club. As we left for the date, I could hear Tiffany and Grazyna giggling behind the curtains in amusement at my date. Was it his bald head, or the silly walk, or both? The venue was amazing, with several floors of fun in the wings of the actual theatre. As he approached me, with both arms outstretched, wiggling his hips to a different beat, Cathal announced he had taken salsa lessons on several occasions. These dance classes were obviously a waste of money. I made the most of the evening and danced like a maniac. After all, this was a great venue.

At 3am, we joined the taxi queue with the other 5,000 or so party goers who wanted to get out of An Lar. Little did we know that we would have to stand for more than an hour on St. Stephen's Green with dance weary feet, looking north for that elusive taxi. I learned a lesson that night; I would always drive my car into town, no matter what, and find parking near to the venue. After all, I was a juice drinker, so there was never a worry of drinking and driving.

The Dublin Horse Show at the Royal Dublin Society, better known as the RDS, was a popular and prestigious international event, drawing crowds from all over the country every August. Cathal received invitations for himself and a guest to join members of the US Embassy in their enclosure for cocktails and an afternoon out.

Even though rain was predicted, as usual, I went off to shop for a beautiful summer hat to wear with my pink and violet dress. Choices were slim, since most of my fancy dresses were still to come on the container from California. Tiffany, Audrey and I went to a hat rental place I had spied on Drumcondra Road to investigate their offering. I tried numerous hats and took photos until the owner decided to sell me a used violet hat for €40. What a deal, I thought. I looked so cute in it. I was now ready for the big day.

Cathal came by bus to meet me and I drove my car to the RDS. We walked to the area where the private enclosure was located, showed our invitations, and entered. The enclosure was beautiful. Drinks flowed like water, and hors d'oeuvres were replenished constantly. We told the American hosts I had recently moved from California and exchanged business cards. They were all married couples and seemed to have difficulty understanding that Cathal and I had only recently met and were on a date. I laughed off their interrogation and focused on the horses and show jumping. I admired the prancing horses and was amazed that the show jumping was continuing, despite the rain. All in all, I was quite impressed that Cathal had brought me to this event. I decided I would come to the RDS every year from then on.

By date six, or maybe seven, Cathal began to expect a return on investment, after our evenings out and entertainment. It finally occurred to me that I had to commit or move on. As I attempted to digest this fact, he announced that his brother would be getting married in Tullamore soon and he could not take me to the wedding. He felt that we did not know each other well enough to introduce me to the family. That was all the information I needed

'Sorry Cathal, but I don't think we should see each other

anymore,' I told him. 'I don't think it will work out'.

And there endeth that story. He left not knowing why I was upset.

In Full Voice

As a 'veteran' soprano and trained musician, I looked around Dublin for a good choir to join. In Trinidad, I had sung with the Marionettes Chorale, an 80 voice choir with a wide repertoire of classical and folk music. In California, I had sung with the Ventura Master Chorale and Opera Society, which attempted very ambitious music and commanded great respect. I wanted to find a similar choir to continue developing my vocal skills. Not knowing anyone to ask, I went online and looked around for information on choirs. I combed the National Concert Hall's website for ideas. I happened to come across an announcement about a concert by the Guinness Choir. That's the one, I thought. I sent an email to the National Concert Hall to get contact information for the Guinness Choir. The box office manager was very gracious in returning my email with the relevant information.

I then wrote to the manager of the Guinness Choir, asking when they would audition for new members. Luckily, they were starting auditions in September, so I was just in time. I prepared a music CV, listing all the choirs I had sung with in the past. I also listed some of the musical work I had performed. I practiced Mozart's Ave Verum for the audition and set off that evening with butterflies in the stomach, but full of hope. I met Eimear, another soprano, who was also auditioning that evening. A young research doctor, with a very kind heart, she chatted away with me while we waited for our turn to come.

I went in before Eimear and with knees knocking, performed

before the musical director. He looked like a typical maestro: tall, thin and slightly balding, with large glasses and a serious face. I was told he had taught music for years at a University somewhere, so I assumed he was a stickler for details. I had to do my best. He turned out to have a kind disposition, despite the veil of grey. After I sang my solo, he asked me to do some scales in order to place me in the right section. And then it was over. I was officially a choir member. Yes, I thought, I'm part of a famous Irish choir. I wanted to jump to the sky and celebrate, but I had no friends to celebrate with. So I just told Eimear. She was also accepted into the soprano section, so I knew I would have at least one acquaintance in the group when rehearsals started that month.

The choir practice was at the old Guinness theatre opposite Guinness brewery on Thomas Street. This building had seen better days and was in a state of disrepair. However, it was free for the choir to use for rehearsals. I enjoyed roaming around the old rooms back stage to observe the faded glory. For the most part, we practised in the hall at the Royal Hospital Donnybrook. The hall had wonderful acoustics and with a 100 voice choir, the sound was amazing. The choir was very business-like, with a manager, a board and a committee. How would I ever get to know any names in that group? It was huge. Luckily, we had a tea break mid-way through the rehearsals, because the Irish always had to pause for tea. I first started connecting with other new members like myself who were awe-inspired, or overwhelmed by the sheer size of the group. There was Ana, an architect originally from Cork: a very pretty girl with dark hair and dark eyes. She told me stories about the trials and tribulations of being the only female architect in a predominantly male firm. And there was Valerie, the friendly red head, who always smiled and always had a kind word.

I sat next to Brenda, the teacher, whose short curly afro defied reason. But then I had noticed quite a few red-heads with hair like mine, which was fascinating. One of my favourite people in the choir, Lucinda, had English parents and her accent was decidedly British. She was very friendly and kind, and we bonded right away. I was fascinated to hear that she was part of a traditional bell ringing group at the famous St. Patrick's Cathedral. I went one Sunday to watch them pull the ropes that played the big bells. During breaks in choir practice, Lu would chew on two or three sticks of cloves. When I enquired why she did this, she said it was to keep the breath fresh. This was much needed when singing for almost three hours. I never forgot that little lesson. I've chewed on bits of clove ever since.

Within a few weeks, we had a performance of Mozart's Requiem scheduled at the Whitehall Church on Swords road. This was a mammoth church, perfect for a large work of music. I could not believe I had just joined the choir and would already be part of a big concert. We used the church for dress rehearsals and actual show time. It was very close to my home, but it took some time to find it on a map, because Swords Road was a long road which changed names as it travelled through different areas of Dublin. Even though the area around the church was a massive construction zone, the concert was a huge success, with not an empty seat in the house.

The Irish builder: A New Breed

After Audrey left and we settled into a routine of work and school, I started my quest to buy a home. The house had to be convenient to work and of course near the bus route to school. I drove around the neighbourhood looking for options. Of course, there was the matter of getting a mortgage in a place where I had no credit history. A colleague at work mentioned that his wife worked for a mortgage broker, so she would have a word with her boss for me. Within a matter of days, I was at Donnelly's Real Estate and Brokerage, signing papers for a pre-approved mortgage. Danny, the agent knew several members at the board of a Building Society. With my steady salary and good down payment, he reckoned it would not be a problem. The irony was that because I had revealed buying and selling two houses in California with the intention of making the lenders feel comfortable with me, I was not considered a first time buyer. That was thus subject to a stamp duty of 6% instead of 4%. Stamp duty was a new phenomenon for me. There was no stamp duty in the United States; property taxes were collected every year. The Irish government was able to squeeze 6% of the selling price. So I had less for my down payment. Unfair taxes, I thought.

Danny was a jovial fellow, with a rosy, round face, to match his round tummy. He was very polite and business-like. He noted that we were born in the same year as we went through the documents. How could that be? I had been holding onto the age of 'thirty-something spring chicken' for years and I was not about to reveal anything more. He was fortunate to have seen my age on the legal documents.

With pre-approval in hand, I combed the popular housing websites www.myhome.ie and www.daft.ie for prospective homes. I loved the Georgian houses, with the beautiful coloured doors and pillars at the side. I also loved the red brick Victorian house in which I lived and searched anxiously for something like this within my price range. Alas, property prices were continuing to rise, so I had to act quickly or risk not finding anything good in my price range.

I combed nearby neighbourhoods and finally found a home on Dean Swift Road, just behind my current abode. It was in the middle of a terrace of 1940's homes. The old lady who lived there had died and her children were selling off the house. I called Ted, the listing agent, who came promptly in his BMW. It was a time when real estate agents were doing very well in Ireland and they created the illusion of urgency, stressing the need to bid higher than the asking price to get a property. As we entered the home, I got the smell of old cologne and aged carpets. The home would have to be given a serious overhaul to become liveable for Tiffany and me. The tiny living room, the fireplace and the kitchen with its metal door and old stove and the brown carpets harked back to years gone by. I saw potential in the place. Everything would have to be upgraded to my liking though.

I planned to pull out carpets, sand the wooden floors, replace the showers and sinks and replace the little tile fireplace with a modern stone fireplace. Everything would be upgraded. The house was one room deep. There were two and a half bedrooms upstairs, with a shower and toilet and a smaller shower room downstairs. Though it was advertised as a three bedroom home, the tiny middle room could serve as nothing more than an office. I would paint the boring walls on the outside vivid yellow to match my sunny disposition. Everyone would know that a Caribbean woman had moved into the neighbourhood.

I bid €365,000, which was €5,000 above the asking price. The real estate agent hesitated and said he was not sure the owners would accept this. He hemmed and hawed making me nervous about my bid. In Ireland, offers were verbal, not written, and acceptance was verbal, not written. This was so different to the United States and other countries where everything had to be in writing, with the date and time recorded.

It was a tricky game of trust and wait and see. Ted promised to call me when he heard back from the owner. I jumped into my car and set off for the office. Before I could even turn onto Ballymun Road, he called back with congratulations that my offer had been accepted. This was faster than I thought. I kicked myself for not trying to bid lower than the asking price, just in case. What a mistake. But at least the deed was done.

I had a young, and from what I could gather, inexperienced solicitor to help with my purchase. Fiona had been recommended by an acquaintance and not knowing any better, I agreed to hire her to take care of my affairs. She pondered on whether a foreigner like me could buy property in Ireland and had to check to see if the laws permitted it. This delayed the process by a week. My previous house buying experience in United States had been swift, so the waiting drove me beyond endurance. As fate would have it, Fiona took two weeks' vacation in the middle of the whole process, creating yet another delay. When I was finally at my wits end, I was called in to sign the closing documents. Finally, I had the keys. The real estate agent and Fiona got their commissions and everyone parted on a happy note.

The real work had begun, to convert the Dean Swift Road house into my home. How would I manage to pull off all my crazy plans? Eddie came to the rescue. He had mentioned he was a freelance building contractor. He told me that he would be doing me a huge favour taking on my project, because he had a 'thing for me'. He would not take on just any project. My project was very small and insignificant compared to his other projects. I was so impressed. I allowed a veil of admiration to cover my eyes. I immediately said yes, he could have the job. I didn't know anybody in Ireland, so why not give him the project. I didn't know what I had gotten myself into, but maybe fate had sent Eddie into my life for a reason. Since the old house was so close to my current abode, we could easily walk back and forth while drawing up plans.

The wall between the bedroom downstairs and the kitchen would be broken and an arch put in to open up the area. All the carpets would be removed and the floors sanded and varnished. The old sinks in the two bathrooms would be replaced with modern bowl type sinks and fancy mixer faucets, with hot and cold water coming from one pipe. In Ireland, this type of pipe was considered exotic and cost more.

Eddie instructed me to put together a folder for the project. Each room had to have its own section in the binder and as I did research into the various fixtures I wanted, prices, stores, models and everything else would go into the binder. This was a brilliant idea and I set to work compiling my data. It was a great way to find out about the stores around the city. I learned who had the bargains and who didn't.

One day, as we were reviewing renovations to the kitchen of my new home, I was overtaken by lust and informed Eddie that I was ready.

'Ready for what?' he asked.

'You know what, I'm sure... And I'm ready now'.

He was overcome with excitement at the unexpected invitation.

'Where will we go?' he said. 'The house is empty. There's no place to sit or lie down or anything'.

'Come on man. There's a kitchen counter. Just improvise'.

After a few seconds' hesitation, he started to enjoy himself and the renovation project was sealed with a kiss.

Eddie promised to bring in another freelancer, Peter Collins, who would be responsible for day to day operations. I was game, but there seemed little choice and I needed help to get the work done before moving in. Eddie said I would have to find labourers. That was a new dilemma for me, because I thought he knew people and was a man around town. Luckily, Grazyna came to the rescue. She knew many young Polish people looking for work. She suggested three people in fact. They worked like clockwork and were very eager to make €100 a day, which could be a month's wages in Poland.

The builders worked right through November and as my lease on the Ballymun Road house ended on December 31st, I had to find some way to speed things along. I decided to tell Eddie that my lease ended on December 15th and I had to move in right away, whether they had finished or not. Building projects in Ireland could continue indefinitely or stop completely if a builder had to go on vacation or happened to get another job in the middle of a project. With the Christmas season looming, I was not taking any chances.

My relationship with Eddie became strictly one of business. Even though he gave the impression of being macho and a ladies' man, Eddie did not have the social graces and charm that I liked in a man. Sex with him was mechanical and uninteresting. When he gratified himself, I wondered if he had finished. I lost interest after only our second escapade. Now there was nothing to tie him to this project except a thin thread of 'duty,' which was wearing thinner with increased pressure.

After a great deal of back and forth with customs in Belfast and demurrage charges at the port, I finally got word that my belongings would be sent by truck to Dublin. All I needed was a place to store them. We emptied the back reception room in the rental home and pulled the blinds to avoid nosey neighbours. When the shipment arrived, I was still at work, so Grazyna and Eddie were charged with showing the lads where to put everything. I came home to find a mountain in the back reception room, touching the ceiling. My favourite little piano sat in the hallway. There was no space for that anywhere. Did I really own all that stuff or was it a mirage. The moving company left a bottle of champagne for me with a sticker that said "Enjoy your new home". The bottle joined the rest of the museum of alcoholic beverages that I travelled around with.

The Search Goes On

I hadn't given up hope of finding a loving partner and decided to try a dating service. This was when I met Quinn. I spotted his profile picture on the dating service and decided to contact him. We corresponded back and forth by email for a few days then exchanged telephone numbers. Quinn was a teacher at a school for the deaf. Well, I thought, someone of such a noble profession would certainly make a good partner. We planned to meet at John Doyle's pub on Phibsborough Road. When I saw Quinn, I was amazed. He had pale skin and dark brown, almost black hair, which he wore cropped short and spiked at the front with the aid of gel. He was around five feet eight inches tall. He was so close to my height that when I wore heels, I felt like I towered over him. His gentle baby blue eyes melted my heart.

'Has anyone told you that you look just like Tom Cruise?' I said to him.

'Yes, everyone says that'.

We had a wonderful time on our date and the conversation was amazing. He was way too much fun. Story after story had me enthralled. He was a Northsider from Artane and part of a very large family of eight siblings. They were all athletic and very good swimmers. He told me that he and his brothers had attempted a relay swim to cross the Irish Sea to the UK. It was a noble and dangerous attempt. He wasn't wearing a jacket and could withstand the cold. He enjoyed teaching his deaf students and was fluent in sign language. I was impressed by his compassion.

Later, Quinn decided that we should walk down Phibsborough Road to another pub, McGowan's. They had late night dancing. Since I was all for prolonging the night, of course I said yes. As we walked, an empty horse drawn carriage passed by. Quinn decided to hitch a ride the two blocks and we hugged each other in the carriage. Oh how romantic it was, riding in a horse drawn carriage. As we danced at McGowan's, Quinn paused a moment to recite a poem to me. He said he had just that moment composed this only for me. Nothing rhymed or made sense, but he was so romantic. I was 'in like' immediately. Before we parted, Quinn invited me to open house at his school in the coming week. I said I might come if I could take the time off, and we left it at that. I had to try really hard to resist the temptation to fall into a hasty relationship like I did with Eddie. I had to wait to let a friendship grow for a few weeks, no matter how difficult this seemed.

Over the following days, I mapped out how I would drive there and showed up for open house. His students teased and laughed as he took me around. Needless to say, he was just as surprised to see me as they were. What woman would show up at an open house at the school for the deaf?

Quinn had a son with one woman and a daughter with another. He was best friends with both women and had no desire to marry either. He brought his children to the weekly Sunday lunch at his parents' home. After school, he was able to collect his children, keep them a while and then deliver them back to their mothers' homes. He played the part of the devoted father well. Secretly, I thought he was playing games with both women, who would cook dinner for him and let him hang around. They were possibly hoping he would change his mind and propose marriage. I did not want to be another addition to the harem and had no intention of sharing. He was so charming; I could imagine how a simple lonely soul would have taken him in and fed him.

At the same time, I had been combing online dating services and came across Sean's profile. He was a mature, educated man, well travelled, and interested in a serious relationship. We wrote email messages back and forth. I enjoyed the interesting tone of his messages. After about two weeks we exchanged telephone numbers and decided to meet for dinner. He impressed by taking me to dinner at Jacob's Ladder on Nassau Street. This was one of Dublin's finest, most expensive restaurants. I had done some research before leaving home. The extensive menu was admirable and the intelligent man before me was even more amazing.

Sean was a mature man in his late 40's and was recently separated from his wife of 20 years. He had a teenage daughter who had just finished secondary school, a son who was 10 years of age and a daughter who was seven. He was six feet tall, of stocky build, and very hairy. His chest hairs stood out of the v-neck of his shirt. He sported side-burns, a beard and a moustache. He had hairy arms, legs, and fingers. Even his back and bottom had dark hair, as I was to discover later on. His calves were larger than most men's calves. They were well developed, like an athlete's. His arms were quite muscular, even though his shoulders were not very broad. His neck was thick and sat precariously on his shoulders. His hair was a mixture of dark brown, red and grey all mixed together. He wore his hair in a pony tail. This alluded to a wild, hippy youth which he couldn't relinquish. Despite the pony tail, he seemed conservative.

Sean was a psychologist with several university degrees, working for the government and also managing his own private clients. He had driven all the way from Waterford in the sunny southeast of Ireland to see me. This man spoke about the history and culture of Ireland with great ease and detailed knowledge. He knew the geography and culture of each region and must have travelled around Ireland a great deal. This was very different to the average Irish person who could tell you more about Canary Islands or the south of Spain than about pre-historic people at Newgrange.

Now, I thought, he would be a good partner. He was someone of character, compared to some of the others I had met until then. But I was not sure if I could like someone older, with so much hair. I would have to get used to that.

After our dinner date, I said I had to go directly home; no drinks, no pub, just straight home. Wanting to prolong the evening, Sean suggested I give him a ride near to where his car was parked. As he alighted from the car, I took one last look at his muscular body and decided he had a lot of potential. He tried to steal a kiss.

'I have found you,' he said.

In that fleeting moment, I experienced the strongest attraction that I had felt to anyone in a long time. I was not sure what the jolt meant but I tried to put the feeling out of my mind. I was not a loose woman and offered only my cheek. Anything more would have to wait. Obviously disappointed, he left, but promised to call. And so he did. I got a call or a text everyday just to see how I was doing. This was a fine ending to November 2004.

The company Christmas party came around and I asked Quinn to accompany me. He looked so cute in his suit. I felt extra proud walking in with him. Everyone ogled him and during the dinner, even my boss, Grainne, came over to interrogate Quinn and take a good look.

'What's your name?' she asked. 'Where do you live? What do you do? Oh a teacher. A noble profession.'

Quinn clearly found the interrogation tiring, even though he enjoyed the attention. I pulled Quinn onto the dance floor so we could have some fun. We didn't leave the event until late.

All Set for Christmas

Not having family in Ireland, we had decided to travel to Poland to visit Tiffany's grandparents for the holidays. That would also give me a welcome break from all the unpacking and construction work. Tiffany's class put on a wonderful musical called How Mrs. Claus Saved Christmas. All the students had amazing costumes and both singing and speaking parts in the performance. Grazyna and I accompanied Tiffany to the performance. I noticed that Grazyna's face was more serious than usual, but could not understand why. We had had a few words in the past few weeks when I tried to monitor her movements. Even though she was 21 years old, I treated her like a child; like my child.

'Where are you going?' I'd ask her. 'Who are you going with? What time will you be back?'

In addition, by that time she had made friends and she realised that working as an au pair paid nothing compared to the money she could make working at any retail outlet in town. So she was not happy.

'After Christmas, I move out. I move in with friend,' she announced.

I was shocked, but also relieved.

'That's fine with me,' I said.

I had heard of a woman called Anne who ran a child care business collecting students after school, so I got her number from a parent and signed up for January.

Thank God I had told Eddie I had to vacate the Ballymun Road premises on December 15th. By then, he actually had most of the work done on the home and we got the construction workers to take all the boxes and furniture back and forth in several trips to the renovated home on Dean Swift Road. Only a few items were left in the Victorian house, to be transferred to the Dean Swift Road before year end. I could now relax and unpack before leaving for the Christmas trip. Since we had two skips in front of the house, I even paid the workers to help me unpack boxes and throw out the wrapping. The skips were hired for the construction rubble and I had to fill them up first before all the neighbours dumped their rubbish in. This was common practice in Dublin. The day my two skips arrived, an old television and broken fan materialised within 15 minutes. The Polish workers hung paintings, unpacked dishes and glassware, put up curtains and drapes. They did not even break a glass. They came at the crack of dawn and worked until 6:00 or 7:00 pm. This was something I could not get Irish workers to do without protest.

Before leaving for Poland, I met with Quinn to say goodbye. He gave me a lovely framed poem he had written, and a fake rose in a plastic box that looked like it was made in China.

'Thank you, darling,' I said. 'That was so thoughtful of you'.

I couldn't wait to get back to him.

Grazyna, Tiffany and I left for Poland the day before Christmas Eve and since I could not yet take vacation leave, I had to return the day after St Stephen's Day to resume work. We enjoyed the Polish festivities, while I wondered what was happening in Dublin. Not much in those days. Christmas was generally a very quiet time and everything shut down. I exchanged the odd text with Sean while in-transit in Frankfurt and in the airport at Gdansk. Tiffany stayed in Poland to get acquainted with relatives until after her birthday on January 4th. She was to return with Grazyna before school started.

As I walked out of the departure lounge at Dublin airport, Quinn was there to meet me. He had found free parking near the employees' swimming pool. It was quite a walk, but I liked Quinn, and we were finally alone. We went back to the old Victorian house on Ballymun Road.

4

PUTTING DOWN ROOTS

New Year's Journey

Quinn helped me move the remainder of my belongings to the new house on Dean Swift Road. I cleaned the old house, returned the keys, and waited for my deposit to be refunded. I got word from the agent that the landlady had claimed the oven of the cooker was not sealing properly. She wanted the cost of repairing this to be taken out of the €1400 deposit. I wrote back, fighting this allegation. The seal was loose when I got the place and it remained in the same condition as when I got it. After going back and forth a few times, she finally conceded and released my deposit. I should have been paid for cleaning up the years of dust from the old wallpaper and furniture around the house. I knew the place had been returned cleaner than when I received it.

New Year's Eve was coming up and I was looking forward to partying at one of my favourite discos, Club M. The dance music was always great at Club M and young people were out to have a ball. We danced and bobbed just like everyone in the crowd. At midnight, everyone was given a complimentary glass of champagne to toast the New Year.

After the party, we went to Quinn's house. It was then that he made his announcement.

'Lindy, I don't think it's going to work between us.'

'What?'

I could not understand what I was hearing. The self professed romantic, with his bad poems and cuddles, was breaking up with me? I could not believe it.

What was wrong?

Escape From Ireland

What had I done?

What had I not done?

I was a very independent woman. I had bought my own home and I had a career. I could handle this I thought. If he didn't like me, there were plenty fish in the sea.

He said we would still go on a planned family trip to Westport, County Mayo. After that, it would be over. I wanted to see a new part of the country, so I decided to go anyway.

We left Dublin two days after New Year's Eve for the long drive to County Mayo. At the time there were no motorways, just long winding roads through many an interesting town. It was one way to see the Midlands. We had to be vigilant in reading all the street signs and directions which were sometimes on lamp posts, sometimes on the sides of buildings.

Having left Dublin after work on a Friday evening, we were stuck in the exodus of country people returning to their homes after working in the big city all week. We reached the half way point at 8pm and stopped for soup and sandwiches at a pub. This pub too was packed. It was on the main thoroughfare and served as a rest stop for many travellers. We were finally served at 8:45pm, when my hunger knew no boundaries. It would have taken a lot more than soup and sandwiches to satisfy me, but I curbed my greed and enjoyed every morsel.

When we finally arrived in Westport, Quinn could not remember exactly where The Castle Court Hotel was located. It was 11pm and I wanted to crash. Westport looked like a lovely town with all its cafés and quaint shops waiting to be explored. However, at that hour, most places were closed except for a few pubs. I urged Quinn to call a relative or call someone who would remember. After all, dozens of relatives were coming to celebrate the 21st birthday of a cousin, so someone would know. Eventually, we got directions to the hotel, but did not know where to park. We drove around a while and then found off street parking at the side of another hotel. We decided to leave the car there for the whole weekend, since the town was small and could be explored on foot.

The hotel offered a special deal to the O'Neill clan, since there were close to 50 relatives. This package included a full Irish breakfast for a few euros extra. Everyone came for breakfast whether on the plan or not. I met Quinn's mum, dad, aunties, uncles, cousins, children of cousins; everyone seemed to be a relative of some sort. Their strong North Dublin accents stood out from the milder western and midland accents of the other guests at the hotel. The kids roamed around as if they owned the place. The hotel had a games room which the teenagers enjoyed and a play room for children, with daytime activities and games. The pool and spa were a welcome retreat. We went to the steam room, the Jacuzzi, then back to the pool, and repeated the cycle all day. It was a really relaxing day and I got acquainted with all the family members, hearing stories about their good old days.

One night, we all crowded into the main salon of the hotel for storytelling, chit chat and songs.

'Sing a song from your country, Lindy', they urged.

I didn't have to be asked twice. I had my usual party piece ready: Mr. John Boulay, a folk song from Tobago. I asked my audience to participate by singing 'Teem Bam' after each phrase and 'Regga, Regga, Regga, Teem Bam' as the response in the chorus. It was the typical call and response folk song of the Caribbean.

My audience loved the song

'Again, again', they urged.

At that point I stood up and did a little dance with the song. They were enthralled. Everyone had a thousand questions for me. 'Where are you from? How long have you lived in Ireland? What are you doing here? Your English is very good. Where did you learn to speak English?' etc. etc... It felt great being part of such a big family for the weekend. My own family seemed very small in comparison. Mercifully, I was able to field all the questions and get another person to lead a round of Irish songs. Gradually people filtered out to their respective rooms late that night.

The next day, we walked around the town to see all the unique shops and cafes. In Co. Mayo, it seemed to rain every day, but there was nothing like a few drops of rain on your head to remind you that God was in charge. Having covered a lot of ground in one day, we decided to spend the following day de-stressing at the pool and Jacuzzi.

At the back of my head was the knowledge that Quinn and I were finished. I was never going to beg to get back with him. After all, there were many more fish in the sea and I had certainly met them in Dublin. The drive back to Dublin was faster than the trip out, since there was less traffic. It still took four hours, so we took turns and stopped at a chipper for supper on the way. Greasy fish and chips could keep you awake during any long drive. When I got home, we said our farewells and promised to remain good friends.

After shedding a tear for a few minutes, I promptly dried my eyes and recomposed my thoughts. I thought of Sean, waiting in the wings, keeping in contact with the hope of another date? I promptly got my mobile phone and contacted Sean. He was my best hope for recovery.

'Hello Sean. How have you been?'

I waited with bated breath for his reply.

'Lindy! So good to hear from you. I got your texts from Germany, Poland and many different places. When can I see you?'

Had a new chapter in my life begun?

Grand Designs

With the New Year came new construction projects. I had the grand ambition of creating a sunroom at the back of the house and breaking down some more walls. I wanted a sun room that would span the full width of the home, 40 feet. We debated back and forth as to whether we needed planning permission to make this happen.

Obtaining planning permission to do any type of construction work in Ireland was a long drawn out process. However, Steady Eddie came to the rescue. He had a friend who was an architect and for a fee, he would say we were well within the limits to make us exempt from requiring planning permission. Within a week, I had my letter on file and we were ready to begin work.

I had visions of the large sunroom hosting a hot tub or sauna, and the huge shed at the back would be tiled with electricity and plumbing installed to create a nice utility room. The dust and madness had started again. The fighting with Eddie for my requirements had also begun. He did not see why I needed a hot tub, and I said that since I was paying for the work, I must have what I wanted. And so it went on. He said that because I was in the middle of a row of houses, I would have to hire a crane to put the hot tub over the top of the house. This was a huge prospect. I said I would hire the crane! The argument went on and on, but he finally agreed to put in the additional electric board to handle the excess current. An outlet was also created in one corner of the sunroom for the potential hot tub.

Eddie brought some bricklayers all the way from Galway to put up this extension, and they were reportedly staying at his home until the walls were up. Then another crew came in to do the plastering. I was told plastering walls was a fine craft and specialists were needed to do this. Most workmen were not capable of doing this and if we did not get in the experts, it would not be done correctly. I believed every word. The foundation went in. Then the walls went up. Beams were placed for the roof and everything took shape.

The next dilemma was what sort of roof to get. I asked for red Mediterranean tiles. I was told I was a nut and had no money for this. We settled on poured tar on a backing. It was used on many an extension and I was told I should be happy to have it. This poured tar looked a bit temporary to me. I had asked for galvanised iron roofing as well, but he said that galvanised iron would look cheap and horrible and that it was only used for sheds. Eddie convinced me he knew everything there was to know about building.

In the meantime, my neighbour Noirin began complaining that my extension was blocking her view of all the backyards. Her view was obstructed by my unsightly brick wall and she was going to report me to the 'authorities'. I was not sure if she would really go so far as to cause trouble, but Eddie advised me to go over with a bottle of wine and try to make peace. I assumed he knew how to deal with irate neighbours. I followed his advice, bought some Chardonnay and went for a chat. Since I didn't drink alcohol, I was hoping Noirin would drink. Instead, she opened the bottle and offered me a drink. I took two gulps.

She was a nice soul and showed me around her home. I

learned about her adult children and how she moved to the area in the 1940's from the countryside. At that time, the neighbourhood was part of Ballymun. By the end of the evening, Noirin and I had made peace and my construction work continued. We even had to go over to Noirin's side of the wall to do some plastering.

The builders smoked like chimneys and their smoke filled the tiny house. I asked Eddie to tell them not to smoke. He said they were expert builders and they could do what they wanted as long as they finished the job. On occasion, I had to leave the house to get away from the fumes. The builders worked steadily. In the midst of all the construction and rubble, I had a visit from one California friend followed by a visitor from Holland. Entertaining guests in a construction site was a bit of a challenge, but not impossible. We had to cook around the builders' schedule so the dust would not get in our food.

Eddie's helper, Peter Collins, brought in another crew to work on the utility room. I wanted electricity and plumbing to run to the storeroom at the back of the house. This room was almost 40 feet in length and apart from the little wooden door, galvanised iron roof, and plastic windows, could have made an ample bedroom. This crew worked into the night and I was able to pay cash when they were finished. The floor was rough concrete at the time and needed tiling, so I was going to get the Polish lads to finish the room with tiles later on that month. Eddie must have spent all the money I had given him, since he seldom came around to the building site during that time.

Instead of fighting with Eddie over why I wanted a Georgian doorway, what colour it would be, and what colour the front of the house should be painted, I decided to source my own material. I got a brass lion knocker at Knobs and Knockers, a fabulous store on Dame Street. I also found a wonderful store selling pillars on Prussia Street, priced them and was ready to purchase. Since Peter Collins was the right hand man, I asked if he would take on this project for me. Eddie had not come around for days and I wanted to get the front door project moving.

'Of course', he said. 'I can put in the new door for €700.'

I withdrew the cash and gave it to Peter Collins.

That was the last I saw of him!

I called him during the day, I called him at night. I got various friends to call him. There was no answer. When I mentioned my plight at the office, everyone told me, "Rule Number One: Never pay a builder until the job is done".

But I did not think someone could rob me so blind. After all, he had worked on the house for at least three months. I had grown to trust Peter Collins, so it was a bitter lesson to learn and one I would never forget. When Eddie finally showed up on the site, he said he too could not locate Peter Collins and was ashamed to know that he was so deceitful.

The last fight Eddie and I had about the extension to the house was about the plastering and velux ceiling windows. I wanted a smooth plastered finish, but he insisted that since the other homes had pebble dash, that was what I was going to have. He brought in two robust lads to finish the pebble dash at the back. One lad's pants kept falling to reveal the builder's bum I had heard about in stories. I was supposed to pay the lads €600 after they had finished the job. I disliked pebble dash immensely and was so annoyed to have to pay for it. Eddie brought in some Velux ceiling windows and announced I would have to cut into the new roof. Someone had to put in the ceiling windows then get blinds for them to keep out intense sunlight. This made no sense, especially as he had to bring a separate person to put in these windows. I screamed and hollered at him to take back the bloody windows to the supplier. I was not going to pay for them, didn't need them. The huge windows covered most the walls, so that was adequate sunlight for me and the neighbours. Using blinds to block out sunlight was not an option.

Eddie left defeated. He disappeared for weeks and in the meantime, I called the Polish lads to complete some of the work. They were able to tile the utility room and install my Georgian doorway. I then got them to paint the front of the house a shocking yellow to match my green garden door.

Eddie finally came around two weeks later and announced he was calling it quits on the job. He was not making any money, so he was dropping off my keys and making a courtesy call. What sort of courtesy was it when a person's building project was not finished? I still had some guttering to put up at the back of the extension, and a block pathway to fill in. I asked around at choir practice to see if anyone knew a builder. My dear friend Valerie offered the services of a builder who had helped with her own home. She warned me that she had had some issues with him in the past and he was an old fellow. But I decided to give him a try, since I had no options at the time. The Polish lads had found full time work and could not come.

Paddy showed up two hours late for work and started by asking me to put on the kettle for some tea. What a fine start. He was wrinkled and weathered, with a stooped gait. Did he know he was supposed to be doing construction work? I then had to toast his gluten free bread since he was a coeliac. I found out all about the woes of being a coeliac while he left a trail of crumbs everywhere he went. Paddy would charge €300 a day since he was an experienced builder and I could pay him at the end of the month, no rush. Well, I was hoping Paddy would spend no more than two days putting in the guttering. This should have been easy. Instead, he spent half the day making a ladder from the remains of wood that the others had left behind. He had no tools and was annoyed because I didn't have sufficient tools for him to use. What builder came to work without tools?

The quality of his work was so poor, he used his bare hands to line up blocks and pour sand in between them. The job took three days and he was ready for his money. I asked him to come back in two weeks, since I had no cash to spare. Sure enough, over the following weeks, with the good Irish rain, the sand washed away. Paddy's advice was to top up the sand when it washed away. I was tricked again, by the worst con artist, I was glad to be rid of all of them.

It had been a torturous four months, but the house and the extension were finally finished and I vowed never to do another thing to the property after that. I even lost interest in putting in my hot tub. All the windows had been sealed into place and it would have been too difficult to hoist the monster over the main house and over the extension too.

New Love

Quinn still came to the house now and then since we were friends. He even rescued us one night when workers were banging and moving material through the kitchen late into the evening and we could not fix dinner. He whisked Tiffany and me to his house for a meal. He steamed sausages, carrots and potatoes in a handy steamer. I learned how to wash dishes the Irish bachelor way: dip in a diluted solution of washing up liquid and dry immediately with a kitchen towel. Why bother to rinse? That was an unnecessary step. Much to my horror, Quinn used the same kitchen towel to dry hands, wipe the kitchen counter and various other activities. Since I was a food safety professional by training, I had to close my eyes and ignore these small transgressions. At least we had had a hot meal and could go back to the house, hoping the builders would have finished work by the time we got there.

During the mayhem of construction work, I had started dating Sean. Valentine's Day was coming and Sean insisted on taking me out for a romantic meal. He did not have to beg too hard. I had decided I was attracted to him. I had never dated a man with so much hair and wondered what it would be like to kiss him. Hair sprang out of his ripped off jeans, which he wore strategically, to attract my interest. I liked this bad boy look. It made him look youthful. We met at the Chilli Club on Anne's Lane for our Valentine's dinner. This was a romantic little restaurant on one of the side streets off Grafton Street. How did a Waterford man know about the most romantic restaurants in Dublin? He had lived in Dublin many years before and was well used to exploring the city, so he knew lots of delightful restaurants. He brought me a rose and a card. I could feel the intense attraction as we sat and chatted together. He held my hand and I loosened my grip just a little. He snapped back my hand greedily.

'How soon can I meet you again?' he asked at the end of the night.

I said I was not sure and would have to let him know when I checked my schedule. I had already planned to meet one other lad, just in case this meeting had not worked out. I let Sean kiss my lips just once and he was delighted. While he hugged me, I pondered on the sensation of the tickling moustache on my upper lip. It would take a while to get used to that.

Sean offered to take me out for another meal and when he came to pick me up, I tested his skills at assembling furniture. I had bought two bookshelves which needed assembling and had had some difficulty with the weight of the planks and lining them up. He was none the wiser and could not do it. I also asked for his help in assembling a kitchen caddy I had purchased from a DIY (Do It Yourself) store. Quinn had been unsuccessful in putting it together; it was a wobbly mess when he had finished. Sean was no better. He laughed, saying he was an intellectual and did not work with his hands. Since I had more University degrees than Sean, I did not find this amusing. He was just not handy around the house. Hmm, I thought, one point off his score board. But his redeeming qualities far outweighed the negatives. He was a keeper, but I would have to pace myself and spread the visits so I could get to know him better.

Meanwhile, I kept my date with the other lad, a character who was nicknamed 'Brian Boru' after one of the historical High Kings of Ireland. Brian took me to Aya Food Bar, a trendy sushi bar on Clarendon Street behind the Westbury hotel. This meal was a great adventure. We were seated at the bar with a sushi conveyor belt, with small plates of sushi which went around the bar. It was a buffet special for couples and we thoroughly enjoyed the little morsels as they went around. They also served tiny morsels of desserts on the conveyor belt and the conversation was brilliant. During dessert, my phone rang. It was Sean calling to say hello.

'Where are you?' he asked.

'Just out and about,'

'Are you with another man?'

Right on target, I thought, but I did not owe him any explanation. There was no spark between Brian Boru and me. We did not keep in touch.

Sean pursued me with vigour and we regularly went for meals and sightseeing. I was completely under his spell, as he was under mine.

He was very willing to share his knowledge of Ireland, its

places and its people. The more I asked the more he would tell. We visited Kilmainham Jail in Dublin to learn about the Easter Rising and the fight for Irish independence. We explored the mounds at Newgrange in County Meath to learn about pre-historic Irish cultures. We also visited Clonmacnoise, to learn about the old Irish monasteries and their history. Every week there was a new place to explore and learn about.

Like any hot-blooded man, he was eager to go on to the next phase.

'When Lindy? When can I have you?'

'I'd prefer to wait a while so we can get to know each other better. Anyway, are you even divorced yet?'

He teased me.

'Does this mean you want to get married?'

I said perhaps I did.

Sean's younger kids were close to Tiffany's age, and in my naïve mind would make a good brother and sister.

'I want to have another child and I won't be using birth control pills,' I blurted out one day

He was shocked.

'You should never tell a man things like that. He would run away from you immediately'.

I told him he could leave if he wanted to. At least he knew what I thought. He did not budge an inch. In fact, he was drawn to me even more. His passion was insane. I told a new friend of mine, Mary, about my beau. She was the mother of one of Tiffany's classmates. She was a sensible, well-educated woman, and I trusted her. Mary told me I should break off this relationship as soon as possible. She warned that separation did not mean very much in Ireland; the ex-wife was still the wife.

Divorce had only recently been introduced to Ireland. A lengthy four-year period of separation was required before filing for a divorce and with young children involved; I would probably be used as the rebound girl to help Sean forget his woes. I thought she was probably correct in her assessment, but it was too difficult to walk away. I wanted him too much. I just could not resist. We ended every date with a passionate kiss and a promise to meet again. Sean would come to Dublin to rugby matches or to meet with clients and he would stay in a Bed and Breakfast in Drumcondra or somewhere nearby, just to be close to me.

As the first phase of repairs came to an end, I decided to have a house warming party, inviting some of my favourite friends from work, choir, and others. From the job, I invited Ray and Mike and their wives and from choir I invited Ana, Brenda, and Lu. I had recently met a Trinidadian couple at a restaurant and was so thrilled to see fellow countrymen that I invited them too. Of course, I invited Sean and I told him he would not have to stay at a B&B that night. The excitement in his voice was unbelievable.

'Are you sure,' he asked.

'I'm more than sure.'

I felt obligated to invite Quinn, since he was still a friend. I also invited his brother, since I had been to his house for a party once. I warned Quinn that I was dating a new man and he would be at the party too. The tone in his voice changed completely.

'Oh. Already? But we just broke up.'

'Well you said you didn't want to date me anymore. What did you expect me to do?'

Quinn did not come to the party.

I cooked a feast for kings and played loud music to create a party atmosphere. Ray brought his fiddle and played Irish music, while his wife did an Appalachian mountain tap dance number for us. The party was a huge success and my guests thoroughly enjoyed the evening. Everyone loved the hard wood floors, the new bathroom tiles, the new fireplace, and my outrageously colourful walls. I had put my stamp on the place. One by one, they filed out. Mike remarked that I had a double fronted house, while his house was only single sided and joined to another. I noted a touch of jealousy in his voice.

When everyone had left and little Tiffany was tucked away in bed, I led Sean to the bedroom. He was a little nervous. I took a shower and dressed in a sexy little negligée. Sean finally had what he wanted; a willing woman and all the time in the world to enjoy her. He kissed me passionately all over my body and I tingled in anticipation. He was the best kisser I had ever met and I enjoyed being held so closely in his big arms.

When we had removed our clothing, he tried but could not perform. He was too nervous or drunk. He apologised profusely, saying that had never happened to him before. The next time would be better. I was sympathetic. I knew in the back of my mind it would be better next time. He was probably overwhelmed with tiredness after meeting all my friends. I was prepared to wait for the next time. We slept soundly and in the morning, he redeemed himself after the previous night's mishap. He was the most sensitive lover I had experienced. He knew exactly where to touch and what to do to make a woman feel special. His maturity and years of experience were big assets. I was in heaven with Sean. I had never experienced such passion before.

Our romance was not without some trials and tribulations. When summer came, Sean announced he would be going to the Canary Islands with his family. He would be gone for a week. I could not believe my ears. My birthday was coming up; one of the most important days in my calendar. I was sure I had told him about this, but he hadn't heard me.

He told me I had nothing to worry about.

'You're going on vacation with your wife and I have nothing to worry about?'

'We're doing this for the children's sake.'

'Will you be sleeping in the same bed?'

'Oh no. We'll have separate rooms.'

I could not believe my ears. I had invested quite a few months in the relationship, but I wanted to walk away.

'Let's go to lunch,' he said.

As if a silly little lunch would pacify my rage, he had deluded himself. We walked around Temple Bar not knowing which restaurant to choose. Eventually we stopped at Elephant and Castle and went in.

'I'm not sure about this menu', I said.

'Please honey, there must be something you'd like to eat.'

I was usually a hearty eater, but I couldn't be bothered.

After lunch, we walked around aimlessly and he tried to pacify me. We popped into a little jewellery shop on Henry Street and he asked about the price of a little gold Claddagh ring. He bought it immediately and placed it on my finger. I started to cry and bawl. I didn't know whether to be happy or sad. He was going to the Canary Islands with his ex-wife and kids and I was stuck in Dublin. Did he imagine the ring would hold me until he got back? Well, I would show him.

'Goodbye. Have a nice trip,' I said coldly when he dropped me back to the house. 'Don't bother to come in.'

He headed to the airport and disappeared for a week. I thought I would take matters into my hands again and try to find someone who was free of baggage. I went out for a very fancy dinner with a man I had met through the dating service some months before. He was a pleasant professional who enjoyed fine dining. But there was no spark or interest on my part. I really missed Sean.

When Sean returned from his family trip, he rang over and over and I did not answer. When I eventually picked up the phone, I said I was very busy and could not see him. He said he felt dejected that he had to drive back to Waterford without seeing me. I felt no obligation to entertain a man who preferred to be entertained by his family.

'I'll see you when I see you,' I said, hiding my sobs.

But he was very persistent and a few weeks later, we made up. For better or worse, the man had intoxicated me and I fell even deeper in love with him.

Tension at Work

My work routine continued. I was assigned the responsibility of managing quality issues related to apples, pears and grapes. The job involved some travel to countries where the fruit was produced. I visited growers in France, Portugal, Greece and Italy. The culture at the company was one of bullying and intimidation. I had never seen this type of behaviour in the workplace and was at a loss as to how to cope with it. People were openly ridiculed in meetings and everyone laughed. I was the subject of ridicule when I revealed some ideas that worked very well in my previous job in California. My colleague became so enraged, she shouted, for the whole office to hear; "If it was so great in California, why don't you go back?"

The company culture reminded me of an old feudal system, with lords and serfs. Management thought they were far superior to the humble plebs. As a manager I tried to connect with everyone, but I did not like the culture. One day, the company owner said openly that she did not like the fact that one factory worker drove an old Mercedes Benz and wore expensive Italian shoes. The owner, part of a wealthy Irish family, who drove her own two door brand name sports car, was actually jealous of a poor Romanian factory worker who drove a banger.

I did something to make folks jealous. I took a day off in August without telling anyone where I was going. In fact, I went to the Dublin Horse Show with my friend Anne. What could be more important than Ladies' Day at the RDS? I made an elaborate hat out of hat material that I spray painted yellow and gold. I put stickers at the front, which read "Dublin Horse Show 2005" in black and gold letters. I got strips of yellow and red ribbon, starched them and curled them and added these to one side of the hat. I also bought two massive feathers, one yellow and one red, to perch at the top of the hat. I chose the colours to match my flame yellow tie-dyed dress, bought in Trinidad.

As the announcement came for the beginning of the competition for Ladies Day, we made our way towards the stage. There was a long queue of hopefuls, since the big prize was €1,000 for the best dressed lady. I had no idea what the judges were looking for. Sponsors gave prizes for the best dressed and the best hat. We filled in the forms and entered the competition to receive a gift bag.

As I crossed the stage, one of the judges, Louis Copeland, joked, "I need sunglasses to look at that dress!" I laughed aloud and told the judges I had made my own hat. The competition continued for over two hours. We went off to get a drink and something to eat, then returned to the stage when the winners were about to be announced. The best-dressed prize went to a lovely girl who had made her own dress and hat in black and grey tulle, a bit like Mary Poppins.

Then they announced, "And the prize for the best hat goes to …" Before I knew it, I heard my name called. I screamed, shouted and ran to the stage to collect my Oscar. It was indeed a great moment. Who would have thought? Anne and her colleagues from work cheered me on. Photographers went wild. My prize included a large bouquet of flowers, €100, and dinner for two at Ernie's of Donnybrook, a fancy continental European style restaurant. I returned home jubilant to tell Tiffany my story. A few days later, I took Little Ms Tiffany out to Ernie's for dinner.

The next morning my photograph was in every Dublin newspaper. A woman from Trinidad and Tobago had won first prize for her hat at the Dublin Horse Show. The Evening Herald also had a piece about the event. If the people at work did not know where and why I had disappeared, they certainly found out in the newspapers. An elderly gentleman who had followed me around even called me at the company to say hello and congratulations. I may have mentioned to one reporter where I worked, and sure enough, it was in a newspaper. Talking too much was one of my problems. When I went to lunch, I discovered that someone had put a newspaper clipping showing my photograph and the article about the Horse Show on the notice board for all to see. I was delighted until I saw the company owner's face when she came to lunch. Her eyes opened wide, but she didn't say a word. I asked her how she was and chatted about sweet nothings. Her eyes said what her mouth could not. She was green with envy and rage.

The owner promoted Mike from a Technical Manager to the overall supervisor of our group. I reckoned it went directly to his head. He felt the need to monitor everything we did and he even dictated letters I should send to clients. I was not used to this sort of micro-managing and was very offended by his antics. He also felt he had to act as chaperon when I visited clients abroad. While it was nice to have company for dinner at the end of a day's work, I had travelled extensively in Latin America and the US in previous jobs and did not feel I needed a chaperon.

Mike even had the audacity to say one day that he could not understand how I had come so far in life. I was so offended by his patronising behaviour. People in the office started referring to Mike as Ming the Merciless, as he screamed and insulted people while patting himself on the shoulder for his self professed brilliance.

I grew tired of his behaviour. When Mike decided to make all managers clock in and clock out like the factory staff, it was the last straw. I decided I would do work during my own time and not during a nine to five slot. Mike scolded me repeatedly for not clocking in and out after breaks. I pretended to forget when in fact I was resisting the new control measures. I became bored and distracted. Even though I had had some adventures visiting clients in remote locations of continental Europe, I had lost all interest in the job and was just going through the motions by year end.

First Steps in Business

In November 2005, I pondered the possibility of starting my own business in Dublin. The economy was booming. Everyone seemed to be spending money on all manner of luxuries that they had never purchased before. Since no Caribbean food had yet made an appearance in Dublin food stores, I thought a company offering Caribbean food would have great potential for success. I signed up for a course entitled Women Entering Business, which was run by the Dublin City Enterprise Board. The course was run on Saturdays and it was perfect for working women who wanted to make that transition from a job to life as an entrepreneur. I was very excited to go to the first session.

The venue was near the Guinness brewery in a building run by the city. One could rent rooms for meetings or even rent office space at a very reasonable rate. The course was made very affordable and we were given coffee and tea. My group had a wide mixture of potential entrepreneurs; a seamstress, a clothing designer, a web designer, a life coach, a potential landlord, and others. We were all a little nervous as we introduced ourselves and our business ideas.

My idea was to create a Caribbean food import business to sell to specialty food shops. Taking the course was instrumental in my future career path and proved to be the most valuable course I had ever taken. We were introduced to marketing, taxation, sales and business planning. At the end of the eight week session we had to submit a business plan and do a short presentation to the group. I bonded with many ladies in the group and kept all their contact information, in case they might be of help with my new business venture.

I also learned about the Dublin City Enterprise Board's Women's Business Network, and started going to their meetings and networking events. Most of the women were very generous in sharing suggestions and giving advice. I was impressed at how much they wanted to see me start my business. When I announced what I planned to do, Regina, one of the jewellery importers, met me and suggested I start by selling at the new farmer's markets. She had quit her job and was selling at certain markets and doing very well. She gave me the name and contact detail for the man who ran some of the best markets in Dublin. I now had most of the information I needed to get started, I would have to try out these markets to see if I could actually make a living doing this. It was worth a try.

I registered the business name, Caribbean Enterprises, and opened a business bank account with the Bank of Ireland. They were offering a fee-free business account at the time. I then contacted some food importers based in London, UK. We arranged with a Dublin shipping company to bring a mixed pallet of Caribbean food and drink to re-sell for a profit. I ordered bottled sauces, chutneys, plantain chips, spice bun, various ginger tea blends and a host of goodies I barely even recognised. I had to pay up front for all the goods since nobody knew me and that was their policy. Nothing ventured, nothing gained. I plunged right in.

Happy Christmas

My first gig was on Saturday 5th December at a market in Malahide. With its marina and lovely cafes and restaurants, it was wonderful for a stroll on a Sunday afternoon and dinner at one of the many restaurants. I was told I would make a lot of money, with so many big spenders around. I set up my little pasting tables and managed to get a spot under another vendor's umbrella coverage. Lorraine was a kind woman who sold various hummus blends and tapenades which she made herself. She also sold a selection of stuffed olives. At night, Lorraine was a jazz singer. What an eclectic mix. However, on the other side of my stall was a fish vendor. His fishy run off splashed onto my boxes and my feet. The smell was unpleasant. Still, I attracted a lot of people to my stand. Patrons had started buying gifts for Christmas and I had arrived just on time with my unique fare.

December 5th was also the date of the company's Christmas dinner dance. I invited Sean to the gala affair, so he came to the market to help me pack up and see how things had gone that day. I had not made much of a profit, since I was unaware how to price products, but I had made some new market friends who were to provide years of wisdom and guidance when I started my business full time.

Sean dressed in a gorgeous pin striped suit for the Christmas party, with a red Christmas tie. As we entered the main hall for the Christmas dinner, we met carol singers and received our mulled wine, warm wine with spices. Many eyes scrutinised my new beau, since they had already observed the last candidate at the party the year before. This one was a distinguished gentleman. The ladies were thrilled to be introduced.

I had briefed Sean about Ming the Merciless, the jealous owner, JG from Yorkshire, and many of the other characters at the office. He laughed as he observed them and compared my detailed descriptions of them to the real thing. Entertainment included a wandering magician who gave out metal puzzles and performed other tricks with coins. I managed to solve some of the metal puzzles, since I had received a metal puzzle magician's kit as a child with instructions. The magician was impressed at my skill. The music blared and we danced into the wee hours of the morning.

Next Monday, during tea break, one of the factory staff said:

'Good looking man'.

'Thanks,' I said. 'I like him too!'

Since I had made friends with my neighbours on Dean Swift Road, I decided to host a small Christmas party and invite them all. The Mulligans a few doors down were the kindest family. The dad was a plumber by trade. I could call on him anytime I had a problem. He would always help, complete the job to perfection, and charge me a decent price. It was the 'friend's' price.

'Ya know I'm takin' care of yuz wid dat price,' he said.

'Yes I know. Thank you so much.'

There was Ms. Kelly who lived down the way. She had swollen ankles and was probably very sick, but every morning she walked out for her morning paper.

'Hello Liddy', she saluted with a wave.

Bless her heart; she never got my name right and I had given up. But she was so friendly.

Vicki and Keith lived next-door, with their new baby Maya. Keith had grown up on the street as a child with a large number of siblings and had inherited the home, moving in with his young British wife. They were a lovely couple and their baby was the cutest baby ever. We joked about how Tiffany would baby sit when she got older.

Olive, who lived opposite, was a Protestant and was raised by English parents. This had been a big thing when she moved to the neighbourhood of Catholics back in the 50's. Poor Olive must have suffered. She kept to herself most of the time. There was Mary, her husband who used a wheelchair sometimes, and their two children, Katie and Kevin. Tiffany enjoyed going to their home to play on the odd occasion. And of course on the other side was Noirin.

I purchased many hors d'oeuvres at the supermarket and

baked them. It was the end of a hectic work week and I had no time to make food from scratch. Everyone brought boxes of chocolates. They were delighted to be invited over and wondered aloud how I could have a party for them when I was new on the street. That was because I loved to entertain and they didn't.

The following day, I hosted a party for the Quality Assurance Department at work. I told them it was potluck and everyone was to bring something. We had so many left overs. A cheeky staff member, originally from Swansea in Wales, pronounced that I could have food for the week with all that. Ming the Merciless was not invited. We had fun chatting and I played dance music but nobody danced. It ended early and I gratefully went to bed at around 10:30pm. At 11pm, there was a knock on the door and then someone rang the door bell.

'Where's dah purty?' said a voice.

Two of the sales guys who had heard about our little get together had come to crash.

'Sorry guys. We finished up early.'

They were drunk and thought they would finish the drinking at our party. They would be sure to tell everyone in the office how early the QA people went to bed. I took all the left over sweets and cakes to the office on the Monday so the staff could finish them off. I did not want all that fattening food in my house, and Mr. Swansea would see I did not depend on the potluck for groceries.

Christmas holidays came and Tiffany and I flew to Edinburgh for a Christmas package holiday at the Holyrood Hotel. I anticipated that Sean would be busy keeping peace with his ex-wife, children and others and I did not want to sit at home, longing for attention. A holiday was in order.

Escape From Ireland

We had the finest time exploring Edinburgh.

5

A NEW DAWN

Birthday Party

Tiffany, my Little Miss, was growing up quickly and so were her friends. We wondered what would be a fitting way to celebrate her 10th birthday at the start of January and decided on a sleepover with friends. For children, a sleepover usually meant no sleep for them and very little sleep for the parents.

Six friends came over for the evening and I prepared a host of appetisers and snacks for them to munch through the night. It was way too much food, and the table was decorated with many glass dishes, stoneware, and party favours. The girls spent the night tramping up and down the stairs, playing music, dancing, telling stories, fighting, putting on makeup – all the typical things little girls did during a sleep over.

As the night drew on, I let them sing Happy Birthday and eat cake and ice-cream and then I went to bed. They had sleeping bags and occupied all of the extension and the dining room, so I was sure they had more than enough space to prance around. The music blared until midnight, after which I begged for them to turn it down a bit. Glass dishes were broken, by accident, one after the next. I should have known better and used plastic or paper for children.

By the time parents came next morning to collect their daughters, they were red-eyed and cranky from lack of sleep. But they professed it was the best party ever and Tiffany had a wonderful time. However, she was not too keen on the cleaning up aspect of having a party. She claimed that she did not think she would want to host a party at the house again. It was way too much work. I thought I was the only one doing all the work, but that escaped her notice.

The Lynching

Tensions on the job continued into the New Year, with frequent temper flare ups. I was tired of being monitored and bullied. I started spending the lunch break in Swords town, running errands or just walking around. Sometimes I clocked in and sometimes I clocked out. I took a welcome break and went to Trinidad. The trip was timed exactly to coincide with Carnival celebrations and I was happy to put on my costume and prance in the streets to wonderful calypso music. The stress that had built up over the past few months melted away.

When I returned to work after two weeks, I showed off photos of myself in my costume. The marketing representative suggested putting some of my pictures in the employee newsletter, which highlighted a different person each month. That may not have been the best idea, but I told her she could if she liked.

One day, I went to a meeting. Ming the Merciless spoke at length about damaged product. He said no one in my department was doing anything to monitor the situation. This led to unnecessary aggravation for our customers and rejection of product. Two weeks later, I organised some training sessions with the Quality Assurance staff on cultivation of the crops we were receiving and factors affecting final quality. It was during a break in one of these training sessions that Ming the Merciless called me to his office. He had a litany of woes and recounted all my transgressions over the course of the past month.

I had used a calling card company to make long distance calls from the telephone on site. I had not clocked in and out as requested. I had clocked in from lunch and then left the premises to go into Swords. He traced all this with my entry code at the automatic gates. One day, they found Caribbean recipes on my computer screen. I had been playing on the internet when I should have been rushing to attend to a crisis with product in the warehouse. What did I have to say about all these things? Nothing. He said that the company had made an expensive mistake in hiring me. I was to collect my bags, give back the company telephone and laptop and leave immediately.

Ming escorted me down to the dungeon of an office while I packed up my things. My colleagues were looking with questioning eyes but did not dare ask what was happening. I suspect Ray knew but had nothing to say. To hell with all of them, I thought. Ming was doing me a favour. I did not know how to feel that day. I felt numb. Was I happy to be leaving a place I absolutely despised? I would miss one or two nice people that I knew there, but realistically I would not miss much. I was on my own in Ireland. What was I going to do? Ming asked if I wanted to keep my work mobile phone number. I told him it was not necessary, I would get another phone.

I called Sean as soon as I got home to give him the news and ask for consolation. He recommended I call his solicitor friend Mick right away to get advice. After all, the company had brought me all the way from California to Ireland with the promise of a job. Could they just ask me to leave like that without notice? Mick referred me to a colleague at his firm who dealt with business law. After speaking with her a few times and watching my pennies, since solicitors charged by the hour, we agreed she would send a letter to the company asking for compensation of up to four months' salary to allow me time to resettle.

The company agreed to this and I met with the HR manager in the lobby of a hotel in the area to sign the departing documents. She told me I was blunt and said what was on my mind. Was that not better than mumbling my problems to colleagues in the canteen? I told her the company favoured men as managers since they did not have to worry about children and the home when travelling for work. She said life was tough. I was determined to show her how tough I could be. After all, I had a Bachelor of Science degree and a Ph.D. from one of the world's finest universities. I had great perseverance and knew how to work very hard to get what I really wanted.

In return for the four months' salary, which I asked to be paid monthly, I was not to work for a similar company for that period. It was called "Garden Leave" and was designed to give me enough time to forget everything I had done there. The HR manager said that if they were asked for a reference, they would say I worked there and no more. That was good enough for me. I planned to carve my own successful path in Ireland.

Lindy's Caribbean Corner

After several unsuccessful job interviews, I realised I had to follow my dream of running my own business. After all, I had four months' salary behind me and plenty of time to decide what to do next. I also had stock that I had purchased in December, and this was the ideal time to start selling it off. I got wind of a new market that was starting in Bray for St. Patrick's Day weekend. The market manager, Dave, was a jovial lad. He made sure all the vendors were well situated and wished us good luck. I dressed in a make believe Caribbean costume with a colourful head tie and did the rounds, meeting all the vendors and chatting. Everyone had ideas about the best markets I should attend in the future and who the managers were.

At the launch of this market, a senator from the Green Party came to visit. Photographers followed him as he made his rounds. Since I was the only foreigner in the crowd, a photographer motioned me to come forward for a photograph with the senator. I was very vain and loved the camera, so I did not have to be asked twice. I held a red pepper in my hand and smiled sweetly, with the senator and another political representative.

The market itself was a disaster, with hardly anyone passing through it. The St. Patrick's Day Parade was on a street far from us and it seemed people did not know about the market, or did not care. We languished in the cold and I had to cover up my Caribbean outfit with a big coat later that day.

I was determined not to be daunted by this first experience. It was perhaps not the best idea to join a new market without history or regular customers. But I signed up for some other ventures and hoped the future would be better. I considered participating in the Friday morning market at Dalkey Castle, Saturday markets in Malahide, and the Sunday market at Dun Laoghaire. That was a full weekend of activities, but it would leave me free to do what I wanted on the other days.

I dug out the business plan that I had prepared in November and looked at the proposal for wholesale activities. I had registered the business name of Caribbean Enterprises as a sole trader, so I could trade using that business name. However, for the markets, I decided to call my stand 'Lindy's Caribbean Corner'. I painted a sign of a woman in folk costume on one of my old pasting tables that had started falling apart and then used that as my market poster.

One kind soul gave me the mobile number of the manager for the Friday market in Dalkey. I called her and after a discussion of the goods I had to sell, she was assured there would be no overlap with other vendors and I was in. I started at the market the following week. This little farmer's market was based at Dalkey Castle. It was a historical site, and the event ran from 10am to 2pm. We had to arrive early to set up and be ready for the crowd, which was but a constant trickle of locals and sometimes a passing tourist visiting the castle for a tour. The vendors of the market were an eclectic mix. There was Franco from Italy who sold various Italian pasta sauces, pestos, pastas, and snack foods in elaborate packaging. Franco charged what he wanted and the people snapped it up. He gave out samples of various pestos and sauces on dried bread and crackers. These were still exotic to the Irish palate. I had to admire his marketing genius.

Other vendors included Janet and Sophie who sold an assortment of handmade bread, Richard who sold fresh fish, Liz who sold chutneys and sauces and Dermott who sold organic vegetables. Cathal sold vegetables for a huge organic grower. Vincent from Noirin's bakery sold cakes and bread, and a few others came and went. The regulars were good solid people, who gave me a great deal of advice on running my business: where to sell, what to sell, how to price product. The advice was endless.

The customers were also very interesting. Some people passed through during their lunch break. Since the market was small, you could never tell who would pass through. Famous Irish stars lived in Dalkey, so we could sometimes count on a visit from an Irish personality. One interesting customer was Hyacinth, who had a dog named Adam. She spoke to Adam as if he was human, and he answered in turn.

'Say good morning, Adam,' she would say.

'Woof Woof,' the dog answered.

'Be a good boy, Adam. Be a good boy or you'll be put out. Sit in the corner and be a good boy'.

'Woof Woof'.

Adam was very obedient. Richard, the fishmonger, always talked to Adam, much to Hyacinth's delight and she bought more fish as a result.

I began to craft my sales pitch, inspired by masters like Franco and Richard. Hyacinth told me quite pointedly that she did not eat spicy food and could not buy my products. I told her I sold, jam, tea, flavoured coffee, plantain chips, spice bun and chutneys, none of which had any chilli. To the Irish palate, anything with too much flavour was too spicy. Hyacinth told me her favourite Trinidadian when she was young was a medical student at the College of Surgeons called Courtney Bartholomew. For some reason, that name was very familiar. Many Trinidadian doctors had trained in Ireland and even to this day, there were a fair number of students from the Caribbean at the College of Surgeons.

I finally convinced Hyacinth one day to buy guava jelly.

'Great on toast,' I said. 'Try it on a scone.'

She bought it and I heard about the purchase for every Friday for the following two months.

I also decided to prepare some cooked snack food and see how that would work at the market stand. So many people sold bread and other goodies. Why should I stick to packaged food only? Cooked products would create a stir because they would be Caribbean style, new and fresh. After all, there was absolutely no Caribbean food in Dublin. It was worth a try. I looked at a few snack food recipes in my Naparima Girls cookbook from Trinidad. This cookbook was the bible of all Trinidadian recipes. These tried and tested recipes were guaranteed to produce an authentic taste and texture. I settled on saheena, a fritter made with the green leaves of the callaloo plant and aloo pie, a fried pie with a spicy potato filling. Since callaloo and taro leaves were not available in Ireland, I used spinach leaves as a substitute and decided to alter the saheena recipe for more flavour. I added diced onions, herbs, curry and black pepper. The recipe was to evolve as the years went by, creating one of the most popular dishes at my stand. I slowly gained a following as I introduced these novel items at markets. People either loved them or hated them.

Visitors to the markets were quite skilled at not buying, but not wanting a vendor to feel badly. They recited well rehearsed phrases which all vendors knew well, like 'I'll catch you on the way back around', 'I just came for a walk, no wallet with me', or 'It's too early to eat spicy food'. Some punters asked me to cut the food up and share it out. This was the boldest request. I told one passerby I could not feed the market today and she was not convinced.

People asked me if I was Nigerian. My sign said Lindy's Caribbean Corner. I sometimes felt I was losing in the Geography lesson. The joys of dealing with the public meant I needed a lot of patience, and then some. The customers certainly had no patience. They wanted to be served immediately. If they had to wait at all, they were likely to wander away to another stand. I had to be swift and polite. Another revelation was that I was expected to babysit unruly children whose parents were content to let them run free in the middle of a market. They tossed the food around and parents turned a blind eye as they chatted noisily about sweet nothings with the same friends they had seen the week before. I was also expected to be a therapist, offering advice on relationships and family matters.

Two weeks after leaving the company, I got a call from one

of my favourite work friends, JG. In the past, we had engaged in many a frivolous conversation to pass time and make the work day enjoyable.

'Ms James', he said, 'What are you doing dressed like that on the front cover of the Wicklow Times?'

'What? I didn't know!'

I had to get a copy of the Wicklow Times right away. Apparently after all the posing I had done with the senator at the launch of the Bray Farmer's Market, I was featured on the front cover of the local newspaper. And as luck would have it, my launch was doing the tour of the old office. I was sure Ming the Merciless would have been quite surprised to see this.

A few months later, I got another call from JG.

'Ms James, are you the only black woman in Ireland? Why has your photo appeared in the grocery magazine advertising Tesco mobile phones?'

Without my knowledge, a photographer had taken a photo of me in my winning Ladies' Day hat, chatting on my mobile phone. This photo was used in a promotion of Tesco Ireland's upcoming mobile phone business.

I asked a kind vendor at a food show to bring me a copy, since she said she had also seen the advert. Sean suggested I make a claim to Tesco for damages. I could possibly make some money. But there had been no defamation of character and quite frankly, it was a very flattering photo. I enjoyed seeing myself in the news. After thinking about the situation, I felt no harm was done. It might even help me to promote my fledgling business.

Irish Invade Germany

Escape From Ireland

The Guinness Choir had planned a concert tour to Passau, in Bavaria, Germany in the spring. I was so excited to be included in that trip. I decided to take Tiffany along so she too could see a new country and have a little fun. She was to be a choir mascot of sorts. The trip was coordinated by a German choir member who had been a tour guide in Passau. Elmer knew everything there was to know about Bavaria and was the ideal person to plan the trip. This was to be my first outing with a group of Irish performers. Every activity was timed to German accuracy: every bus, every tour, hotel accommodation and concerts. All we had to do was show up on time and perform.

Tiffany and I observed the travellers with great interest and amusement. We assigned nicknames to all the characters and used them as code to chat about them. Elmer's friend, who sang a solo, we called "Moo-oondie," because we were amused at the way he pronounced the Latin words 'Peccata mundi'. We called another choir member Tourist, because he wore a floppy hat, Bermuda shorts and sandals with socks. Who wears sandals with socks? But Tourist was delighted with his attire and wore variations of this whenever we had a casual moment and were not performing. Nora was very, very short, so we called her Little Lady. Clodagh had lips with an interesting shape. She usually wandered off from the choir and had an eccentric way of dressing. We called her "Liptoy". Aisling and Colette were two sisters, so we called them "The Twins", even though they did not look alike. They were so friendly and they loved Tiffany to bits.

On the first day in Germany, we visited the Erdinger brewery. What a fitting place for a crowd of Irish who loved to drink. The brewery was amazing. Erdinger was the only company to filter beer through ice. The tour ended with a trip to an onsite pub where we were given free beer, white sausage which appeared to be made with fat and flour, large pretzels and mustard. These were German favourites, but unfortunately I did not like beer and the sausages were not appetising. I asked for non-alcoholic beer and had a laugh and chat about this and that with friends in the choir. We had a night time concert on that first day and it was not easy to stay awake. Some choir members were a little tipsy after the brewery tour.

We performed in a church near Erdinger and then very late at night went over to the parish hall for food and refreshment. Then there was the long drive to Passau. By the time we got to the Achat hotel, everyone was suitably exhausted. Elmer gave instructions.

'We meet at 9:00 am for ze boat cruise. Do not be late.'

Luckily all meeting times were written on a detailed schedule distributed a week before we left Ireland.

I overslept and found myself rushing down to the lobby at the eleventh hour. Many had the same fate. Elmer shouted at us, but he might as well have been talking to himself, since everyone was engrossed in conversation.

'When I say 9:00 am, I mean 9:00 am German time! Not Irish time,' he yelled.

Most of us thought it was hilarious. Did he have to be so specific? After all, we were bound to get to the lobby eventually.

We did a bus tour around the town of Passau and learned about the history of the town and the region. It was the most beautiful town we had ever seen. Many old buildings that survived one flood after the next as the Danube overflowed its banks year after year. We could not wait to explore every street on foot. We then boarded a delightful flat boat for a cruise up and down the river. We sang on the boat as if it belonged to the Guinness Choir. The weather was magical for spring. Not too hot, not cold, and very sunny. We could not ask for more.

We had rehearsals for our concert at the great cathedral and got to hear the amazing, newly refurbished pipe organ. Our concert had been advertised in the series of concerts to celebrate the new organ. Our rehearsal was also featured in the local newspaper on the morning of the concert. With rehearsals done, we explored the town. Round and round the choir members went. We were enough to fill up the little town. On every street I saw at least one person that I knew. The afternoon of the concert, we roamed around again, shopping, eating and exploring the wonders of Passau.

The concert was glorious. I looked at the frescos on the walls and ceilings as we performed. Some were beautiful and some were bloodcurdling, with images of death and murder. Not what one would expect in a holy place.

The next day, we had a tour of Austria planned. The Austrian border was a stone's throw from Passau so we were very fortunate to get onboard our tour bus and be in another country in such a short time. We visited Trappist monasteries where monks sold numerous alcoholic beverages: liqueurs, spirits and other potions. Why was it that the religious focused on making money and alcohol? I thought, as we were guided to gift shops at every venue. It was a strange revelation.

We had the pleasure of lunch in an open beer garden and the good weather was perfect for a massive Austrian lunch, washed down with pints of beers for the drinkers. The food was full of flavour and very delicious. At one Trappist monastery, we even saw the bones and embalmed body of a saint in a glass case. I found it horrific to see the bodies of saints and martyrs. We sang in another Trappist monastery, where we experienced the delight of watching a statue of the angel Gabriel stabbing someone in the eye. I tried not to look at the image and focused on my words, pitch and diction.

Alas, the time came to return to Ireland. On the final night, we all enjoyed a buffet dinner and sing-along in the hotel dining room. The crowd went wild, with various solos and group numbers. Two girls had even bought traditional Bavarian costumes to sing a German folk song and wow the crowd. The prizes on offer were ceramic beer mugs and I really wanted one of those! A few people at my table were encouraging me.

'Go on, go on,' they urged. 'Sing a song from your country'.

I didn't have to be asked twice. I had my usual party piece ready: 'Mr. John Boulay', the folk song from Tobago. My audience loved the song. 'Again, again', they urged. I did a little dance, shaking my waist, my hips, and my head with the song. I won my ceramic beer mug, which I placed in my china cabinet, never to be used, like all the other souvenirs from trips gone by.

We had great drama on the plane journey home. Changing airports with over 70 en route was always a joy for tour organisers, but everyone thankfully arrived in one piece and we had much to talk about for weeks after our trip to Germany.

Ireland Supports Trinidad and Tobago

Tiffany and I had visitors for a few weeks in the summer. My mother, my sister, and her two sons came for a visit. My mother had started showing early signs of Alzheimer's disease. She could not travel alone, even though she absolutely loved international travel. My sister, Colette, also loved travel and could not wait to see Ireland. Her sons were aged 16 and six. Her younger son, Khadir, could not sit still. He was always on the go: singing, dancing, darting here and there. He would fall and bounce back up like a rubber ball. There was no stopping him. He had to be monitored closely in airports in case he ran off. Colette's eldest son, Amiri, was at least six foot three inches tall, very skinny, and very aware of his good looks. His appearance around Dublin certainly created a stir. He was Mister Friendly and collected an entourage of followers everywhere he went. All the teenagers on Dean Swift Road became his friends immediately.

I never knew we had so many teens on my street until Amiri James, or AJ, arrived. I was known as AJ's aunt; I had no name. Teens visited at various times, day and night, looking for AJ to go down to the city centre. Colette and I were worried about his staying out late in a city he did not know. But AJ was as cool as a cucumber. Sarah from a few doors down got teased for "fancying" Amiri. Poor Sarah must have only said hello once, but it was misconstrued as a sign that she "fancied" him and that idea stuck.

Colette rented a car in the airport, since I only had a two-seater and could not accommodate my clan. We did some sightseeing: Powerscourt Gardens and Powerscourt Waterfalls, Dalkey, Bray and other Dublin and Wicklow towns. We also took a day trip to the National Aquatic Centre, where we tried out all the slides and tubes and attractions. The family complained that my house was too cold, and Dublin was too cold. I had forgotten to warn them to bring jackets. Even though it was June and temperatures were over 30ºC in Atlanta, where Colette lived, Ireland was never very hot.

'Turn on the heat, you cheapskate!' they clamoured.

'No, it's June!'

'We're never coming back again if you don't turn on the

heat!'

'That's fine with me.'

I threw a Bar B Q party and invited my favourite neighbours and other Dublin friends: the Hennessy's, the Callally's, and a new Trinidadian family I had met recently. Everything was fine except the Bar B Q grill, which was still in the box. I started assembling the grill during the party and it never quite stood up correctly. Those little kettle grills were not always reliable and I did not know how to assemble it. I called on one of the guests for assistance so we could get the meat over the charcoals, but as a time saving measure baked everything in the oven so it was cooked by the time the grill was assembled. The party was great fun for the kids, who bounced on Tiffany's huge trampoline for hours.

On one fine Saturday morning, the family decided to come with me to the Malahide market to see what I was doing in my new enterprise. I had been very sketchy in describing my business, since selling at markets in the Caribbean was always frowned upon by people of our background. Trinidad was a very class conscious society. If you had as many university degrees as I had, you never got your hands dirty. You were supposed to sit in an office somewhere and order people around, making a lot of money. I was worried the shock of my market role would kill my poor mother. I talked about trading at venues, plans for wholesale operations, promoting Caribbean food, being the first in this country to run this kind of business, being a pioneer; everything but selling at farmer's markets. As I prepared cooked snacks my sister said, "Let me help, Let me help."

But as I cooked, she kept scolding me.

'That's not the way to make aloo pie,' she said. 'Saheenas don't look like that. Why are you only using one baking tray for coconut drops? Shouldn't you buy more?'

By the time we got to pie number 30, she was tired, said I had great patience and sat down to relax. She vowed never to do that type of work.

I had recently hired Paul, a jovial Jamaican lad, as a helper. He had the gift of the gab, needed to make some money, and did a great job at charming the ladies and chatting with the lads to make sales. Paul met us near the Malahide marina and we set up the tent, put up the flags and set out the tables and the goods. Setting up took longer than usual, since the whole family had followed in the rental car and everyone wanted to help, even Mammy. I had to beg them to take a walk around and look at the other vendors who sold delicious cakes, jams, and other goodies.

'Leave Paul to set up please,' I urged them.

My nephew wanted to try selling and started singing a Jamaican folk song as a couple approached the tent, but he only managed to scare them off. I had had enough. I took the family off for a drive up the coast and a visit to Howth. Anything was better than scaring off the customers. We let Paul do the remaining sales that day and I returned to pack up and collect the proceeds.

The going rate at the time varied for helpers. I asked several market vendors what I should do. They all agreed that selling my own produce was the best idea.

'Nobody would do it as well as you. Don't waste your money'.

But I wanted to do two markets in a day. Janet, the bread lady, said the more markets she did the more money it was possible to make. Since I could not be two places at one time, I offered to pay Paul €70 a day, and he was satisfied.

The Trinidad and Tobago football team had made it to the

finals of the World Cup Football competition, hosted in Germany in 2006. Since I had not planned to go to Germany for the game, I decided to enjoy the games right there in Dublin. Just the Saturday before, the Trinidad team played against Sweden, who was part of the group. I had the opportunity to talk for a few seconds on RTE radio, inviting Caribbean people and anyone who wanted to support Trinidad to come and watch the game at The Botanic House on Botanic Road, Glasnevin. The event turnout was great and I made some new friends, even though Trinidad lost the match.

The biggest game of all was approaching: Trinidad would play England. FM104 had my favourite morning radio show, The Colm and Jim Jim Breakfast Show. I listened to them religiously every morning. Colm and Jim Jim had decided to support Trinidad and Tobago in the World Cup Football match against England and put together a lavish party. It was sponsored by a brewing company and hosted at The Village Pub on Wexford Street, Dublin. I called the radio station and won tickets for the event. I ordered seven tickets, because of course Sean had to come to the party with my family.

When the evening came, we all went down to Wexford Street. There was a big party atmosphere, with Brazilian dancers and drummers outside. Did the organisers not realise that Brazil was a slightly different country to Trinidad and Tobago? Oh, never mind, I thought; the atmosphere was fun. We went inside and I made sure I introduced myself to the radio hosts, told them I was from Trinidad and handed them two music CDs they could use to play authentic Trinidadian music.

There was free beer and hors d'oeuvres, sponsored by the brewing company. With the Trinidad and Tobago flags and a host of decorations, it was almost as good as being home. At the front door outside, I tried to sell Trinidad wrist bands,

T-shirts, flags, and chains Colette had brought over from the States. They were all made in China, just like souvenirs from most parts of the globe. Colette protested against my market vendor attitude and was too embarrassed to watch me. She stayed inside.

The hosts had competitions and prizes during half time. That day I had my hair wide open in the biggest afro anyone had ever seen. The hosts enjoyed this immensely. I ran up to answer a question and I won a DVD player. I think it was because of my mad afro. The hosts introduced the crowd to my family; we were highly visible in our Trinidad and Tobago T-shirts! Mammy enjoyed the attention and little Khadir did a dance. Sean was amused by the little fellow's antics. Khadir was allowed to go wild in the pub since everyone else was going wild. It was so encouraging to see all the Irish out supporting a country they knew little about.

The game resumed. We screamed, "Foul! Foul!" when the other side scored a goal, as if the referees could hear us. Would Trinidad ever recover? I could not breathe in anticipation. But it was as if the team had given up. The game came to an end.

'No! No! This can't be!' the crowd yelled. 'They cheated. There was a foul. The referee didn't see it!'

The party went on with music and dancing and people were reluctant to leave.

My family returned to Atlanta the following week. Colette protested about having to keep them all together as a unit.

'I have to be the guide dog for all of them!'

With Khadir running helter skelter, Amiri checking out the girls and Mammy wandering off in the opposite direction, the trip home was going to require patience. I heard the airport stories two days later. The pile of passports had been forgotten on a table by accident in the Dublin Airport food court, and Colette had had to walk back to find them before going through security.

Hot Summer in Tramore

We had arranged with Sean to spend a week in Tramore during the summer of 2006. We enjoyed this time away immensely.

Finally, we were enjoying a real summer in Ireland. It was so hot that we swam with Sean and his kids until almost 9.30pm one night. It was magical. Best of all, I was able to spend a lot of time with Sean. I called my sister to tell her about the hot weather. She did not believe me. We learned about many of the small beaches near Tramore Bay. According to Sean, these beaches were only known by the locals.

At the Guillamene swimming point people would run and jump into the water. There was also a platform for diving. When the tide was in, it was perfect for diving. When the tide was out, you could walk out on the concrete, barnacle covered platform, which went deep into the water. Tiffany and Sean's daughter, Nuala, enjoyed swimming out to the other side of the cove.

We went hiking one day with Sean's friend in the Comeragh Mountains. I complained most of the way about not being athletic and not wanting to walk far. We parked at a paved area and started our ascent of the mountain trail. The terrain was beautiful and the children found interesting treasures along the way. We saw the skeletal remains of a dead mountain goat. The great horns and bones were intact along with its fur.

'Are we there yet? Are we there yet?' clamoured the

children.

Sean's friend knew the trails to get to the lake and we could see a waterfall in the distance. A few other people were hiking that day, but not many were on the mountain.

At last we reached Lake Coumshingaun. I was so warm after the hike; I decided to take a swim in the lake. This was a first for me: swimming in an Irish lake. But the weather was warm enough for a swim. I wanted to show that a Caribbean woman could actually survive a cold swim.

During this holiday in the sunny Southeast, we were also introduced to interesting towns in County Waterford and Wexford. We went to Faithlegg and took the little car ferry from Passage East in Waterford across to Ballyhack in Wexford. The ferry ride was delightful and just 10 minutes later, we were in Wexford. We passed the haunted mansion, Loftus Hall on the Hook peninsula. It was rumoured to be the most haunted house in all of Ireland and had a permanent hole in the roof. We then visited the lighthouse at the Hook Peninsula and jumped along the flat rocks, since the tide was out.

Sean decided to throw a Bar B Q and invite friends and I offered to help prepare the food on one condition, that the house be cleaned thoroughly before the guests arrived. The house was a typical bachelor pad. It was full of dust. Sean's belongings were strewn all over the living room. There were dishes piled around the kitchen and what looked like last year's chicken in the refrigerator. I took it upon myself to clean the refrigerator before preparing appetisers for the dinner. Sean was supposed to set up a Bar B Q pit in his Mediterranean style garden, lovingly created with clay gadgets, a pond, and some decking and miscellaneous furniture.

As I removed items from the refrigerator, I realised the task would take longer than anticipated. I was not allowed to toss glass bottles into the bin. Sean was very serious about recycling. Every bottle had to be rinsed and placed in separate containers; cardboard had to be placed in one container and food waste in another. I did not finish until 5pm. With guests asked to arrive at 6pm, I was happy to be on Irish time, since this meant 7pm, or better yet eight-ish!

But everything was ready on time and as dusk drifted in, we lit lanterns in the backyard. I was introduced to many of Sean's friends. It was all about introductions that night. I was examined by a few of the ladies to see if I was suitable. When the guests left, Sean and I hugged in the romantic lamplight in the back yard and he said he was so happy to have me as his partner. His friends all liked me. Acceptance by friends was very important for Sean, so I was happy if he was happy.

PooBee to the Rescue

Towards the end of the year, I wondered if my new enterprise would allow me the opportunity to make enough money to pay the mortgage and live a worry free life when the four month salary dried up. This caused a bit of financial panic. I decided to take in a lodger with the hope that the extra income would help in some way. The idea of having a stranger in my home was disconcerting to say the least. I came up with very clear and restrictive criteria to keep my sanity intact: a quiet female, no partying. I had a living-room that was seldom used since I had the large sunroom installed in the back of the home. This could readily be converted into a bedroom. There was also a shower room downstairs that would work well for a tenant, since I seldom used that shower. The tenant could share the kitchen space with me. I reckoned everything would work fine.

On a trip to the new Tesco superstore in Finglas, I

discovered a nearby furniture store with the best prices in oak furniture. I bought a bed and mattress, chest of drawers, night stand, two wardrobes (one was to store my market supplies) and a table with two chairs. When this furniture was delivered, I set up the room for viewing. The room had a working fireplace. What more could a tenant want? I decided on a price of €400 a month for the room. This was quite reasonable compared to other places I had seen advertised. Would €400 a month actually help me? I had no idea. It turned out to be more trouble than it was worth!

Since we lived close to Dublin City University (DCU), I put up a few fliers around the campus and waited for a flood of enquiries. But there was no flood, just a trickle of phone calls. One student who visited did not like the fact that she had to share the kitchen. I wondered what mansion she had owned before coming to my home. Another candidate mentioned being on a government allowance and I would have to claim the rent from that. I did not want to have any problems with a third party for my rent and decided against that option. A very quiet, mature woman came to enquire about the room. She had recently arrived from Eastern Europe and had a job as a night cleaner at DCU. She wanted to live close enough to work so she could safely walk home at night. Dean Swift Road was ideal. I weighed my options and decided to accept this woman.

Having absolutely no experience in screening and managing tenants, I asked for a copy of her passport and a reference from her current employer. I called the supervisor who managed her group and the woman at the other end of the phone claimed she was a quiet and reliable worker. A mature person who didn't speak any English was way better than a prattling 20-something from the university. The student might invite 1,000 friends for a party every weekend. The decision was made.

My new tenant settled in quickly. She owned just a few suitcases and decided to buy her own sheets and pillows. This was fine with me. I offered a duvet. She had worked as a purser on a big ship in her country during the days of Communism. She was used to being dressed in uniform and working in a strict and regimented environment. I learned a great deal from her about Eastern European culture and life under communist rule. Her friends and relatives had also been affected by the Chernobyl nuclear power plant explosion, with many succumbing to various forms of cancer over the years. It was a sad story indeed. So many Eastern Europeans were flooding into Ireland at that time with the hope of finding jobs and a better life. The word had spread like wild fire that Ireland was the land of hope.

My tenant was so shy, she would microwave frozen dinners, then run swiftly to her bedroom and close her door to eat quietly. I offered her the use of the table and chairs in the dining room if she wanted, but she was content with the table in her room. She would boil potatoes sometimes to go with her small meal. But as soon as they were boiled, she would wash up swiftly and run to her room to eat. Little Tiffany found this quite amusing to watch. I asked her not to snoop around and give the lady her privacy.

A small group of my tenant's fellow countrymen would meet occasionally in the city for drinks and socialising. It was after one of these gatherings she attempted to explain about the good time she had had at the Poobee.

'Where did you go?' I asked her

"The Poobee, Poo Bee'.

Her red face was so jovial. Her enthusiasm was infectious. I asked her to write it down for me. She wrote "P… U… B…"

'Oh, the pub!' I exclaimed, as light dawned.

And so from that day forward, Tiffany and I referred to the tenant as PooBee, but behind her back of course. She was much too lovely to be addressed by such a nickname.

PooBee sometimes asked my advice on which blonde hair colour dye to use. I had no experience with hair dyes, since I was fortunate not to have any grey hair and loved my dark brown hair colour. However, one of her hair experiments was disastrous, resulting in her hair turning more grey than blonde. I have to say, it looked horrible.

PooBee had a very good friend who came to visit occasionally. She was a very well dressed, mature woman. She had the most stylish shoes, jackets, and accessories, and must have been a real fashion plate back in her country. She spoke even less English than PooBee and I could not communicate with her at all, except to say that she looked lovely. Yet when those two got together, they talked nonstop; laughing loudly at whatever was absolutely amusing. The joke could have been on me, I would never have known. It was good to see PooBee occupied and happy with her new friend. One day they put on bikinis and sunned themselves in a small corner of the backyard, out of the view of nosey neighbours.

My gardening skills were less than nil, even though I enjoyed looking at flowers. I bought bulbs of the most gorgeous flowers as seen on the paper packs and attempted to create an oasis in the middle of the 100 foot back yard. This was Sean's grand idea, but he did not help with it. I had many blocks left over from the building project. When the sunroom was put in, the blocks which formed a small patio at the back had been removed. They were saved in a pile at the far back wall. I decided to build a circular Great Wall of China, and then put in various coloured perennials and bulbs that would grow into lovely flowers every spring. PooBee saw me struggling one day, as I attempted to form my Great Wall.

'I like garden. I do it,' she said.

She did not have to offer more than once. I was delighted not to have to work on a task which I did not enjoy. Before I knew it, PooBee and her friend were pulling out weeds, bringing blocks and planting bulbs. They worked for hours, prompting a great deal of peeping from the neighbouring windows as everyone tried to figure out what was happening in my yard. I am sure the neighbours made up their own stories, as neighbours in Dublin tended to do.

As the weeks went by, all I had to do was water the plants and pull out a few weeds. I reaped the benefits of having skilled gardeners who were around all day and worked in the evenings.

Farmers Market Frenzy

One of the biggest events in Dublin was the Festival of World Cultures in Dun Laoghaire. The food market at that time was managed by the same woman who managed the weekly markets in Dun Laoghaire. I wanted to participate and asked her early for a spot. The fee was €450 for three days and I thought it was expensive. Little did I know the value of this event. I rented a tent and a large van to transport all my goods, tables, pots and pans, and ingredients. My plumber neighbour helped me create three sinks for washing up and a host of other paraphernalia for the event. I called up Paul and another Jamaican lad nicknamed Chicken to help. I loaded the van and was on my way.

The food market was hosted on Haigh Terrace, a very narrow roadway. It was made narrower with a double row of tents which were set up for traders. After unloading the van, I had the adventure of trying to turn around a 16-foot van and get out, with other vans doing the same. I found a little gap ahead to try to turn. I had to go backwards and forward at least 15 times to turn that monster of a van. A large crowd of on lookers gathered and offered useless advice.

I started sweating. There was no hope of turning the van. More people had gathered to watch.

'Turn left now and lock the wheel'.

'Go forward to the right, then back up'!

Jaws dropped and hands went on the hips as they drew closer to watch. I took off my cardigan. It was way too hot.

'Would you like me to drive the van for you if you don't know what to do?'

'Women drivers take forever. Yer takin' too long! Others have to move their vans!'

And so it went for what seemed like an eternity.

The market manager passed by to caution me that I should not bump into anyone, because they did not have insurance to cover such injury. It was not what I needed to hear.

But at last, I was able to turn the van and drive out the lane, to a huge round of applause. Why couldn't everyone mind his own business? This I could not understand. Yet, there was a sense of community. I should have been grateful.

I set up a mini kitchen and tried to cook the aloo pies and saheenas on site. The cookers were too slow and it was a disaster. The crowd had no patience to wait. The following day, while Paul and Chicken watched the stand, I cooked at home and wheeled my boxes of pies through the crowd to sell at the stand. As soon I arrived, the crowd swooped down. Everything was gone within minutes.

'Two pies, three pies! Sold to the man in the red T shirt!' Paul yelled.

He was very good and people rushed forward to get their pies. Chicken was brilliant at attracting the young girls because he was cool and had a Rastafarian hairstyle. I continued to cook slowly on site and an RTE TV crew came and asked permission to film me. Who would refuse free advertising? I was extra expressive and acted the part. The presenter asked a few questions and tasted a hot pie, to the crowd's delight.

'Mmm…' he said, 'This food could really catch on in Ireland!'

The crowds cheered. Poor Tiffany was cowering on a chair in the corner. Too many people, too much noise.

The traders near me wondered why they had not been filmed. Yuki sold cooked Japanese vegetables and noodles next to me and a long queue formed when he started cooking. They blocked my stand and even knocked over and broke a few items. It was very annoying. I was thankful when he ran out of stock and the crowd dispersed. I did not quite know yet how to prepare large quantities of food and even though I gave the illusion of an expert caterer, I was learning on the run. The following year, I hoped to be more organised and capitalise on sales.

On Sunday, the last day of the event, Paul disappeared for more than an hour. I asked Tiffany to do a scout around to see if she could find him. She reported back that he was dancing in the middle of a huge crowd that surrounded Mr. Whippy's ice-cream van. The van actually housed a mobile DJ who played the loudest and most impressive selection of reggae, dance hall and old school Caribbean classics. All the Jamaicans and wannabes were in their element. Did Paul not realise he still had an apron around his waist and the pockets had all the money we had earned that day? When he returned he said he was keeping an eye on the apron. Just as pick pockets in the massive crowd could have been keeping an eye on him, I thought. We were lucky; the apron was too dirty to attract attention.

Paul, Chicken and I were able to do more markets throughout the summer, and connect with even more vendors. The process of gathering business advice and networking continued for months. I signed up for the Thursday Donnybrook market on Anglesea Road; Friday was Dalkey, Saturday Marley Park and Malahide and Sunday Dun Laoghaire and Howth. I was on the most tiring treadmill and did not realise it, because business appeared to be booming. I imported a full pallet of Jamaican goods: condiments, sauces, spices, bun, jam, plantain chips, flavoured coffees and teas, cocoa balls and chocolates.

I bought a drink called Irish Moss and Babba Roots herbal tonic. These were reputed aphrodisiacs in Jamaica. Babba Roots was supposed to enhance male performance and I advertised this. The foul smelling concoction sold out, much to my surprise. Irish men were obviously interested in high performance. One middle aged Italian passed through the Dun Laoghaire market on a Sunday afternoon with his adult daughter. He bought two bottles of the tonic. I asked her why he would buy two.

'I don'ah wanna know. I don'ah wanna know', she said.

We all laughed hysterically.

Gearing Up for Wholesale

Farmer's markets were good to generate cash, but I had the

brilliant idea to start wholesale activities. If I could get specialty food stores to buy my products, then the volume would be greater and in turn the income would be greater. I decided to order another pallet of products and increased the range. I had Walkerswood brand sauces and jerk marinade from Jamaica, Fish Tea Soup, Cock Soup, plantain chips, ginger tea crystals and herbal tea blends of Dalgety teas and blends prepared in London. The mix of product was amazing.

I decided I would dress in a dark green suit and place a sample of each product in a small rolling piece of luggage. Next, using a new company letter head, Caribbean Enterprises, I prepared a product list and order sheet. I printed receipts, put together information in a portfolio and prepared a list of potential stores to visit. I focused on the outlets in and around the market area of Moore Street in Dublin. There were a few Asian food stores, African food stores, and a Muslim Indian store. These would be the first stores I had to visit.

I wanted to look professional. In the sales section of the course I had taken in 2005, they had told us to look professional, say "We" and make the business seem larger than life. I practiced my speech repeatedly. What was I to say to these people? My stomach fluttered. Should I call first or just show up? I thought it best to just show up. If I called they could tell me not to come.

Early next morning, I dressed in my suit and dragged my bag to the front door. I decided to take the bus into town rather than attempt to find parking. I went for a drink of water, then went to reapply the make-up. My face had to look lovely. After all I was going to be talking to possible buyers. I changed my shoes. How could I possibly walk around town in such high heels? What was I thinking? Good sensible shoes were the key for a lot of walking. They had to look good, but be sensible.

I then tried to find a bracelet that would match, but gave up. All I needed was a wrist watch. Who would be looking at my bracelet anyway? They would be looking at the products. I put in two extra bottles of pepper sauce into the tiny suitcase, so I could give them samples to taste. It was still manageable. I could still roll the bag. Then, as I was about to step out of the front door, I felt a drop of rain.

Oh well, I thought, there was always tomorrow. I could rehearse my sales pitch better and go another day! I ran upstairs, took off the green suit and settled contentedly in front of the computer to check my email. The truth was, I was too nervous and lacked the courage to take that first step out. My procrastination tactics had driven me to insanity. I could not walk over the threshold that day.

The following day, I convinced myself that come hell or high water, I was going into town with my bag of samples and my portfolio with order sheets. I had to sell to someone. That morning, it was actually raining, but a few drops of rain could not be the reason for a failed business. I put on a raincoat and left at 8:30am. I did not turn back once. I walked up and down Moore Street and saw my first target, an Indian store laden with all sorts of goodies, cheap sauces and spices. How could I compete with their low prices? At least my products were a different brand.

'May I speak to the person responsible for buying?' I asked the shop assistant.

'Mr. Khan not here. He back in afternoon.'

What was I supposed to do? I decided to leave a product list with prices, my home made business card and two sauce samples. If he could not see me, he could always taste a sauce. 'Please tell Mr. Khan I will call tomorrow,' I said

I had not decided whether I would visit again or just ring the store, but I had to do something. I gave a price per dozen and a price for six, in case they did not want to take too many.

I next went to a Nigerian store on the street and asked for the boss. A jovial fellow came out, looked at the products and right away decided he was willing to try a few in his shop. This shop had a mixture of frozen fish of all description, root crops, hair products, packaged foods, calling cards, Nigerian movies, and everything else people needed to feel like home away from home. They called themselves an Afro Caribbean Store. The word Caribbean was just thrown in for good measure, to attract buyers who would rather visit the Caribbean than Africa. I could not find any Caribbean products except maybe fresh fruits and vegetables that could be grown in any tropical country. At least with my products on the shelves, they could be true to the name.

I agreed on the products and quantities to deliver the following day and offered thirty days' credit to push the sale. I asked what was a busy day for his customers and if he wanted me to do a product tasting in the store. He laughed at this idea and I said that was fine. If they didn't need a product tasting, why bother.

I walked down to Middle Abbey Street where there was a very big Chinese grocery with all manner of food products, Chinese and others. I asked for the manager and showed him my products and the price list. He went through the whole list.

'That one too expensive. That one way too expensive.'

By the time he was finished I felt deflated, and was wet from the rain too. I promised to come back with new products and prices. How was I to cover my exorbitant shipping costs of $400 plus Value Added Tax (VAT) for a pallet? I could not meet expenses, much less make a profit by selling cheap. I was going to have to find a cheaper way to bring products across from the UK.

The next weekend I asked if people had any ideas on shipping costs from the UK. Some had suggestions, since they brought ingredients and packaging from the UK. I looked into the alternatives and made many telephone calls the following week. That would be the key to dropping wholesale prices.

I visited another Nigerian shop, which also called itself an Afro-Caribbean store and spoke to the head man himself. I explained I was just starting in business and wanted to have the chance to sell product in one of his four stores. He was kind enough to give me the history of his rise in business from one store to four in a few short years. But he said he was not willing to buy any products from me. He would provide shelf space in his store on Parnell Street and I could be paid for anything that sold. That was a fine agreement. It was better to have product out in the public eye rather than sitting at my home. So I delivered a few hot sauces to his shop and hoped for the best.

6

ESCAPES AND ESCAPADES

The Real Ireland

Sean and I planned a long weekend away to get a little rest and relaxation. I could hardly wait. Summer had been very hectic with markets and festivals, and I was due for a mini vacation. We looked at the options for short breaks around Ireland and decided to go out west to the Aran Islands.

Sean got the number for a woman who rented out a refurbished, self contained, traditional cottage. I had fallen in love with the cottages I saw while touring the Burren in Co. Clare and could not wait to spend time in a relic from the past. The mud and wattle white washed walls, and thatched roof were calling out to me. And to at last spend some time alone with my beloved Sean was beyond my wildest dreams.

I had to get a babysitter to stay with Tiffany during my four day break, take her to school, collect her from school, and organise her meals. Babysitter.ie came to the rescue. It was a new website which linked baby sitters with parents. I called several potential candidates who lived in our area and created a list of reliable sitters. There was Samia, a French student who studied at DCU. She was a little shy, very respectful, and very assertive about her rights and earning requirements. Tiffany bonded well with her. Petra from the Czech Republic was a bit stern and her English direct and literal. Petra had been working part time at a hotel restaurant and wanted to make extra cash. I asked how she would put Tiffany to bed:

'Go to bed!' she said.

That was certainly direct, but it evoked the wrath of Tiffany, who said she was not a baby and did not need a baby sitter.

There was Rana, a beautiful Romanian woman, quite soft spoken but firm. She had left her own daughter in Romania to come to Ireland for work and more opportunity. She was certainly the ideal candidate for a substitute mammy. Tiffany would not be able to play games with that one, but Rana could certainly keep her entertained. Sandra, an articulate vegetarian from Galway, was finding her way in Dublin. To work or to go back to school, that was the question? And there was Sarah, our neighbour's soft spoken daughter, but she was only fifteen and too young to stay overnight with Tiffany. I settled on Rana for this particular excursion and would subsequently get help from all the other baby sitters on occasion.

Sean and I left early for our trip away to Inishmaan, the biggest of the Aran Islands. We drove to Galway and then north to Rossaveal where we caught a little boat over to the island. I thought we were going on a big ferry to the island, but it turned out to be a boat seating no more than twenty people. As the boat pulled up to let passengers disembark, we saw a few of the island people leaving. They looked a bit rugged, dressed plainly and spoke in Irish. The sky was overcast as usual and it looked as if rain would pour from the heavens at any moment. I was hoping it would hold up for the evening and the whole weekend so we could explore the island properly. But one never knew with Irish weather. We had brought our food as well as raincoats, jackets, swimming gear and summer shorts. We were prepared for four seasons.

When we got there, we saw a derelict boat, a few curraghs (traditional island boat made of wicker and tar, typically used as fishing boats). We walked up the hill on the main road which Sean remembered from previous trips with his family. We had been instructed to collect the keys to the cottage at a house down the way, but we were not quite sure which house. There was not a soul on the road. A rugged terrain of rocks and grass with a few homes dotted here and there, it was hard to imagine how people made a living on the island. We passed a pub on the way. It was the only pub on the island. We would have to go over for a drink in the evening to meet the locals. Since it was autumn, very few tourists, if any, would be around. We decided the island would be ours to explore.

We called the owner a few times and found out that the keys had been left with a cousin whose house was behind the house on the front road. With that cleared up, we located the cousin. She gave us the keys and fresh towels and said if we needed anything, just call in. When we got to our cottage further up the hill, the view was spectacular. Across the rocks we had an unobstructed view of the Atlantic Ocean. It was the most beautiful, peaceful place I had been in years. We sat on the front bench and took in the view from our idyllic cottage. I felt very happy in the arms of my true love, with not a care in the world.

Surprisingly, the rooms of the cottage were larger than I had imagined. There was a fireplace in the decent-sized living room which opened into a little kitchen. A doorway led to a warm bedroom, with a queen sized bed covered with a hand embroidered duvet. The owner had left little wild flowers in a vase, so the room looked very beautiful with its rustic furnishings and cotton frill curtains. Another bedroom in the loft had two twin sized beds and would have been ideal for children. Without delay, we jumped into bed. Why waste a beautiful bed? We made love over and over that night, enjoying each other and wishing that this time would never end.

We had such a good time, we forgot to eat. We awoke famished and set about making breakfast from the supplies we had brought to the island. There was really no place to go out for a meal, especially once the summer season had ended. After breakfast, we decided to get dressed and walk around to see the island. We stopped at a restaurant down the hill. The owners, Louisa and Terry, said they were closed for the season but offered to prepare dinner just for us that night. It was kind of them. We then went to explore the prehistoric fort left by ancient inhabitants of the island. We climbed up and down the rocks and imagined the ancient ceremonies that would have taken place long, long ago on the island. We then took a long walk to find the beach which Sean remembered was close to the little airport. We saw a few cows eating grass slowly in patches of land well marked by little stone walls. On one occasion, we passed an old man who held one arm behind his back as he walked up the hill.

'Slan', we said.

He gave a barely-audible 'Armph.'

We finally found the little beach that Sean had raved about. It was spotless. There was not a soul in sight. The sand was beautiful, full of small pebbles and the tide was out, so the water was clear and shallow. This was our beach to explore. We lay in the cold sand, hugging and kissing and revelling in the quiet, unspoilt moment. Could life get better than this? Would we really have to go back to the mainland?

We walked back very slowly to the cottage by another small roadway so we could get a glimpse of some of the other cottages. One was supposedly where the author and playwright John Millington Synge hibernated while he wrote Playboy of the Western World. We got dressed for dinner at the restaurant. The meal consisted of produce grown right there on the island: roast potatoes, vegetables seasoned with fresh herbs, fresh fish. Everything tasted so fresh. Where would they get groceries so far from the mainland? What would happen during the winter when they could not grow anything? I had so many questions. They were great talkers and told us a little about their life on the island that year.

We asked if the pub would be open and went there to have a drink. It was a traditional Irish pub, perhaps built in the 1700's and re-furbished several times over the years. The bartender spoke in English and in Gaelic with a few locals who came in for a pint. A funny character came in, ordered a pint and sat at the end of the bar, smiling at us. He had a rugged face, weathered by time. He had a large nose, a few warts on the face, a wrinkled brow, and large beady eyes. He wore dark brown trousers and a farmer's shirt. He stared and stared, as we chatted with the owner, who was behind the bar.

Eventually, the strange man said:

'Where'd ya get har?'

'What?' Sean asked.

'Where'd ya get HAR?' he repeated.

'In Camden Town.'

The whole pub laughed.

'I saw one of har kind in Connecticut.'

By then, the owner was suitably embarrassed and told him to shut up in Irish. I was amused by the whole scene, since I did not understand anything that was going on. I just looked at people's body language and tried to guess. In the end, the strange man settled in a little corner to drink his pint and reflect. I didn't know one black woman could cause such a stir in the little pub.

We spent one more day on the island and again walked

around meeting the locals. We met an old man who lived with his brother. He seemed not to understand our questions or conversation too much. He was harvesting potatoes for winter when we passed. He said he grew all his own vegetables. It must have been a quiet life for those old fellas, with very little social interaction from the outside. I decided that the island was a great place to unwind and for an occasional visit, but I probably could not settle there. I would miss the bright lights of the city.

The next morning when it was time to leave, we rang the cousin about payment. She said to leave the money under the mat. In Dublin city that would not be an option, but we guessed the people of Inishmaan were more trust worthy. We were able to get the light aircraft returning to the mainland next morning.

It was again fascinating for me that passengers were weighed and balanced around the little craft based only on weight. Since Sean's weight was different to any of the other five in the craft, he had to sit at the back of the jet. As we drove back to Dublin, we reminisced about our time together on Inishmaan and promised to return again soon.

Home Alone at Halloween

I wanted to share my fondness for partying and dressing up with Sean, but being as mature as he was, he thought it was all rubbish. At any rate, we planned to skip out of the house at Halloween and go into town just to see how the folks were dressed up. I decided to dress as the naughty school girl in a mini skirt, long sleeved shirt and Tiffany's school tie. I could not get a baby sitter to watch Tiffany that night. Everyone I called seemed to be busy doing something. I decided that since she was a sound sleeper, we could skip out for an hour or two and return with no fuss. She would never know we were gone. But it was as if she knew something was going to happen. She could not seem to fall asleep as early as usual that night.

'Sean, are you leaving soon', she asked.

'Oh yes. I will be gone shortly.'

At last, she went off to sleep.

I placed pillows under my duvet and lined them up to create the illusion of a sleeping mum. How deceitful one can be when planning a night out. I felt like a guilty teenager.

As soon as she stopped stirring, we tip toed quietly out the house. I was draped in my most conservative trench coat, which covered my naughty costume.

We went to Break for the Border. People were dressed as devils, smarties, clowns, nurses, Frankenstein and various other characters. One lad looked at Sean and said?

'I know who you're supposed to be. John Travolta!'

That was brilliant, since Sean was wearing a light jacket, not dressed up in any way, just being himself. He was Travolta for the rest of the night.

We danced and walked around, upstairs and downstairs, checking out the crowd. The time flew. When I finally looked at my phone, I saw that I had missed almost 10 calls from my house number. The ringing had been drowned out by the loud music. There was even a call from Phil, the neighbour. I panicked and asked Sean to take me back right away.

I called Phil to find out what was happening and she put Tiffany on the phone.

'Mommy, where are you?'

'I'm coming right away. Don't worry.'

'I woke up and I couldn't find you, so I went to ask the neighbours.'

We drove like maniacs to the house.

Good Lord, just what I needed. The whole street was looking for a missing mother. They would think I was a negligent tart! When we got to Dean Swift Road, a small group had gathered in front of my house. Since we had used my car, Sean decided he would just run to his car and drive back to Waterford. The coward! He did not want to be around to answer their questions and face their questioning glares. The accomplice in crime was running home with his tail between his legs.

I covered myself carefully in the trench coat and went to Phil's house to collect Tiffany. She gave me a big hug and said she was worried about me. I apologised to Phil and Mary, who lived opposite. I told them I had just gone over to a friend's house nearby for a short visit and I thought Tiffany was sleeping. I advised Tiffany that the last thing she needed to be doing was walking around on the street looking for me at night. It was not safe. The gypsies could take her away. She said she thought the neighbours would know where I was. All was well that ended well, but it was a night I would not forget.

Cashing in at Christmas

Christmas time was always busy for traders. They tried to make funds to live through the winter which was known to be dead for sales. I followed everyone's advice and signed up for the Christmas Craft Fair at the RDS. The rent was €1,000, which was a lot for me to put out for my first big event. Everyone assured me that I would make back the money and more in the five days.

The fabulous food hall was full of the most beautiful chocolates, sweets, chutneys, Christmas pudding, cookies and many gift wrapped food related items. Having no experience, I set up my stand like a farmers' market stall and only learned by observing the others what I should be doing. The first day was the 10% discount day, with many invitations going out for this day. We were busy for the scheduled opening hours of 10am to 10pm. Many schools visited that day. How was I going to survive for five days with so many long hours of work?

Friday was the day when all the country people came to shop. The wealthy farmers came from the midlands and spent large sums of money. They were the best shoppers we had. Luckily, I had asked Samia, one of the babysitters, to get a friend to help me sell on one of the days. This enabled me to cook some saheena and aloo pie. Other traders were selling ready-to-eat snacks, so I brought mine out on day two and noticed an increase in sales. Saturday was rugby day. The snobbish South Dublin crowd passed through, looking down their noses and complaining. They were not generous in spending and left most traders frazzled with the efforts of trying to sell to people who were impossible to please. Many of the ladies were spending time at the RDS while their husbands attended the rugby game. They had no interest in shopping.

Sunday was the last minute crowd. They hadn't been able to come all week and waited until the end to dash out of the house. These were mad shoppers looking for Christmas bargains. The luckiest came near the end when goods were heavily discounted and they came with cash. So I had to save energy until 6pm on Sunday. The last day of the show, selling to the last customer, it was still possible to make money.

What a harrowing experience it was. Still, the five days went swiftly and profitably and I learned from other traders how to decorate my stand and how to create gift items from small pieces. I had met many traders from the UK and Northern Ireland. They came annually to Dublin, where the streets were paved with more gold than in the UK. They made their money and looked forward to the following year. They were my new RDS family.

With the Craft Fair at the RDS done, it was time to think about celebrating Christmas. Since Tiffany and I had not yet established a Christmas tradition, Sean invited us to spend Christmas with him in Tramore. I knew he was not fond of celebrating the holidays. He could not see what the fuss was all about, and blamed it on his mother who never gave him and his siblings Christmas gifts. Christmas was my favourite time of year. I was not about to let his killjoy attitude ruin it for me. I would fuss about a huge Christmas meal and buy everything I needed to make a feast. He could eat or not eat if he chose.

I bought a leg of ham, a leg of pork, a leg of lamb and a turkey. I also bought pigs' feet to make souse. This was a popular breakfast dish in Trinidad, made with pickled pig's feet, onions, cucumbers, herbs and a little mustard. I would try to make pastelles, a corn patty stuffed with minced beef. I also purchased lots of chocolate. One Irish traditional token for children was to buy a selection box, a mixture of popular sweets and chocolates in a cardboard box. The term was unfamiliar to me. The Irish also enjoyed Brussels sprouts, melons and mince pies at Christmas time. I did not fancy eating bitter Brussels sprouts on Christmas Day. Mince pies were way too dry for my palate. I would have to re-create my own Caribbean Christmas meal or suffer. At that time, everything was shut down for the holidays, so I was careful to take as much as I could remember. There was only a very small grocery close to Sean's house with basic supplies.

I bought gifts for Sean, but had no idea what to buy for his children. They had been trained to appreciate only expensive gifts and to despise the less expensive. I had no intention of wasting money on expensive meaningless gifts, so I bought a girly magazine for one, a poster calendar with rock stars for the other, and a little handmade necklace for the oldest. If they thought I was a cheapskate, they could fling the gifts in the corner and I would not have invested too much. This is what they did with the dozens of CDs Sean bought for them.

Sean was shocked when I arrived with my car full of food.

'What were you thinking woman?'

'I was thinking of recreating a Trinidadian Christmas meal in Tramore. Will you let me?'

'Do as you please. You know I'm not a big fan of Christmas.'

Still, he helped me unload the goods.

I cooked the big feast on Christmas Eve, because his ex-wife had informed him that the children would be having Christmas dinner at her house and Sean didn't want to make waves. The brats turned up their noses at my "strange" food. The evening was saved when Sean's good friend, Colm, showed up for a visit with his twin sons. The strapping lads were about 19 at the time and had hearty appetites. Even though they had previously eaten a meal at home, they demolished my cooking. I felt very happy that someone had enjoyed my food. We sat around, chatted and watched TV until late, then retired for the night.

On Christmas morning, the tradition in Tramore was to go for an early morning swim at the Guillamene, regardless of the temperature. I had heard about this custom, so I wanted to witness the exercise in the flesh. When we drove to the Guillamene car park, it was filled to the brim and overflowing. We were lucky to get a spot when someone drove away. We watched the brave swimmers: men, women, and children, as they jumped into the water and jumped out again, shivering. They were actually enjoying this frigid experience. I could not understand it. After a while, we returned to the house for breakfast. I prepared ham and eggs and souse, which had been pickling overnight. I had not made this dish in ages and settled to enjoy.

Sean was horrified as I sucked on the toes of the pig's feet.

'Don't make such a disgusting noise when you're eating,' he said. 'I can't stand the sight of those feet! Go in the other room!'

He made such a commotion. I gave in and went to the other room to eat in peace.

Afterwards, I found out that in the past, Irish people also ate pig's feet; a dish called crubeens. He may not have had this in his life but I was determined to find a restaurant that actually served Irish dishes. I heard that Rockett's restaurant, on the way out of Tramore near Garrarus beach, was the only place for miles around that actually served Irish food. We decided to go out there for a meal one day. The place was plain, with wooden tables and chairs. The extension had plastic tables and chairs. I ordered boiled bacon and cabbage with colcannon. Sean and Tiffany ordered fish and chips. Everything tasted great and at last, I had found a true Irish restaurant.

Sean had to go into work two days that week so Tiffany and I found ways to relax and amuse ourselves. It was on one of these days that his mother, Geraldine, came to the house. At last I could meet the woman he never wanted me to meet. She visited his home every Thursday to clean, as she put it. He thought the cleaning was her excuse to see him. As I walked down the steps that morning, a tiny wrinkled lady with glasses turned the corner of the living-room door. We were both startled.

I smiled and said.

'You must be Geraldine. Hello. Nice to meet you.'

She smiled, shook my hand and said she had heard about me. I wondered what she had heard.

"Anyway,' she said, 'There's work to be done. There's work to be done.'

She proceeded to the wash room, grabbed a brush, put on an apron and started sweeping and dusting. She swept the kitchen and washed the dishes in the sink.

She sang away merrily. I remembered the song 'All Kinds of Everything' from my childhood.

Geraldine then moved on to the living room. Sean had bought two parrots and they created a mess with the bird seed. As they chatted, she answered back. The parrots did not know what they were in for. Geraldine could give them a chat for their money. She cleaned up the bird seed and overflow, and then sat down for a rest.

By this time, Tiffany had woken up and came down to see what the commotion was about. Geraldine gave Tiffany a big hug and we all chatted. She told me how much she loved Sean. He was her wonderful son and I should take care of him. I promised I would.

I called Sean to let him know that Geraldine was there. He was horrified.

'Quick. Leave the house right away! Go shopping or something!'

'No', I said. 'Ger and I are having a great conversation about you. Contrary to what you have said, she is a very pleasant woman'.

We continued to chat until it was time for her to leave. I gave her some pieces of Caribbean Christmas cake that I had made. Sean had told me she had a sweet tooth. She left the house, swinging her walking stick in the air.

On New Year's Eve, we went to the local pub, and sat in our usual corner. I decided to liven things up a bit by wearing an outfit the locals would think was outlandish. Giving them something to talk about, I wore a little pair of hot pants with fish net stockings and high heeled boots.

'Oh Lindy, you look sexy,' said Sean. 'What will they say at the pub?'

'They'll say I look sexy of course.'

The man was perpetually worried about what 'they' would say. Who were they anyway? I had to give them something interesting to talk about. I imagined the conversation and chuckled to myself.

Close to midnight, all Sean's friends rushed home to wish their kids a Happy New Year. A group of drunken friends and neighbours knocked on the door and came in to continue drinking and chatting. Sean brought out beers and spirits. As the only sober person in the crowd, I was a little bored. The conversations did not make sense. Then they started singing. Someone must have remembered I sang in a choir and called for me to sing. I tried to sing a few lines but the cigarette smoke choked me, so I calmly retired upstairs and told Sean he could come up after his guests left. I fell asleep quickly, so I didn't know what time the partygoers retired.

Tiffany and I spent the remaining days of our holiday visiting tourist sites. A drive to Cork city for shopping proved to be a big adventure, because the rivers overflowed and we had to drive through flood waters on the way back. We visited Hook Peninsula and a few Wexford sites, taking the Passage East car ferry.

Alas, it was soon time to return to Dublin. Sean was getting cabin fever and I had to get back to Dublin to regroup and make a business plan for 2007.

'What will I do without you?' Sean said to me. 'You are my soul mate.'

7

NATIONWIDE COVERAGE

Motoring Ahead

Winter was always very quiet in Ireland. The wind howled, the rain blew horizontally and income was not certain. I decided to step up my wholesale activities significantly by visiting as many fancy food shops nationwide as I could. I got good advice from Janet of Janet's Country Fayre. She said I should buy the Bridgestone Guide and be sure to visit as many of the shops listed on the guide as possible.

To get a distributor or not: that was the burning question. Some said I should, others said it was not worth the expense. Their mark-up would be exorbitant and I would make no money. I decided to drive around the country with samples and order sheets, taking orders and delivering products. This made my winter very busy. Unfortunately, providing 30 days' credit and in some cases, 60 days' credit, did not immediately generate cash.

I found myself with the dilemma of an unreliable car which needed a gear box replacement. Instead of doing repairs, I decided to sell it off cheap or trade it in for another vehicle. The Hyundai Coupe was very popular in Dublin at that time and I wanted one. Not practical for markets, but cute nonetheless. I visited a new area of shops and car dealerships near Swords. The whole area had only recently developed from grassland and a lot of enterprising hopefuls moved in.

I walked into a Mazda dealership and asked for a Hyundai Coupe. The manager was very friendly and accommodating. What a welcome change to some other dealerships. As luck would have it, they even had a black Hyundai Coupe which had come in recently and the price was €14,000. I would have to get a loan for that. The dealer offered financing. He called my bank and with my savings on file, I had no problem in securing a car loan. I tried negotiating a better deal with the garage and managed to shave off a few hundred. This I used to get new mats and a sun visor.

I traded in my old scrap and drove away with a sleek black Hyundai Coupe. When I collected Tiffany at school that afternoon, she was so proud.

'Tiffany, is that yer ma's car?' asked her friends. 'Deadly. Yer so lucky.'

She walked with head held high, nose in the air, and could not control her excitement.

'Mommy, this is the best car ever.'

It felt great to have a sporty car without the hefty bill. To be sure, every curtain on the street twitched as I parked my car in the driveway. My neighbour Mary and her husband were notorious for manning the windows, watching as people came and went. One day, she came out to quiz me on my new vehicle.

'Every time I see that black sports car, I get jealous'.

'Well, why don't you just buy one?'

'Well, er...ah... ya know...er...ah...'

I waited.

'We have enough bills to pay with the cars we have now.'

I thought to say, 'Mind yer own business', but I was too polite.

New Set of Wheels

After a while, it became apparent that my Hyundai Coupe was a toy car and not suitable for markets. Funds were coming in regularly by summer time, so I then decided to get a van. I had no clue what to examine in a van and felt quite vulnerable. I decided to ask everyone's favourite Italian trader, Franco, the Don of Dublin. Franco boasted that he had bought two reliable vans which hadn't cost more than €5,000 each. He knew a lad called Tony in Drumcondra, who was friends with a wholesale dealership that sold old business vans at minimal prices. All I had to do was hook up with Tony and I would be sorted.

I rang Tony, got directions to his house and set out one morning for negotiations. It felt like a shady mafia deal to me. The houses in that block, a stone's throw from Croke Park, looked very quiet and deserted at that time of the morning. They were small brick houses with very small gardens, and everyone seemed to have left for work. When I spotted the house, I decided to call Mary, Tiffany's classmate's mother, who lived not too far away on Clonliffe Road. I gave her the address. Then I told her I was off to negotiate a deal for a van. If she had not heard from me within an hour, she was to call to make sure I was still alive.

I walked up to the grubby little door, rang the doorbell and waited for an answer. A stocky fellow with strong arms answered the door. He said he had been expecting me. I sat at the edge of the chair and described the type of van I was looking for. He said he would check and get back to me. He would get a finder's fee, the company would sell off their excess stock, and everyone would be happy.

He asked what sort of business I needed the van for, and then told me about his own cooking skills. Then I heard about his trip to South America, his girlfriend who went back to South America and how his heart was broken. It began to feel like a therapy session. After about 10 minutes, I looked at my watch.

'Oh well. Have to run,' I said. 'I have so many appointments.'

The truth was, I had absolutely nowhere to go that day, but I needed to make a speedy escape. The next day, I got a call to go to the wholesale dealer, so we could check out the goods. Patrick was the contact, and if he was not there, Donal was the contact. Tony had heard they had two small vans that would suit my needs. We had to go quickly before another person snapped them up. Apparently, this dealer ensured the vans were working well. Since they were used in business, they had to be in good working order all the time. I had nothing to worry about.

When I arrived, I saw several vans in the yard. Some were covered in the dirt of years, others shiny and newish looking. We looked at the interior of three vans and I imagined how my goods and gazebo would fit in them. We then looked at one white van that was a possibility. This was a six-foot Honda van with ample storage space. In the front had comfortable leg room and a stick shift, which is what I wanted. This van was also within my budget of €5,000.

I tried to negotiate a few hundred off since the van needed the annual DMV certificate and that was a cost for me, not to mention the insurance. I had to pay cash to get this deal. There was no credit with this company. That was fine for me. I told them that if I could get a few hundred off, they could have their money in a day or two. The deal was struck and I drove frantically to Bank of Ireland for a chat with Fergal, the bank manager, to get a business loan. I had already opened a business account, which they advertised repeatedly to small traders, so I thought I might as well benefit from the fees I was paying.

I managed to get an appointment and was carried away as I

gave a speech about absolutely needing a van to run my business. I was well rehearsed. I had to travel all over the city. I had started selling wholesale to shops. My small car was overcrowded with goods. I would deposit cash into my business bank account every week. He would be able to see my progress. By the time my speech was finished, Fergal, a reasonable man who had many more important meetings during the day, had the check for €4,800 prepared and made out to the dealership. I was out and ready to shop.

I returned the next day to the van dealership to purchase the van. It was a 2002 model, but the mileage was still reasonably low, which was good, because my plans for wholesale activities involved treks around the whole island, so I planned to generate a lot of miles. My sales agent gave me the address of the nearest DMV where I could go to have the van evaluated for the road worthiness test. He said I should have no problems and I certainly hoped this was true. I did not want to face another trip to a garage.

I now had two vehicles in front of my house. As I pulled up with the white van, several curtains twitched. I could imagine the talk, about this strange Caribbean woman and her two swanky vehicles.

Markets and Media

One day, a brilliant article was written about my business in the *Sunday Independent*. My photo had been taken at the Donnybrook Farmer's Market on Anglesea Road, posing with various Caribbean products. Other traders wondered why I was being photographed and not them. It was because a journalist had called the Dublin City Enterprise Board looking for someone to interview about being a female immigrant entrepreneur. My name was put forward. The journalist was called to do the interview. Then a photographer was sent to the Donnybrook Market. A small photo appeared in the front of the Business section, then half a page within the business section. It was a well written article and good advertising for a fledgling business. My first newspaper appearance prompted a flurry of media activity around my business. There was nothing better than free advertising and I got great advice to copy articles, laminate them and plaster them around my stand at markets and festivals. People respected the media. If I was good enough to appear in a newspaper, then my products were good enough to purchase.

On Easter Sunday, RTE sent a reporter to interview traders at Dun Laoghaire market. This was for their Easter special on The Spectrum, a new multicultural radio program. I babbled on and on about the virtues of my wonderful imported Caribbean products, the delicious flavoured coffees, the tropical drinks, ginger beer and teas. My product selection had increased tremendously and there was no stopping me.

RTE contacted me to do other radio segments on The Spectrum. I recorded a hello to my dad from overseas on Father's Day, a Christmas letter to a friend from overseas, and a Caribbean Christmas cake recipe which appeared on the RTE website. I was not sure who was listening to these little chats on the Spectrum with host Zbyszek Zalinski. However, I was paid a small allowance for my time spent recording at the studio. It was free advertising.

A reporter also came to the house to watch me cook dishes, taste them, take photos and learn more about the Caribbean. I spent a whole morning with this freelancer, but the article never appeared anywhere as far as I knew. Not all writers could sell a story. However, I did have a wonderful article written about my fare in the *Sunday Business Post* and a photographer came to the house to get a shot. At that time I had a Caribbean beach mural painted on a full wall in my sunroom. An Irish friend had painted the mural to create a home away from home in Dublin. The reporter wanted a story about how difficult it was for foreign entrepreneurs to get funding to start a business. I had used my own funds to get started. I had no difficulty to report. No matter how many different questions she asked to support her angle, I did not entertain them. I told her it was easy to start the business and a lot of support was available through the Dublin City Enterprise Board and government agencies. Free or very cheap training was available for small businesses. She managed to write a reasonably accurate account of what I had told her, but it was overshadowed by her underlying goal for the story.

Spreading My Wings

Since I now had my own van, I set a goal of putting products into specialty food shops which were opening all over the country. I drove nationwide to sell wholesale to shops and at festivals. Rural Ireland was uncharted territory for me and I found myself in the quaintest towns looking for business. I was sufficiently thick skinned by that time to tolerate rejection. "No, not today", meant a real possibility and a follow up. "I'll pass on this", meant a firm maybe. The Irish were never very good at saying no. Some did not want to hurt the feelings of the bold Caribbean woman who had driven all the way from Dublin to try to sell foreign products. A few kind shop owners indulged me in conversation and bought six bottles of this and six of that in support. To me, it was a start and a foot in the door.

My travels took me to Northern Ireland. I visited The Yellow Door in Portadown, Sawers in Belfast, Fountain Centre, and Cargoes Cafe on Lisburn Road. Other shops on Lisburn Road either had excess product or could not see themselves selling my stock. The store owners and managers were a delight to chat with. I learned a lot just observing their range of products. I went to a Chinese wholesaler, but had to reduce my product prices, since they sold at very low prices. They were willing to try some of my products, but called me back to reclaim those that had a short shelf life. It was a big learning curve for me in terms of delivering product and trying to get paid for them. With all the long distance driving, I wasn't sure I made any real money. Since all my goods were paid off in advance, and usually on my credit card, I had to find creative ways to make back the money.

Sometimes market customers who wanted goodies for parties or events would buy cases of product from me. But that was sporadic. I got an order for boxes of curry sauce from Belvedere College, a private school in Dublin. The boys were preparing a curry meal for a graduation event. That was a unique opportunity. It came about because one of the teachers had tried my products in the past and wanted to offer a nice dinner at the school.

I managed to get some items into Dublin's fancy food shops: Caviston's in Glasthule and Donnybrook Fair in Donnybrook. I did a number of product tastings in Caviston's and got to meet the whole family, including the grandfather. He would pass through occasionally to chat with customers and old friends. On the first occasion, Tiffany and I did product tasting in a little corner and some people bought because the child was cute. I called it the sympathy purchase. When she was not around, the products did not move as swiftly. It was the same in all the stores, and dust would sometimes settle on the bottles, which made the shopkeepers very annoyed.

A brand new food store called Fresh - The Good Food Market opened its doors on Malahide Road near the airport. This was swiftly followed by a branch in Smithfield and one in Grand Canal, near the newly constructed Dublin Docklands. This market was aimed at the yuppie 20-and 30-somethings. They were moving into newly constructed concrete and steel apartment buildings. I was fortunate to pass through the Good Food Market one day when one of the owners was there. I did some name dropping, since a manager at another store had told me they were opening up. I referred to him and a conversation we had.

As a result, I was able to get a large number of items into the Malahide store. I promised them product tastings, fliers and shelf talkers and chatted up Simon at the butcher's counter, persuading him to sell my sauces during Bar B Q season. He was a jovial ginger, who talked volumes of meaningless banter as he sold beef and pork. Simon asked me on a date to the cinema. I had to turn him down, but we both got a good laugh out of it. I went back at the weekend to deliver the products and place them on the shelves. I spent the day chatting with customers and doing product tasting. This time I took PooBee, who was bored at home. Simon tried to make a pass at PooBee, but she did not understand a word he said. He had to give up.

I went to every new branch of the Good Food Market. I asked to speak directly to the man in charge and gave him a list of the products that other branches had accepted. When they asked who had authorised this, I used the name of the owner, and was able to get a limited range of products into the various stores. I was probably mixing up their planograms (plans used by retail stores to place their products). However, when a store is new, there is some flexibility and I made the most of this. The hard part was driving around doing the merchandising: determining what sold, what did not sell, and how I could get the store to order more? It was too hard and I was buckling under the challenge.

I decided to go to the midlands and try my luck there. Rumour had it that a new fancy food shop had opened on Main Street in Tullamore. I went to have a chat with Fergus, the owner and placed a few products in the store. I did a product tasting and then moved on to the next challenge. I visited a few shops in Athlone, but no luck. Sean told me about a wonderful café and food store in Nenagh, County Tipperary. I passed through for a visit, left samples and a price list and promised to call again. The owner was away on holidays.

Next, I decided to tackle County Galway. There was a large independent supermarket in Galway, with a branch in the upscale neighbourhood of Knocknacarra and one in Creboy. I visited the country branch, but I reckoned it was too conservative for Caribbean food products. It was not easy to meet the managers, since everyone was too busy or away on business. In Galway city, McCambridge's in the town and Morton's in Salthill were the most likely targets, so I went for a visit.

The owner of Morton's, a relative to the folks in Dublin, was willing to try some of my products. I took in some of them and hoped they would sell. At that time, there was no motorway to the west. It was still under construction and I could not see myself trekking three or four hours to do a product tasting, I promised to send fliers and recipes to help customers figure out what to do with the sauces. The flavoured coffees and ginger teas were self explanatory.

After leaving samples with an assistant manager at McCambridge's, she went on vacation. The last I heard, she had broken a foot and had to go on leave. So I was out of pocket for my samples. I had to start all over again in negotiations with a newly hired manager, who had no clue about me or my products. As a small business, all this was really tiring and costly. I started to appreciate markets and festivals more and more. I could get ready cash on the spot. No credit, no bulk sales discount, just cash. One instructor at a business workshop told us: "Cash is King."

Sean was a source of unending information of which shop

would be a good bet and which would not. He frequented an amazing Asian food shop on the quays in Waterford City, buying numerous bottles of 'joy' to prepare amazing meals at home. He would frequently cook for me when I visited and he truly made the most wonderful meals. Surprisingly, Sean's tolerance for hot, spicy food was higher than mine.

I took samples of all my products to the Asian food store and spoke to Patel, an Indian man who was the owner. He was very kind and said he would try some of each. He had adventurous Irish customers who would visit frequently in search of foreign food. The store was a gold mine of ingredients from India, China, Thailand, and even the Caribbean. I was happy to sell my products there.

The owner asked me if I could source Brazilian food products, because there was a small Brazilian population in the Waterford area , looking to his store for food from their country. I confirmed that I could. In fact, I had no idea where to get Brazilian food and had to start looking. I combed Dublin magazines, newspapers and the internet and finally came across a Brazilian restaurant off Lower Camden Street. I set out there one morning with clip board and order sheets in hand.

The young woman who ran the business was a lively, talkative character. I thought I chat a lot, but she out talked me. She explained all her products and her pricing scheme, giving information about various regions of Brazil. She told me more than I could possibly imagine. I placed an order for products and she wanted to be paid right away. The products were expensive and I wondered how I could possibly make a profit reselling them to Patel. I added a few cents onto everything and hoped for the best. Realistically, if I had factored in my time to travel to Waterford, the price of petrol and the long wait to get my money, I was actually running a charity. I decided to display some of the Brazilian products at the Caribbean market stalls and hoped people would buy. Some people were still asking me if I was from Nigeria, so Brazil would add to the confusion of countries.

I went around Kilkenny City visiting a few shops and again a brilliant Asian food shop took some of my ginger teas. The owner was a shrewd Chinese trader who had been in the business for years. He asked why he should buy my products when he could get them from the UK for less. This was a fair question, to which I had no clear answer. I guess he just decided to help my business. I had set a goal of conquering 100 fancy food shops, with at least one in every county. My quest continued throughout the year, visiting new shops, negotiating with established stores and dealing with rejection. I had a few small successes along the way.

More Market Madness

At the same time, many markets and managers were coming out of the woodwork. The markets were either very good, or very, very bad. Everyone claimed to be a market manager. They would rent a site, print a flier, invite vendors, promise hundreds of buyers, and collect rent from the traders. It was a no brainer as a business enterprise, and promised quick income from unsuspecting traders. I was very gullible and tried many a new market, much to my detriment; wasting time and money.

One of the most interesting markets was a market introduced in Ballymun as part of the Ballymun regeneration project. The brand new buildings of the Ballymun Civic Centre housed health offices as well as other government offices. The city wanted to generate a buzz by inviting market traders to sell their goods right inside the foyer of the new building. Best of all, there was no fee and the budget was so good, they were able to pay a market manager. The first experiment worked; office staff came during their breaks to buy goods.

The following month, the organisers decided to put us outside. They created banners and charged a fee of €30 for the day. This was still reasonable by any standards. It was a stone's throw from my house, so I decided to set up a stand with pies and some curry lunches. I invested in containers and did vegetarian curry and rice. We had a small trickle of visitors throughout the day. Everything was fine until school was dismissed. Then we had the nightmare of fending off brats from all directions.

A group of 10 boys targeted my stand and I put on a brave face.

'Run along now,' I said to them.

'Miss, Miss, do you know Bob Marley?' they cried.

'Yeah. He's me brudder!'

They laughed hysterically and as I laughed with them, two or three went behind my back, stealing some of my Caribbean drinks. I only realised what had happened when I counted the stock at the end of the day.

As I worked feverishly to sell products at every market in Dublin, I also attended a number of agricultural shows and music festivals. I was advised by Vincent, a market colleague, to go online and check out all the agricultural shows, pick a few and sign up. I had nothing to lose and it was a way to get my business known outside of Dublin. I signed up for the Athlone Show in County Meath, Tinahely Show in Wexford, Tullamore Show in Offaly, The Iverk Show in County Kilkenny and also the Electric Picnic, which was one of the largest music festivals at the end of every summer. It was indeed a huge financial commitment to send off €200 or €300 here and there in application fees. However, nothing ventured, nothing gained. The first was the Athlone County Fair. People were friendly and curious enough to come around and buy products. I wondered what I was doing there selling Caribbean products, next to granny's best jam and the judging of the county's cows. However, it was a day out, a chance to interact with people in rural Ireland, and also an opportunity to make some money. I did not leave empty handed. Poor Tiffany had to endure the long day and we sometimes wandered away from the stand to see one or two of the other tents, which had various beautiful displays of crochet and handicrafts.

The agricultural shows always had rides and stalls selling sweets for the children, so Tiffany would usually find something she liked. I did not understand the judging of cattle, horses, dogs, sheep, or any other animals. It was amusing to see people strut around with the ribbons they had won. I heard that the Tinahely show was popular with Wicklow people, so I signed up and luckily got accepted. I tried to map out the journey to this remote site and found two ways to get there. There was a road through Tallaght and one through the countryside. The site was also accessible via the N11. I decided to go down the N11 on the way to the event and then come back home the other way for an adventure.

I invited my Caribbean friend, Pamela, to join us at the show. Pamela was teaching at one of the universities in Dublin, and like us did not have any family in Ireland. I thought it would be a good chance for her to see rural Ireland. Even though we had a two seater van, I imagined Tiffany and Pamela would be able to squeeze into the passenger side with little effort. The journey was only going to take an hour and a half. I was so wrong. It lashed rain, then the sun came out, then it got cold, and so it continued with no sign of letting up. When we finally found the show site, I checked in and got a map leading to my location. I was stuck between people selling dishes and others selling car mats. Just driving into the event, we had to pass a host of vendors trading large volumes of bric a brac: toys, T-shirts, hats, ceramic household goods, Tupperware, utensils and other stuff.

When the rain let up a little, Pamela and Tiffany went off to see a stall with snakes and then the dog obedience show. Many pooches were presented with their ribbons, and the proud owners strutted around for the rest of the day. It had rained so much that summer that rain gear was in style at the agricultural show. The ladies had the most exquisite rain coats and hats, with matching umbrellas and rain boots. The rain gear companies must have made a fortune. There was gear in every style: pink or purple, spotted or floral, paisley or plain. I wore a tie-dye Caribbean dress and got soaked to the bone. It was not the weather for tropical clothes. One or two Caribbean customers passed by with their Irish partners and they were very excited and surprised to see me. They promised to visit me at future events and I added them to an email contact list I kept to announce upcoming events where I would be trading. I sold teas, coffees, sauces, snack foods, and all my usual market fare. Of course, I was awake at 4am to prepare a hefty supply of aloo pies and saheena, so I would have snacks to sell. Nearby traders bought the snacks since it was a long trek up the hill to get food.

The income that day was mediocre, but I paid Pamela a token for taking time to help me and also for entertaining Tiffany. We had a dry sunny spell as soon as it was time to pack up. Then the rain came again, but this time with hail stones. We had seen it all: four seasons in one day. As we made the journey back to Dublin through country roads, it was a lot longer than what I saw on the map. We turned this way and that, following my worn out road map of Ireland. Why hadn't I just gone back on the N11? I was too tired for adventure and the other two were numb with tiredness. It took us almost three hours to find our way out to Tallaght on the N80. Getting onto the M50 was indeed a joyful moment.

I asked Pamela how I should get to Goatstown, where she lived. Although she had bought a car and taken the Irish driving test, she had no clue how to navigate the roads of Dublin. There must have been a faster way to get to Goatstown. She did not know the way. By then, I was too tired for exploration at night. I drove the long way around, which I knew. In total, it took a full four hours to drive home from the Tinahely Show. Needless to say, I collapsed into my bed without unloading the van. There was enough time for that the following day.

Sean had told me about the Iverk Show, a small agricultural show in South Kilkenny. According to him, all Waterford's wealthy farmers loved to go to that one and I could probably make money. I asked Paul to help me for this event and he came the day before to assist in the frying of saheena, aloo pies and a new item, beef pies. They were made with a spicy minced beef filling. I had run out of ingredients and had to go and buy more. Then I had to go to collect Tiffany from school. I was happy to have Paul to help and he liked to cook.

The next morning, a Thursday, we left early for the event. The Iverk Show was always on a Thursday. I was sure no-one would come to a show on a weekday, but the traffic entering the grounds was unbelievable, even though we were early. We parked behind the food tent and unloaded our food. There were so many tents, all hosting the usual county competitions: the best baking, the best jam, the best knitting, sale of work, art and craft, needle point. The food tent had a mix of bread stalls, cheeses, jams and chutneys, and my Caribbean fare.

'What's that yoke?' people asked. 'I'll have one for a laugh.'

I put out crackers and bowls of sauces for tasting and people ate heartily.

'I like that one. I don't like that one,' they exclaimed. 'Ooooh, nasty. I like that one".

"Would you like to buy the ones you like?' I said.

I had to be assertive with the tasting crowd. They would taste you out of house and home and not buy. Paul and I wore colourful clothes and the event photographer took our picture for the show's website. He gave me the web address so I could check it out when it was posted up. Sean came to the show after work to visit and see how we were progressing. It was only 20 minutes from his house.

'Please stay over after the show, baby,' he begged.

'No I can't. Tiffany is with a baby sitter in Dublin and I have to take Paul back home anyway'.

A few of Sean's friends passed by to see me and purchased goodies in support. This was nice of them.

The Public Health Inspectors of Waterford City were responsible for checking on food vendors at this event. They were notorious for having more extensive requirements than in other counties. Since I started my business and registered with the Public Health Office in Dublin, I had traded without trouble for a long time. That luck was to change at the Iverk Show. I watched as the inspectors confiscated cheeses at the stall next to mine.

'You can't put out cheeses in this hot tent all day long,' they told the owner.

The poor girl had to remove all her cheeses. This did not make sense. They were hard cheeses and hard cheeses were sold at markets all over Europe. This was not true for

Waterford city, where they made their own rules. The next victim was Mary, who sold bread, olives and salads on the opposite side of the food tent. They told her to put away this and that and she argued and argued about what she usually did every week at farmer's markets. She put away the items and as soon as the inspector left, she took them back out. They next came to my stand and I smiled as sweetly as I could. But it cut no ice.

'You have product in boxes that are not chilled,' they said. 'You have beef pies at room temperature. That is a hazard and we will have to throw them away.'

They then went on to the potato pies and then the spinach and onion fritters. They decided that they did not recognise any of these products as food. They asked if I had garbage bags. I said no. That was a problem too. Why would I have garbage bags to throw away product? I had taken hours and hours to make them. In addition, I had to pay a helper to get the work done. When they left, I called Sean, who had been browsing. He met me at my van. I wept and wept. I blew my nose in his shirt while he tried to console me. Sean didn't mind. I was his baby.

'At least you were able to sell a few of the pies in the morning,' he said. 'You'll be all right'.

I had left Paul at the booth to rearrange everything, so I needed to return. I calmed down and returned with renewed energy to sell Caribbean aprons, potholders, cookbooks, and other bric a brac, which had so far served as decoration. We continued selling until the end of the show.

Awards Season

My first award in Ireland was one that I had to buy: the

Bridgestone Award. Everyone who was given the honour of a place in the coveted Bridgestone Food Guide of Ireland happily put out the money for the heavy metal plaque and the opportunity to advertise in the guide. I was featured alongside restaurants, guest houses, and other market traders. I got the award for innovation and introducing new products to Ireland. John and Sally McKenna, the creators of the guide, combed the markets and food shows spotting new talent. I was not even aware of who they were when they passed my stand. But I had become very skilled at explaining the virtues of all the products on offer. Paul had the gift of the gab too. No matter which of us they had spoken to, they got a great answer. Chicken was more concerned about making sure the display was neat. He did not call out to people, shout at them or engage in meaningless banter. He had a more serious character.

I won my next award at the Women's Business Network of the Dublin City Enterprise Board (DCEB). It was the Female Rising Star Entrepreneur Award. Every year, applications were sent out to members of the business network to get nominations. A few colleagues urged me to apply, so I did. I remember rushing to the podium to collect my Oscar, a framed certificate, and being absolutely speechless. My photo appeared in newspapers and on the DCEB website. This was a bonus for business.

8

RIDING THE LOVE ROLLERCOASTER

Sean's 50th Birthday Party

In August 2007, the love of my life was due to celebrate a milestone, his 50th birthday. We tried to decide what we should do to celebrate this great milestone. He knew he wanted to do it in style, but was not sure exactly what to do. I volunteered to cater and planned a massive event at his home. We would use my gazebos and fold up tables. Sean's friend Colm also had a massive gazebo. Rain was certain, no matter the month. Even if it was a dry night, the tents wouldn't go to waste. We decided on a Hawaiian party theme and looked at party decorations and outfits for the party. At that time, Ireland did not seem to have stores dedicated to theme parties. These businesses were to come in later years. We were limited to ordering decorations and costumes from the UK. We ordered garlands, grass skirts, coconut shells and other paraphernalia to create a luau atmosphere. In addition, I always had a stash of decorations from house parties I threw when I lived in the US. I also owned an authentic Hawaiian grass skirt, which I had purchased on a past business trip to Honolulu.

Sean bought a blue and white floral shirt and a straw hat, and was ready for the event. He sent out invitations to neighbours, cousins, old Waterford friends, work colleagues, and friends from his old boarding school. He was very excited to see friends from boarding school, since many of them would be turning 50 that year and were having parties. We planned the menu and used my membership at Musgrave's Cash and Carry to buy volumes of food for the party. We may have overdone the shopping, but we spared no expense on olives, cheeses, wine, meat, fish, and ingredients to prepare the feast. We decided that instead of buying cakes, we would make them from scratch.

Sean's half sister, Oonagh and her family were visiting from America that summer. She was one of his father's daughters from a first marriage. When her mother died, Sean's father had married Geraldine who adopted the girls. Oonagh was celebrating her 60th birthday, so it was going to be a double celebration. There were so many visitors staying at the house. Among them were Sean's children, Tiffany and I, my Caribbean friend Pamela from Dublin, Sean's cousin and his daughter. Peter, Sean's friend from boarding school, was also staying over for two nights. To say we had a full house was an understatement. Sean wasn't worried about feeding the tribe. He left me in charge of the kitchen and invited his children's friends, the triplets, to stay over too.

I started preparing the meal for the birthday dinner the day before, cooking and refrigerating anything that could be made in advance. With so many children to feed, I also had the task of setting the table, serving the food, and clearing up after them. I cooked for at least 14 hours. Tiffany and Nuala made two birthday cakes and started to ice them. Sean's relatives came by and asked to help, but we did not have spatulas.

'How can you ice a cake without spatulas? Why are you using knives?' they asked.

At that point, my nerves were frazzled.

'Go sit in the living room,' I said to one. 'Here's a cup of tea".

The last thing I needed was instructions on which kitchen implement to use when we were running out of time. This was a bachelor's kitchen and we used whatever was available. By nightfall, I was extremely short tempered and snapped at anyone who came close. I had to ask two neighbours to store food in their refrigerators for the following day. We had run out of space.

In the middle of all of this, family and friends came to visit to see how preparations were going. I told Sean I could not fix cups of tea. He would have to entertain the visitors. There was too much work to be done. His friend Eoin came to help and I left the lads to work on erecting the gazebos, putting out tables and chairs and helping the brood of children to decorate the gazebos.

'She's a bossy woman', Eoin said. 'I don't like her'.

I didn't like him either; moody and brooding all the time. As far as I was concerned, if he was not helping, he could go home. Sean's old boarding school mate, Peter, arrived that night. He was a short, skinny man with balding brown hair, a moustache and long nose. He wore a bowler hat and looked around with beady eyes. As I cooked frantically, I played Techno music to keep me going. It stopped my tired knees from buckling. Peter decided that he did not like that music and he would change the radio station. I asked Sean to kindly take 'yer man' away somewhere so I could do my work in peace.

'She doesn't need to listen to that crap,' said Peter. 'Let me find another radio station.'

I wondered why he didn't just go to bed. It was late. But it turned out he didn't sleep much. It was my lucky night.

By midnight I had to stop. The only tasks remaining were to make salads, bake the humongous salmon, and put everything outside. We had too many hors d'oeuvres and crisps. Of course I had to make saheena and aloo pies for good measure. The guests would probably have been full on appetisers alone, but I didn't care. I wanted Sean to have the best feast ever for his birthday.

The next morning, we were able to relax. It felt good to have most of the work done in advance. And of course, it poured out of the heavens: Would we ever get a break? Some of the paper decorations got wet, which was unfortunate. We went to the train station to meet Pamela and go to the Tower Hotel for a spell before returning to lay everything out for the party.

Pamela was a bit cautious when dealing with the Irish. She had suffered intense bullying at her job in Dublin and had had a nervous breakdown. She thought I was very brave to go out with Sean, to stay in his 19th century stone house, and to socialise with his friends. But in my world, everyone was the same until proven otherwise. Poor Pamela's eyes were bulging with wonder and amazement at everything and nothing. When we got to the house, she was assigned the little bedroom which Tiffany usually occupied. Tiffany was sharing with Nuala, Sean's daughter.

We covered the tables with our plastic Hawaiian table cloths and laid out the appetisers, serving utensils, glasses, drinks, Hawaiian plates and all the other themed table ware and decorations. Then we hung up garlands of flowers and balloons. The gazebos looked smashing. Sean set up the stereo and speakers. I hoped it would be loud enough. I had been thinking so much about food and decorations, music had not made an appearance on my checklist. Sean took care of the booze. An Irish party could never have enough alcohol. We dedicated a whole gazebo to a table of alcohol and other drinks.

I wore a floral bathing suit and tied on my authentic Hawaiian grass skirt. Tiffany and Nuala wore children's grass skirts and coconut bra tops. Then we waited for guests to arrive. We had said 6:30pm, but that was wishful thinking. The first family arrived from the house opposite at 7pm. The kids were dressed in Hawaiian costumes, and even the youngest child sported his coconut shells. He was cute as a button. They had kept a lot of the food for us in their refrigerator, so it was good that they were early; then I could start to heat sauces, rice dishes, and meats.

By 7:30pm, friends started trickling in and at 8pm we had many guests. Brooding Eoin did not observe the dress code and wore a three piece suit. Most other guests were casually dressed. Tiffany and Nuala were assigned the duty of placing garlands around the necks of arriving guests, and greeting them with "Aloha!"

Cillian, Sean's old childhood friend from Waterford, made himself the designated DJ and controlled the stereo. He played mostly what he liked as he chugged beer, Guinness and other libations. Everyone drank happily and drank plenty. I announced that dinner was served. I was a nervous wreck, as I took heated food out of the oven, removed empty trays and replaced them with full ones.

Just when we thought everyone had come, one of Sean's cousins arrived with Sean's mother, Geraldine. He had not really invited her to the party, but his cousin thought it fit to bring her. Geraldine was very ill at this time and needed assistance to walk in. She was delighted to be there and people brought her food and then dessert.

'Lindy made all this food,' they told her. 'She made the cake too'.

'It's delicious,' said Ger. 'It's the best cake I've tasted. I really like this cake.'

At one stage, as the music blared, Ger rose from her chair, put her walking stick in the air and did a little jiggle. It was funny to watch, and I felt happy the poor old soul could come out to enjoy her son's 50th birthday. It must have been one of life's happiest moments for her. Sean's brother, his wife and two adult children were also at the party. They praised me repeatedly for the good job I had done in preparing such a feast. They said he was lucky to have me and I was special.

As everyone got drunker, a few rows broke out over the music choices and I had my own bone to pick. I wanted to hear Caribbean music, Sean wanted to hear Gypsy Kings and everyone else had requests. But Cillian played what he wanted to hear. I was allowed two songs and I got everyone to dance the limbo under a decorated broom stick. It was good fun. When I attempted to do the limbo an hour later, Sean objected and I went to a corner to sulk. I had spent 14 hours cooking and I couldn't even get a song in. That was wrong and I would let him know about it.

Then came the time for birthday cake, speeches and acknowledgments and the music was turned down. We sang Happy Birthday for Sean, and he cut his cake. Then we sang Happy Birthday for his sister and she cut her cake. I stood in a corner near Sean, eating my cake and relaxing. The meal was a success and I could finally exhale.

'Speech! Speech', everyone yelled. 'Let's hear what you have to say.'

Sean started by thanking all his friends and family, who had come out that night to celebrate with him. He thanked his old mates from boarding school, his mother and his family from the States. Then, to my horror, he thanked his ex-wife who could not be there that night, because she had gone to visit friends in Connemara. Were my ears deceiving me? Where was I on the list of acknowledgements, having spent 14 hours on my feet cooking and at least three weeks preparing for the event? I felt hurt and dejected. Sean was performing like a puppet for his friends as usual and being politically correct because they all knew his ex-wife. Mary's warnings about dating separated Irish men came back to haunt me just at that moment. I had been with him for almost three years, but this did not seem to matter.

Finally, Sean thanked me for preparing all the food and helping to put together the party and everyone cheered. The crowd continued to drink, and since the music was not to my taste, I settled on a sofa and chatted to a few people. Sean had bought a new living room suite and carpets. He was creating a lovely home for himself. It became apparent that he was not preparing to include others in his home. He said one day that he would create an en-suite bathroom out of one of the his- and hers-closets in his master bedroom. I should have walked away at that point, but I was blinded by 'love'.

A brawl started between moody Eoin and Sean's brother. They were both artists and both very drunk by 2am. The brother's family then became part of the argument. I was too tired to care and decided to go to bed. Most of the guests were filing out and the die-hard drinkers weren't going to leave.

'Baby, stay and party with me,' Sean pleaded.

'Sean, you're too drunk. Entertain the rest of the guests, I'm going to bed.'

Cillian had to be torn away from the stereo. He was too smashed to know what music he was playing and Sean wanted to select his own music. Eventually, Sean told a handful of guests who were still there to let themselves out. Apparently, the argument between Eoin and the brother's family had not ended. It was going to come to blows. Eoin kept knocking on our bedroom door, telling Sean he was afraid to walk home because 'they' were out there waiting to beat him up. Sean went out to calm down the arguing factions, trying to make peace and send everyone home. The brother and his family were waiting for a taxi to get back into Waterford City. Nobody was sober enough to drive.

They had a lot of time on their hands and enough drink in them to fight everybody.

Eoin came back and knocked frantically on the bedroom door.

'They're going to beat me up! They're going to beat me up!'

I wished they would get on with it. He was such a coward, and he was disturbing my sleep. He obviously had no regard for us. We were tired and just wanted to get some rest. Sean had to crawl out of bed to see what was happening and I had no idea when he returned.

We were awoken at 7am next morning by the sound of bottles being thrown into bags, and the driveway being swept up. It was Sean's old boarding school friend Peter, who could never sleep and had decided to clean up the mountain of mess. While we were happy for the help, we did not imagine having to wake up so early. Sean had a hangover and every bone in my body ached. As the noise grew louder, we had no choice but to get up and get moving.

Sean went out to tackle the yard with Peter, and I was designated chef. I decided to make ham, eggs and toast. I scrambled a dozen eggs and opened a pack of sliced ham, and it still did not look like enough, since we had kids, visitors and others who had slept over. I had to make more of everything. With so many hands on board, we were able to clear up everything, then take Peter and Pamela to the train station in Waterford City. When all the visitors had left, we could finally sit down, relax, and open all the birthday gifts. This was one of my favourite activities. We spoke about the event for hours and hours. Sean's 50th must have been the biggest event in Tramore that night. We wondered if Moody Eoin ever made it home in one piece.

Holidays and Trips

For Easter vacation, Sean and I decided to go for a four day weekend to Westport, County Mayo. Tiffany was coming with us, so we decided to rent an apartment. We settled on a self contained holiday apartment on the outskirts of the town centre of Westport. We took some groceries, and planned to purchase fresh fruit and vegetables when we got there. Sean drove to Dublin to meet us, then we left early next morning for the four and a half hour drive to Westport.

The town was buzzing with activity, as Easter was the beginning of the tourist season for this area. We walked around and admired the many cafes and restaurants and visited a fancy food shop that looked like a good prospect for my range of products. I had not thought about doing sales in Westport. We met the store owner, who chatted for half an hour non-stop with us about the virtues of good packaging. I looked at the ingredients of some of the UK brands that were stocked in this store and many similar shops around the country, and the detail was in the packaging. These products contained many preservatives, colour compounds, extenders, bulking agents, sugar, high fructose corn syrup, and saturated fats, but nobody cared.

One morning, we rose early with the goal of climbing Croagh Patrick. I had heard about this mountain since moving to Ireland. Faithful Catholics used to do an annual pilgrimage to Croagh Patrick and some even climbed on their knees as penance. I was not doing any penance. For me, the climb would be penance enough, since I was not athletic. We started the climb with a few sandwiches and snacks. We also brought bottles of water for the climb. I had heard there was no form of refreshment along the way to the top, so we had to bring everything. It could take the average climber one and a half hours. However I was in no hurry to climb to the top, I wanted to take in everything.

As we set off, Sean assured me that he would not be waiting; he had done it before and wanted to get to the top quickly. Since, I could never keep up with his pace, I told him to go ahead; it was no race. He was being very childish and I had no patience with his behaviour that day. I asked Tiffany to stay at my side since we had not been there before and I didn't want her to be snatched away. We were warned to bring enough gear for four seasons in one day. It was a timely warning. It was fairly chilly as we set off. There was a bit of fog and we could not see the top of the mountain. Many others had decided to start early for the climb as well, so we had some company, but it was not crowded.

The paths were rocky in some areas, and we had to jump over small gaps along the way. However, the ascent was gradual, making the hike very pleasant. We chatted with families as they passed us and sat down to have a little picnic when we needed a rest. What was most exciting was to look back and see the islands in Clew Bay. They seemed to change colour as we ascended the mountain. As the fog burned off, it became very hot. The sun cut into the rocks and my skin. I had to take off most of my layers.

We came to a plateau on the ridge where the walk was level. There was an old set of toilets and the ruins of a stone structure. By that time, Clew Bay was out of sight and we were looking at the fields at the back of the mountain. The rolling hills and plains went on for miles and the beautiful shades of green made the view equally impressive and calming. After our second rest, we continued to another area that was considered the most difficult part of the climb. The top of the hill consisted of large sharp rocks. I had no idea where to pass. I followed a few different people, just looking to the top, the final goal of this journey. We had purchased carved walking sticks that were supposed to help us balance when climbing up the hill and walking back down.

By the time we were making our final ascent, Sean had already reached the summit. He kept sending messages through people who were going back down, that I should have courage and soon I would be there. Total strangers were coming up to me and saying: "Sean said good luck. Keep climbing." He could have stayed with me and told me everything himself. I was really annoyed with him.

When we finally reached the top, it started to snow. I had to put back on every layer of clothing. It was dark and overcast. We could barely recognise the islands in Clew Bay and the back of the mountain was obscured by fog. We walked around the little church at the summit. There was really nothing to do but observe the tourists who had made it to the top. We chatted with people, asked where they had come from, and took some photographs. I had forgotten my camera, so I had to make do with some blurry shots on my mobile phone. However, the memory of this climb was etched in my mind forever.

We had taken three hours to climb to the summit. Before I could celebrate too long with Sean, he decided to hike back down the hill. Of course he was not waiting for me. Tiffany decided that I was too slow as well. She said she would hike down the hill with Sean and reach the bottom before me. I told them to go ahead. I used the time walking downhill for meditation and reflection. One hiker told me to use the stick to guide me and meditate as I walked. I paused again to take in the beauty of the surroundings. I was able to take in the panoramic view of Clew Bay, studded with its 365 islets. . It was a welcome reward after such a strenuous climb. When I finally got to the parking lot, Sean and Tiffany presented me with a certificate from the gift shop that said:

'This Certificate is presented to Lindy James for climbing to the top of Croagh Patrick'.

It was a lovely gesture and I decided to keep it, along with my other Irish tourist certificates.

We drove back to Dublin by a long scenic route, travelling south to Connemara via Doolough and Leenane. On the way, we passed through Doolough Valley to see the famine monument. The valley was deserted and bare. All we saw were the mountains and lakes. Not a living soul was visible for miles around. Ireland had such a rich history. Through Sean's eyes, I began to love the country more and more.

Aran Islands Revisited

In the autumn, we decided to visit the Aran Islands once more. This time, we planned to take Nuala and Tiffany, so they could enjoy the clean fresh air and see an amazing part of Ireland. We booked tickets on the tiny airbus that flew back and forth to the island. Tiffany and I had spent a day in Tramore and we were to drive in Sean's car the next day to Galway. The night before we left, Nuala's mother decided that she should not go, because her uncle was driving down the next day from Galway with his wife and newborn baby. Nuala absolutely had to see the baby or she might not see them again. What an excuse to destroy a well thought out holiday with the kids. Sean was agonising over the whole prospect of not being able to take Nuala on the trip, and I was shocked at the crazy woman who was obviously grasping at straws to hold his attention.

Eventually, they reached a compromise. We could meet the brother at some point along the way so Nuala could see the baby. Sean agreed to this idea reluctantly, wanting to keep the peace with everyone. I had hoped that by now, everyone and their brother knew that Sean was dating a Caribbean woman. The brother must have been told. Now he could see me for himself, if Sean would allow the scrutiny. We left Tramore early next morning for the long drive to Galway. In the end, we did not stop on the way to meet the brother and his new born baby. Apparently, they now planned to drive down another weekend to visit relatives in Tramore. It was amazing how easily Sean became distressed by incidents like these. He could be pulled back and forth like a puppet. I found it sad to watch, even though I was an outside observer in his family's antics. He was a good, kind man.

The long drive to Galway was fun and we stopped on the way in a little village called Gort in County Galway, where many Brazilian lived and owned shops. I learned that many Brazilians had immigrated to the area to work at meat processing plants. Who would have thought County Galway would be full of Brazilians.

When we got to the Connemara Airport in Inver, we went to check in. There was a limit to the amount of luggage one could carry and the plane could seat no more than seven people. After getting weighed in, as if we were participating in some competition, seats were assigned. I got to sit next to the pilot because I was the same weight as he was. Poor Tiffany was placed in the back and was not very happy.

'That's not fair, Mommy!' she moaned. 'How come you get to sit with the pilot?'

I asked the pilot if he needed assistance during the 10 minute flight over to Irishmaan. He laughed heartily and Sean kept a close eye on the proceedings from the back. We landed in the little airport and then had to find a way up to our favourite cottage, which we had booked weeks in advance. Not a soul was in sight. But the one worker who was in the airport said he knew the cottage, he knew the owner, and he knew the cousin who had a van. He rang up the cousin, who came swiftly with his van to taxi us to the cottage. Thank God he was available. It would have been a long hike that evening with two moaning children, after travelling so many hours from Tramore.

We unloaded our bags, asked him to come back for us when we were leaving in four days and got some more info on what was open and what wasn't. The key was under the mat. This time it was easy to get in. The children loved the cottage. It was like a fairy tale. They ran around, exploring every room; upstairs, downstairs, choosing beds in the loft. They loved the quaint bathroom which had a vintage bathtub. It was a happy scene, which was to last a mere 15 minutes, until they discovered the TV only had four stations and it was black and white.

'Oh no! What will we do without TV?' they exclaimed. 'That's not fair. You've brought us to a place without TV.'

'Well', Sean said in his wisest tone, 'That's why it's called a vacation. We are getting away from everything. We can play cards, board games, read magazines and talk.'

And those girls prattled into the wee hours of the morning while we snuggled in bed. It was our favourite bed, in our favourite cottage, on our favourite island of Inishmaan. Who could ask for more?

The next morning, we set out to explore the island. There was a friendly donkey in an open enclosure as we walked down the hill, so we said hello to him. We picked tiny flowers that were still growing between the rocks, and we found what turned out to be the only supermarket for miles around, They sold only one brand of flour, and one brand of margarine. We bought eggs, cheese, bread, and a few items to make supper.

We had spotted a sign advertising bike rentals while we were driving uphill the previous evening. When we went back to enquire, we knocked on the door and it opened, but no one was there. There was no chance of bandits on the island. Perhaps everyone knew everyone else. We visited the house next door and the woman said "He's out, he'll be back soon." We decided to walk down to the pier and look at the curragh boats. The tide was out so we were able to walk onto the tiny beach. We peeped into little buildings on the shore. There were a few abandoned holiday homes.

We then decided to go back to Mr. Bike Rental and thankfully he had returned. We all got bicycles and rode around the island, uphill and downhill. We saw no-one else on our travels. We rode across to the side with the airport to see if we could find our beautiful little beach which we visited the year before. We had to park the bikes and walk through some sand dunes. Eventually we came across our beach. Sean and I hugged, but we had to be careful of the roving eyes of children and be on our best behaviour. It was getting late and the crew would be hungry soon, so I suggested going back to the cottage for dinner amid protests from the children.

'We can always come back out after dinner,' I promised them.

I cooked chicken, potatoes and vegetables for supper. Afterwards, we went back down the hill to explore a pre-historic fort that we had seen along the way. It had a large central area and sturdy walls made of stone that you could find all over the rocky island. We had to hike up a hill to get to the fort. I complained about hiking and Sean was losing his patience.

'You'll love it when you get there,' he said.

I guessed I would if he said so, and kept hiking. It was really a spectacular sight and from the top of the walls, you could look out to the ocean. We walked around the fort wall and played games. The children played hide and seek until it started to get dark.

'Time to leave', I said. 'I do not want to be stuck up here in the dark.'

We climbed down the hill and eventually reached the main track. We went to visit the pub where we had met the strange man who stared at me the previous year. The pub was empty. We ordered juices and took a look around. The walls were full of photographs of years gone by, a few paintings and bric-a-brac. We sat around for a short while and then decided to go home. No adventures this time with the locals.

After three days of exploring the island, it was time to go home. During the long drive home, the children slept. They were tired from hiking and riding bicycles all weekend.

Trip to West Cork

My exploration of Ireland continued when Sean asked me to come with him for an overnight stay while he visited a client in West Cork. I could not pass up this opportunity. We set off early in the morning and after bypassing Cork city, we took another road towards Clonakilty. We walked around, exploring the town's fancy food shops. I toyed with the idea of trading at some of these shops. I took contact details at one market place and explored some more shops. Sean bought me a signed print of Freddie Mercury.

We then drove on to Skiberreen and explored some of their little shops. Even the Supervalu stores in Clonakilty and Skibbereen had exotic food that you would never see in the average Supervalu around Ireland. The palate of West Cork was indeed different. I heard quite a few British accents and learned that there was a boating community that loved to eat foreign foods. It seemed like the ideal spot for me to do sales. The fuchsia flower was used as the symbol for West Cork and every town was announced by a big sign with an image of a fuchsia and the name of the town. Fuchsia grew wild in this area, pink, purple, red, white, and a combination of colours. West Cork was another very beautiful part of Ireland and felt more tropical than other areas, with many tiny islands off the coast. We drove all the way to Ballydehob, so we could see all the little villages along the way and check out the cafes in each town.

We had a reservation at the Islander's Rest hotel on Sherkin Island, so eventually, we drove south along a country road until we came to Baltimore. It looked like a fishing village, but there were quite a few pubs and restaurants, so it was the ideal holiday village too. A few little islands could be seen very close to the mainland and small ferries were in operation, taking holiday makers across the bay. While we waited for the ferry, we walked around the quaint village, admiring its colourful houses and pubs. The refurbished Baltimore Castle caught my attention. When I read the sign outside I absolutely had to go in for a visit. It was bought by the McCarthy family. My Granny was a McCarthy, so I had to visit my namesake's house.

I chatted with the girl at the entrance and signed my name. She was the daughter of the owners and I told her I was a McCarthy and had come to claim my heritage. She looked at me as if I were mad but said that it was an interesting idea. They were always happy to see long lost cousins and I should have a look around. Sean didn't bother to come in; he went off to have a beer. He was not fascinated with castles the way I was. I walked upstairs and downstairs. The owners had done an admirable job, putting in flooring and using antiques to recreate a beautiful castle. From the photographs on the walls, the castle had been in ruins when it was purchased.

I bid my cousins farewell and went out to get the ferry. As we boarded the ferry, we saw an Irish television celebrity getting off. We figured Sherkin Island was popular with celebrities. We unloaded our bags and walked up the track to the Islander's Rest Hotel. It was a basic hotel with no real interesting features, so we went downstairs to explore the garden and paths around the island. The pub had interesting old photos and paintings and the yard was decorated with installations, and pretty evergreen plants. Sean remembered a good restaurant near the hotel. We walked up the track to find this place and sat out on the patio to have dinner.

After dinner, we walked down the track, looking at old farm homes, modern holiday homes and a hippy style art store that sold wind chimes and other bric a brac. We chatted for a while with the owner and found out about a beach we could walk to, but it was a bit of a hike. We walked along the dirt road until we came to a small sign that said Beach. We followed this path a good way into the undergrowth. Eventually, it opened onto a little beach, with smooth stones and some patches of sand. We wanted to claim this beach for ourselves, just like our romantic beach in Irishman. However, another couple also had the same idea, so we were not alone. We said a quick hello and walked knee deep in water near the shore. The water was cold but still refreshing. This island had more vegetation than Irishman and a very tropical feel with the lush evergreens.

The next morning, we went for a swim at our little beach and afterwards, we checked out of the hotel, returning by ferry to the mainland. On the drive back to Tramore, we stopped to visit art shops in Clonakilty and had a chat with some of the artists. When Sean went to his appointment, I took the opportunity to browse and window shop. It was a very relaxing break from work.

Ireland Comes to Trinidad

Sean decided to come with me to Trinidad for the Christmas holidays. He insisted that he would do his duty and attend

Christmas dinner at the ex-wife's home on Christmas Day "for the children's sake", then he would fly out on St Stephen's Day. That was fine with me. We would have almost 10 days in Trinidad for fun and adventure. Sean had not been to my country before and I welcomed the opportunity to show him some of the sights. We were also celebrating my mother's 75th birthday, so it was a grand family occasion.

My sister, Colette, who was also on holidays in Trinidad, came with me to the airport to collect Sean, who had endured a long flight, with stopovers in London and Barbados. All he wanted to do was go to a beach, strip and get into the water. We could not convince him that it was night time and we were not close to any beaches at the airport. We decided to take him for a dip at Dean's Bay, Carenage. This was a place we would never go because the water in the Gulf was supposedly polluted and the sand underfoot was muddy from the silt deposited by rivers. Luckily, the changing rooms were open. Sean stripped and ran into the sea while we sat watching him in amazement. When he had had his dip in the dark, he changed and returned to the car refreshed and ready for a night out.

We stopped at Don's roti shop for a beer and some rotis, or curry wraps. We would usually pick up rotis and drive away. It was not somewhere people of our background would want to hang out. But this idea was foreign to Sean. When he saw a man fall over from drunkenness, he said he felt right at home. My God, I thought, I was going to have an interesting time keeping an eye on Sean in Trinidad.

Over the next few days, we took him to the really pretty beaches and some of the many classy pubs and bars. Sean felt very insulted when he was turned away from a pub on Aripitia Avenue, one of Port of Spain's trendiest streets. They had a strict dress code. Sean argued with the bouncers but they would not let him in. We had to go to a more casual bar down the street and Colette and I had to listen to his moaning for hours.

Sean looked visibly uncomfortable being around so many black people and he tried to keep a brave face. It was amusing that every time he saw a white person, he would engage them in conversation and then ask them if they were from Ireland. We took him to a big pre-Carnival party, which was held in a very wealthy neighbourhood, with huge mansions everywhere. He protested saying it was unfair that so many people could splurge on wealthy mansions and fancy cars when there was poverty in the world. I wondered which country did not have rich and poor.

'Where are you from,' Sean asked another party guest, who could have passed for Irish.

'Right here,' the man said, in a strong Trinidadian accent.

'Well where are your parents from?'

'Right here, man'.

I felt a bit embarrassed by Sean's behaviour when he saw a red head dancing in the crowd and asked her if she was Irish. She was actually a British tourist visiting her Trinidadian friends.

Sean finally settled down when we flew to Tobago for a few days and stayed in a hotel. He could have the comfort of an air conditioned room, which was not available at my mother's house, and the mosquitoes gave him a break. His skin was polka dotted from the mosquitoes at my mother's home, since they liked to feast on fresh blood. In Tobago, the tourist island of Trinidad and Tobago. Sean saw many German tourists and others from Europe. He felt easier around his own kind.

We rented a car and travelled all around the island, beach-hopping and eating. We visited my father's cousin, Phyllis. Both she and her husband were retired and all their friends were retired. They would throw weekly lavish parties at their home which had fruit trees in the garden. My father was also visiting Phyllis at that time and he had an opportunity to socialize with Sean. We ate, drank and drank some more.

When we returned to the hotel, my heart was heavy, because I was leaving my sweetheart all alone in Tobago. I had to go back to Trinidad and pack up my things, since my flight left from Trinidad. Sean would have two extra days in Tobago and his return flight to London left from Tobago. I was anxious about leaving him on his own. He was 50 years old, but I felt as if he was my child. We hugged and kissed for a long time. I did not want to let go. Eventually, I managed to pull myself away and boarded the ferry back to Trinidad, looking longingly at the shore.

Looking for a House

I was so in love with Sean and I assumed he was in love with me. I decided this was the ideal time to buy a house in Tramore. I loved the coast in the summer time. It reminded me of the Caribbean. I thought that rather than driving long distances to see each other, the best solution would be to move. I would be near to my sweet heart all the time.

One night, Sean went out for a reunion dinner with his boarding school friends in Dublin. These were always drink fests. When he returned to my house from the party, I was awoken by the sound of pebbles being thrown at my bedroom window.

'Lindy. Oh Liiiiiiindeeeeeee'.

'Man. What are you doing?'

I ran downstairs and let him in before he disturbed PooBee and all the neighbours. He staggered into the bedroom with a big smile on his face. He stripped and headed for the wardrobe, thinking it was the toilet. Thank goodness I was wide awake and vigilant.

'Come this way, you silly man'!

He held one hand on his chest, imitating Napoleon Bonaparte. I chose that moment to ask him how he would feel about my moving to Tramore.

'I'd be delighted,' he beamed.

The next morning, when he was sober, I said.

'You have to help me look for a home.'

'Uh, what? Oh, Oh yes. You mentioned that. Oh yes.'

He promised to look around the neighbourhoods in Tramore and get back to me. I looked on Daft.ie and Myhome.ie and put together a list of places to view during my next visit to Tramore the following weekend.

Tiffany, Nuala and Seam came with me to the viewings. At Moonvoy Landing, near the racecourse, we saw a large, modern four bedroom home. It was almost new and selling for a fraction of the price of houses in Dublin. We visited a seven bedroom house on Lower Branch Road. This 19th century residence was ideal for a Bed and Breakfast business. Upstairs and downstairs we tramped; around and around. Too much work, I decided. It would be a monster to maintain. It had been on the market for many months too, so nobody wanted it.

We then visited a 19th century home on Upper Branch Road. It was at the end of a terrace of five houses. As soon as I walked in, I loved this house. I felt an instant jolt, as if struck by lightning. I also developed an instant headache and a strange, overwhelming feeling. The house had 10 foot high ceiling, with coving and polished wooden floors. There were three working fireplaces with a marble fireplace in the main bedroom. The kitchen had large flag stones on the floor. The banister of the staircase leading upstairs was made of beautiful varnished wood. All the rectangular Georgian windows had the original wooden shutters which closed with large metal clasps.

This house was the most beautiful we had seen that day, with so much character. From every room, we had an unobstructed view of Tramore Bay. No trees or houses would ever block that view because the other side of the street was actually the back yard of a terrace of houses on another level. The four of us ran up and down the stairs. The attic was converted into a massive lounge or family room spanning the full width and depth of the house. Its skylight windows let in light all day and could open to let in fresh air. The back yard was terraced into three levels. The lower level had flag stones and as one went up the steps to the second level, there were gooseberry bushes. On the top level, there was a huge apple tree and a shed as big as a bedroom, which stored garden supplies and other bric a brac.

Nuala and Tiffany screamed with delight. Nuala said her mother had bought a new house down the street for a lot more money than mine, and it was not half as beautiful. I told the agent we all liked the house and we would be making an offer. In typical agent fashion, she said I would have to hurry because several others were looking at the house. I was not sure if that was true, but I told her I had to sell my house in Dublin first before making a move. About two days later, Sean told me his ex-wife had scolded him for taking Nuala to look at houses with me and he was not to do this again. Nuala had read the flier for the house and told her mother about the cost and everything, I could imagine the rage.

9

MOVING TO TRAMORE

Getting Ready to Move

I now had the task of selling my house in Dublin. By 2008, the property bubble had burst and I was selling in a very tough financial climate. When I asked my tenant, PooBee, to try and find other accommodation, she announced to me that she was in no hurry. She had heard from friends that houses were taking a very long time to sell and was prepared to dig her heels in and stay. Well, I thought, it would not be an easy task showing the home to prospective buyers if the tenant was not willing. I employed Ted, my former buying agent, to sell my home for me. He told me I would have to pay almost €400 for the advertising costs. On the day we had arranged to take photographs of the house for a brochure, PooBee decided she did not want her room photographed. We wanted the curtains downstairs to be open for the photo of the front of the property and she protested.

'It's my room,' she insisted. 'My room!'

PooBee had obviously been speaking to people who were advising her on her rights as a tenant.

I had already made contact with Danny, my favourite mortgage broker, to see what could be done to get a loan for my dream home in Tramore. Mortgage loans would be difficult to arrange since I was self employed. I was told I would have to get a special type of loan since I was high risk. This did not look promising. However, I followed the advice of an entrepreneur I had met in the Women's Business network, and kept a vision board with a photo of my dream home on my dressing table. I looked at this every day and imagined myself living in this house.

A move was, as always, a monumental task. I managed to get a quotation from a moving company based in Waterford to help me with the move. They had storage facilities at their base just outside Waterford city. I would need storage if my home sold before I was able to buy my dream home. They offered to pack all the small items for an extra cost, but I decided to pack them myself, so I would know where everything was located. I began to get rid of some furniture that I had purchased in California by advertising on eBay. A monstrously large leather sofa and love seat were the first to go. It took great effort to squeeze the sofa through the tiny doorway of my Dublin home. We had to try several different angles to get the sofa out, even after removing the large cushions. I decided I would buy a whole new living room suite to create an antique look in my new Georgian home.

I sold off an old patio set, coffee table and chairs from 1920's California and other worn items. I hired a large skip and started to slowly fill it with items we did not want. It was a long, tortuous process. I also had to beat my neighbours and others to the skip, so it would fill with my rubbish rather than theirs. After I returned the skip, I realised that there was a bulk pick up day courtesy of Dublin City Council the following week. This was free of charge and I could have saved myself the unnecessary expense.

Bulk pick up day usually attracted Travellers, who rummaged through to see what they could salvage and sell. It was a bit frightening to see these characters grabbing at items and crowding our small street. I put out an old vacuum cleaner I had brought from California. I'd managed to use it by hooking it up to a step up transformer.

'Does dis Hoovah wook?' asked one of them.

'Of course it works.' I replied.

The idea of having to vouch for a free item was annoying to say the least. And it had worked in California!

Tiffany had accumulated over a hundred stuffed toys and dolls and we needed to part with some of them. She was 12 and no longer interested in these toys anyway. I removed the ones with the best memories and stories and calmly placed the other toys on the pavement. They disappeared within seconds.

In all the weeks of packing, Sean never came or offered to help. One Dublin friend told me plainly that he should help me and if he didn't, he was obviously not interested. I ignored her advice and ignored his behaviour, assuming he was just busy. After all, he was the one who had spotted the perfect property for me. He had taken me around to look at a few places. Surely he wanted me to move to Tramore. Another friend, who had property in Dublin and Portally near Dunmore East, advised that after selling my Dublin property, I should only rent in Tramore to see if I liked it. Selling a property was going to be too complicated if I decided to move. Unfortunately, I never listened to the voice of wisdom and reason.

Every time we heard about a potential buyer for my Dublin home, we would clean up all the rooms, put out the fancy linen and duvets, put out fresh flowers in vases and bake bread or cake. It was thought that the smell of fresh baking would encourage buyers. This exercise was particularly difficult after a weekend of working at markets and events. The kitchen had to be cleaned thoroughly after all the cooking. Food boxes and market gear had to be stored in the large store-room in the back yard. This room was off limits to visitors. We would tell them it had plumbing and electricity for a washer and drier and that was it.

At last, Ted announced we had an offer on the house. I had asked for €535,000 when I heard one house on Dean Swift Road with similar renovations was going for €600,000. According to Ted, the offer of €500,000 had come in from first time buyers who had fallen in love with the property. In previous years, you could be guaranteed offers higher than the asking price, but not in 2008. Ted told me I was lucky to get any offer. I pondered on it for a little while, wondering whether to accept or not. I called around to a few people for a second opinion. Finally, I accepted, after my wild eyed agent told me repeatedly to take it. I was eventually able to persuade PooBee to move out, so we could finish our packing and clean her room. There was a lingering odour in that room. It seemed to have never been opened to let in fresh air. I mopped and scrubbed furiously so I would be ready in time for the moving company.

I also had to sort out temporary housing in Tramore and a school for Tiffany. Finding a school was more difficult than I imagined. Tramore had two primary schools and they were both bursting at the seams. Each classroom had over thirty students. Temporary trailer classrooms had become permanent fixtures. One Irish language primary school had vacancies, but that was not an option. There was only one girls' secondary school and one boys' secondary school. I had managed to purchase a book which showed national and county school rankings. Unfortunately, Tramore schools scored well below the national average and I felt I was setting my child up for early failure in life. But I thought, whatever was available, we would make full use of it.

An Irish Funeral

In the middle of my packing frenzy, Sean's mother died. She was in her 80's and even though he claimed not to be fond of her, it was still a very sad time. She had battled lung cancer in her last days and it was a swift demise. I heard that the ex-wife was in the hospital room too when she died. Of course she would have been. Geraldine had known her for many years. I wondered why I could not be the one there to support Sean.

Sean said his mother was very common. She was tight with money and gave his children expired sweets and gifts from a discount store for Christmas. What an odd way for him to describe his mother, especially when she was trying to make amends by coming to visit him every week. I knew she loved him in her own way and was unable to show it. This should have been a warning sign for me, but I usually ignored warning signs and plunged into many a relationship for the experience. He said her house was old and dirty and he would never take me there. This was extremely annoying but I could do nothing about his decision and had to respect his wish for privacy.

I had listened to Sean's long stories of how he and his older brother never got along well. According to Sean, his brother owned property around Waterford city and did not do much of anything. He claimed his brother was jealous of his education and did not want to speak to him. He was tight with money and never seemed to have any. There was clearly a lot of ill feeling between them. They had to get together to plan the funeral, but they could not speak to each other in a civil manner when it came to dividing the spoils: a tiny house with very little furniture or value.

Sean paid all the funeral expenses. He said he would not wait for his brother. I dropped everything I was doing, pulled Tiffany out of school for two days and took the long drive down the N11 to Waterford. We were about to witness the rituals of an Irish funeral for the first time.

In my past experience, a funeral took place on one day. The mourners got together after the funeral to sit around and chat, have some food and a drink, then leave. An Irish funeral was a two day affair. Close family and mourners met at the funeral home for the removal. This was followed by drinking in the pub. The next day was the church funeral, burial, then soup and sandwiches in a pub, followed by more drinking. Ger's funeral was a reunion of the Power clan in Waterford. Power was a popular name in Waterford city. Every second person seemed to have the last name of Power. Sean informed me that it was derived from the French Huguenot name, de Pouvoir.

Tiffany and I arrived at the funeral home that night when most of the family was already assembled. I went past Sean's children and ex-wife, who were seated near the entrance and said a quick hello to them, ignoring the ex-wife's puzzled stare,

We proceeded directly into the main chamber, where the body lay in the coffin. I sat next to Sean. Geraldine looked so peaceful in the coffin. They had given her a good grooming. The hairdo and make up made her look very respectable. The attendant began a long speech about what a great person Geraldine was. One of the Power cousins rattled off 100 Hail Mary's. I had never heard the Hail Mary delivered so swiftly in all my life. I was on the verge of laughter, but everyone was solemn, so I had to try to compose myself.

The attendant, who resembled a gangster, was tall and dark in a dark suit, with greasy hair slicked back. He claimed to have a ring given to him personally by the late Pope John Paul II. He rambled on about the virtues of this ring and how powerful it was supposed to be. Then he touched Geraldine's forehead with the ring.

'I am touching her head with the sacred ring,' he proclaimed.

I almost burst out laughing. I knew Ger had no time for

priests or religion. She despised all the rituals and had stopped going to church years earlier. I imagined her jumping out of her coffin and giving him a whack on the head with her walking stick. That would have been a fit ending to proceedings at the funeral home. The attendant said one Hail Mary and the cousin another 100 Hail Mary's, again proclaimed at top speed. This prompted hasty, muffled "Amen's" from the audience. At last, mercifully, the chanting stopped.

Everyone then went on to The Vic, a popular Tramore pub. I followed the crowd over there, found a seat with Tiffany and ordered juice. Before we knew it, the ex-wife had settled at the table right next to me.

'Hello Lindy,' she said cheerfully. 'Thanks for coming to the funeral'.

Even Tiffany was jolted by her extreme friendliness. It was 'over the top'. Out of the mouth of babes, Tiffany asked me if the woman was ok. Realistically I thought she was not, but assured Tiff she was only being friendly. We had one drink, and then went back to Sean's house for a rest, so we would be refreshed for the funeral next morning. He confessed to me how genuinely sad he felt at his mother's death and regretted not making time to get to know her more in his adult life.

Sean's half sister had come back from America for the funeral. She was given the spare room. She expressed her grief too at Geraldine's death, even though she had been worked like a slave by Ger the wicked step mother. We heard stories how Ger made her wash clothes and dishes by hand every day when the family ran the pub and bed and breakfast. Oonagh had been anxious to turn 18 and run away to England to study and become a nurse. Now, returning to Ireland for Ger's funeral, she sobbed repeatedly. The stepmother who did not seem to love her was dead.

The next day, the whole town of Tramore turned up for the funeral. I saw the old Nigerian lady who Sean used to transport to choir practise. She pulled me over to sit with her right in the front row. This was usually reserved for close family. Wow, I thought, the ex-wife would be furious. But she was busy taking care of children in the choir pews and arranging the reading of the lessons. Sean's old aunt, who ran a one room pub in town, was escorted by a relative into the church and placed in the pew just behind us.

'Who are these people in front of me', she asked. 'They're not relations!'

Ger's sister was well known around the town for her sharp tongue and acid wit. I kept my head straight, looking very interested in proceedings. Sean was in rare form, chatting and joking with friends and doing the rounds throughout the church. He greeted people here and there. There was no sombre mood at this gathering. It was going to be a party all the way. The priest went on and on about Geraldine in a dreary voice, describing her as an upstanding woman in the community.

Just when the worshippers had had enough, the service ended and everyone made their way across the street to the burial site. This was quite handy. There was no driving anywhere. Ger was to be buried in the same plot as her deceased husband. Tiffany and I walked ahead and stood near enough to where the coffin would be put in the ground, so we could get a good view. The faithful sang hymns and the priest said more prayers.

We felt someone pushing past us to get to the very front, and sure enough, it was the ex-wife, pulling one of the daughters forward. We snickered at the drama that unfolded: the claiming of territory. Sean's brother, his wife and their daughter cried continuously. I had never seen people cry so profusely for a grandmother's funeral. From what I was told, they had never been keen to entertain Ger one day a year: Christmas Day. Perhaps it was the guilt of being so nasty to her that made them cry so much.

The faithful moved on to the Silver Slipper pub. Poor Sean would be stuck with that bill. Everyone poured into the pub and formed two camps, the Powers and the others. I sat with the others and Sean sat with me. The ex-wife sat with all the cousins, remembering old times. I enjoyed watching the people and the drinking frenzy. By 2pm, Geraldine was long forgotten and the drinkers were already planning to eat Chinese buffet for dinner and continue drinking. Sean's friends came to the pub and those who had to return to work had one drink and left. At 3pm, I decided to call it a day and return to Dublin. After all, I had things to do and Tiffany had to return to school. One day off for the Irish funeral adventure was enough.

It took us five hours to manoeuvre onto the M50. Poor Tiffany was bursting and had to use the bathroom. I eventually pulled off the motorway at the first exit I could find, and drove to a housing estate. Since it was already dark, I asked her to relieve herself on the ground at the side of the car. I then started to use my homing pigeon skills to move in the direction of the Grand Canal. I knew I was in South Dublin and had to drive north but I did not quite know where I was going. By a stroke of luck, we ended up at Harcourt Street and from there I found a way to the Liffey. The years of driving around had paid off.

We arrived in Glasnevin at 8pm. What an ordeal. The funeral faithful were no doubt very drunk by then.

Whirl of Activity

Since we were moving in April and Tiffany would only have one term left before going on to the girls' secondary school, I thought it wouldn't matter which school she attended. I managed to get her a space at a small country school in Fenor, just outside of Tramore. The class had a few students from different class levels in one room. They were taught by the Principal who also had to carry out administrative duties. This was a big culture shock compared to the large and organised Dublin classes at St Columba's School in Drumcondra. As we collected Tiffany's academic records and said farewell to the teachers, principal and secretary, the principal said:

'Tiffany is a lovely girl. She's a credit to you.'

I made one trip to bring down valuable items like certificates, jewellery and documents, which would be stored in the spare room at Sean's home. The room and the staircase leading to it were full of my junk. It was also a good time to try to seek temporary housing, since the buyers of my home were moving in any day. I contacted a real estate agent who specialised in rental property, and managed to get an apartment at Apollonian Suites on Gallwey's Hill. These holiday apartments had a spectacular, unobstructed view of Tramore Bay. The rate was low since it was low season and the town was practically empty. I figured that if I had to feel homeless, I might as well have a place with a view.

A week before I moved house, I got a call from the Dublin City Enterprise Board. They had sent out my name and business contacts for the filming of an episode of Capital D, a TV program which featured interesting people around Dublin. Always appreciative of free marketing opportunities, I gave a definite yes when the caller asked if I was a chef. I could be a chef if a film crew wanted to come to my home to film me cooking Caribbean delicacies.

Boxes were piled everywhere and I had to locate cooking

utensils to get ready for the occasion, pushing a few boxes into corners or into the store room. I prepared a corner with a well-dressed table of all the products I had been importing. This was going to be a wonderful opportunity to show off the business and I was determined to make the most of it. The reporter and camera crew came early. I instructed them to please ignore the boxes as I was in the process of moving. Luckily the rooms were very clean and walls empty from packing and showing the home. The countertops were also bare so not much preparation was needed.

I decided saheena would be an ideal item to prepare. I prepared a batter ready for cooking and showed the basic method of preparation. The reporter had to remind me to look at her, not the camera. I was never camera shy and enjoyed the experience thoroughly. The crew filmed my display table. I had done my own stage make-up and hair, and wore a colourful dress. I spoke with confidence of the virtues of Caribbean food and my love of cooking was evident. I tried to put in a plug for all the markets and events I had frequented. My guests left with servings of saheena and I was overjoyed at the chance of free TV exposure.

The Big Move

Moving day was full of mixed emotions. I had spent a lot of time and money to create a home in Dublin with my stamp on it. And now I was abandoning everything for an unknown future. I went around and said farewell to my favourite neighbours. Olive, who lived opposite me, even invited me over for tea. I had lived there for three years and had never been invited for tea. Kathleen down the road even confided in me that she had cancer.

'Goodbye and good luck, Liddy,' she said, still not getting my name right.

I recorded their names and telephone numbers and

promised to keep in touch. Olive volunteered to keep some of the many packaged juices I could not squeeze into my van at the last minute. I could not give the movers any food products which I planned to sell, since I didn't know when I would have my own residence and be able to take my belongings out of storage.

The movers were a father and son team with one helper and they managed to pack and wrap all the furniture well enough. I wrote a massive cheque for the move and spent a few hours cleaning and mopping so the new owners would find a clean home when they arrived. I collected Tiffany from her last day at school at St. Columba's, drove around to the bank, the real estate agent and all other last minute details, then took off for Tramore. We arrived in the evening and settled into our little apartment in the Apollonian Suites. Even though the place had been cleaned, I had to give all surfaces a clean with bleach to be satisfied. The kitchen cupboards were full of dishes and cutlery. I brought my own linen and put away the linen they supplied in a closet.

On our first evening in Tramore, Sean said he could not come to visit. He was busy. I thought this odd for someone who was supposed to be my closest friend, but took the time to off load my van, unpack and get settled. The next day, I drove Tiffany to the little school in Fenor. There was no way to get to this school except to drive the child there or hire a taxi. Two private buses took children from Tramore out to Fenor daily, but they were already overbooked. Sean came over during the day, tripping over boxes and suitcases and acted as guilty as a child who had stolen candy. He said he would come by another day. The next evening, he popped in, leaving his children in the car. I offered for him to bring them inside.

'No, I don't have to force them to like you!' he shouted.

That was a strange reaction.

The following day, I asked him what was going on. He said I had made his daughter cry when she heard I had moved to Tramore. She told him she would never visit him if I moved into his house. And furthermore, his ex-wife had told him the children would not be comfortable having a black stepmother driving them around to activities. I was fine in Dublin; a safe distance away, safe enough not to appear real. But as soon as I moved to the town for good, I would feel the family's full rage.

'Don't you think your ex-wife's remarks were racist?' I said to Sean.

'She has a point. I've never seen the child so unhappy.'

Obviously the child's head was filled with stories.

Conquering New Markets

I decided to go about my business as usual and settle in with or without Sean. I had signed up for trading events and needed to determine how I would use the tiny kitchen in the apartment to bake and prepare items to sell. I had also signed up for markets in Waterford and Dungarvan, so these were pressing matters. A few days after the move, I participated in a Dungarvan Festival put on by the French European Market. I was not French, or European, but felt I could babble in basic French if anyone were to ask me a question, so I managed to get a stall.

At the market, stalls selling exotic sausages made of deer and ostrich and smelly cheeses of different colours abounded. The traders cut samples of their food and gave them to curious onlookers. I was surprised that some customers had seen me on the Capital D TV show the week before. The marketing effort had paid off. To some of the passers-by, I was famous.

My display stand was not sophisticated or well presented like some of the other French traders who were doing this business for years. I had a flat table and the bottles and packages were difficult to see. The market manager, in true blunt French style, did not hesitate to tell me how unprofessional my stand looked. I was to go around, observe the others and come up with something better. That was my first experience working with French traders. It was an interesting weekend. The same French CD played repeatedly, while a monsieur on the accordion amused passers-by with the same routine several times during the day. He was next to my stand, so it did attract a crowd who would then purchase from me out of curiosity. However, by day three, I was tired of his routine and wished he had picked another spot in the market. The event was packed and I made new friends. I even met two customers of Caribbean descent, who had moved to Dungarvan via the UK with an Irish spouse.

I decided to join the French European Market for future events, since they had a list of annual events throughout the south and the midlands; uncharted waters for me. I would sometimes take Tiffany on these mad adventures. One time, we participated in a large Garden Show which took place around Belvedere House and Gardens near Mullingar in County Westmeath. We were able to tour Belvedere House and Tiffany and I stayed overnight at a local bed and breakfast. It was a fine old house and gave us the opportunity to discover a new part of the country.

One of my most interesting experiences with the French market was when I participated in a Horse Trading Fair in Ballinasloe, County Galway. I mapped out the journey online. The route looked straightforward. I left Tramore in thick fog at 5am and had to contend with poor visibility all the way through the small roads of Tipperary. It was only later that morning that the fog burned off, promising a sunny day ahead. This was good news for the organisers, who were sceptical after the previous days of rain. When I finally found the market manager, I learned we were dispersed among all sorts of other traders. Since I was not one of the 'regulars', I could not sell on the main thoroughfare. My spot was on the outer street.

I was placed between a man selling vegetable peelers on my left, and some ladies selling saddle wax and other horse fare on my right. The market was full of Irish Travellers, English Travellers, and many Roma gypsies. The Romas sold balloons and whistles and would braid little girls' hair, weaving in coloured thread. They circled continuously and my nerves were frayed from guarding my goods and cash pan after a few hours. I managed to befriend one of the kind ladies in the stand next to me and asked them to keep an eye on my stand, while I ran to the portable toilets and back.

'Take yer money with ya!' warned the lady. 'You never know'.

I took her advice.

I had a visit from the health inspector, who seemed lenient enough, taking notes and asking questions. Since health board standards varied from county to county, I could never tell what to expect. A health hazard in one county would be overlooked in another. From a practical standpoint, I had mainly packaged food and snack foods. But I had also made some saheena and aloo pies. In Waterford County, everything was a hazard, so inspections gave me the jitters. But here, I managed to pass and the inspector eventually moved on to other stands.

Mr. Vegetable Peeler invented the most innovative sales pitch, which drew in a host of onlookers, both children and adults.

'Look how easily I can peel this potato,' he said. 'With this gadget, I can make curly fries and wedges too. Even curly carrot spirals.'

The crowd went "Ooooh" and "Aaahh" during each presentation. At the end, a host of unsuspecting souls bought vegetable peelers for themselves as well as gifts for friends. One never can have enough cheap and cheerful vegetable peelers in the home. The gadgets were so slight that you could break them immediately if you pressed too hard. That thought never occurred to anyone because of the skill of the demonstrator.

I tried out my own sales pitch: "Caribbean sauces and seasonings. Come try a sauce!" Before I knew it, I had made €600. Not a bad result from selling foreign food to Travellers. I was a curiosity at their festival. A mad hot sauce was certainly worth trying for the craic. I was thrilled when a young Jamaican man passed by and noticed all the Caribbean flags at my stall. He stopped and chatted for a long time. I told him that I had started my business two years before, and I was promoting Caribbean food around the country. He was suitably impressed and would have chatted for a while longer, but his young Irish partner, who was heavily pregnant, scowled at me and urged him to move on. She latched on to his arm as if to prove he was her property and gave me the evil eye. Since I had no interest in her property and saw her distress, I sent him along, saying I hoped to see him at the next festival.

At 6pm, it was time to pack up. The Roma gypsies were closing in. Many lived in an apartment just opposite where I had set up. They circled the area as nightfall came. The whistles, shouting and games around traders began to increase. Luckily my saddle wax friends helped me take down my tent and stayed a few minutes extra so I could collect my van to load up. I drove out of the town as swiftly as possible, not bothering to run to the toilets before the long drive. I hoped to find a roadside pub on the way. I lost my way getting out of Ballinasloe and never made it back to the route I had taken through Counties Clare and Tipperary early that morning. I had hoped to find the exit to Tullamore off the N6, but there was so much construction at the time for new motorways. I missed that exit as well. I eventually ended up in Dublin after two and a half hours and then had to drive another two and a half hours south to Tramore. I was so tired from the long day, but could not stop to rest. I wept half the way home, calling Sean sometimes to console me and let him know where I was en route. It was after midnight before I arrived home. The only consolation was that I had actually made money at a very unpredictable event and had stories to tell.

My New Home

After the sale of my Dublin home, the proceeds were put in one of my bank accounts and I now had to endure the games that surrounded the purchase of the Tramore home. The owner had completely refurbished the house to its former glory. The style was Georgian with large rectangular windows. They all had latched shutters inside.

The asking price was €490,000. It was so long winded, going back and forth through agents who were sometimes not available. I called the owner directly one day and offered him €450,000. There was no response at the other end of the receiver. He hesitated and hesitated. If I was smart, I could have held my ground. However, feeling wealthy because of the €100k profit on my recent sale, I said, "Oh well, what about 465k?" He said he would get back to me soon. Of course, he accepted it.

It was a happy day when we finally moved into the new

home. The moving company came and all my furniture was reassembled. I got into an argument with the mover's son when I noticed how badly cracked my antique wardrobe appeared. He said that it was like that when they dissembled it. We went back and forth. He then charged me extra for having to move my piano up a flight of steps. According to him, I didn't tell them they had to climb a flight of steps during the delivery.

The view from my window was what I loved most. Sitting on my bed and seeing the full expanse of Tramore Bay, unobstructed by trees or buildings, was worth every penny. As all the furniture had been delivered, I made a few trips to Sean's house to collect the remainder of our belongings. Sean had been generous enough to allow a delivery of two pallet loads of Caribbean packaged foods in his front yard. The place was a mess, with boxes and boxes of sauces, seasonings, spices, snack foods, jams and jellies stacked precariously, hidden under tarpaulin. They were all removed gradually and piled sky high in a large store room at my home.

The difficulty of bringing anything into my house was the flight of 15 flagstone steps to climb before reaching the front door. Even rolling out the wheelie bin was a challenge. I had to roll it one step at a time to reach the pavement. Because the entrance was flanked by two large concrete posts, I almost bumped into pedestrians a few times by mistake. I learned eventually to run down the steps, see if the coast was clear, and then make the trip down with the bin. Bins had to be deposited on the other side of the street for rubbish collection and could not be left on the street all week, or you could be fined by the City Council. I had some spectacular spills. Sean was sympathetic and offered to help me move my rubbish, but the help didn't often materialise.

10

TASTE OF THE CARIBBEAN

With stocks dwindling and high freight costs, I wondered daily why I could not just make my own products. After all, I was a food scientist. More than that, I was a great cook, creating my own recipes all the time. My dilemma was where I should make food products and what I should make. I also had to create a brand that was easy to recognise. While chatting with customers and friends at the Dun Laoghaire Farmers market one day, I got an offer to create a brand relatively inexpensively. My friend Daphne knew a lot about branding and marketing products, having run several businesses for years. One of her retired friends, a graphic artist, agreed to sit down with me and come up with a concept for my brand and new products.

We toyed with ideas of the Caribbean: movement, dance and music. We thought up names like Caribbean Spirit, Tropical Food, Caribbean Taste, and a host of other options. We wanted to capture the spirit of the Caribbean in bottles and packages. We had to sell the idea of the sunny tropics in rainy Ireland. Why not use a dancer in folk costume, as well as a man playing the steel pan. I was not fond of the stereotypical palm trees. They could represent anywhere from the Philippines to Hawaii. Alan, the graphic designer, drew the dancer and steel pan musician. He crafted the words 'Taste of the Caribbean' into my first logo. We also had to decide on colours. Colourful labels of my imported Caribbean products worked well in the Caribbean. However, on the Irish gourmet scene, they looked cheap and distasteful. We used a beige back ground, with words in magenta, and black and brown outlines for the characters and the first 'Taste of the Caribbean' logo was born.

A friend, Lynne, produced her own brand of sauces and chutneys and traded at the Dun Laoghaire market. She offered to manufacture my sauces at her commercial kitchen in Dublin. I sent her the recipes and she calculated a per bottle price for manufacture. I ordered small 110 ml cylindrical bottles for the extra spicy sauce, which Tiffany called Bad Boy Pepper Sauce. Tiffany was always creative with ideas and names. I also had a delicious recipe for Jamaican Jerk Bar-B-Q sauce, adding bananas for thickness and flavour. All my ingredients had to be fresh and the products were free of artificial preservatives. I also devised a pasta sauce, thickened with chopped green mangoes. It had an exotic taste and rich texture. I called the product Rasta Pasta Sauce.

We started with these three sauces and planned to add products as time went by. It was very exciting when I went to Lynne's kitchen to get the first batch of sauces made. She had purchased all the ingredients. Bottles and caps were stacked into crates. The kitchen was large, complete with commercial cooker and hood, and steaming ovens. We chopped and cooked, bottled and capped. It took forever. We steamed capped bottles in a water bath as an additional sterilisation step and some were turned over to ensure the cap was sterilised with hot product. The facility had to be vacated by 7pm each day. We had to leave everything and return the next day. We had cleaned as we went to avoid a buildup of debris around the kitchen. This made it easier to clean up at the end of the day.

In the weeks of all the cooking and bottling, I also produced a cookbook of Caribbean recipes. Sean helped me come up with the title "Caribbean Cooking for Culchies". The term 'Culchie' is used affectionately for Irish citizens from outside 'the Pale' or Dublin. Since I was now a country woman living in Waterford, I filled the criterion. I took a gamble that the title would be a hit rather than a cause of offence and sent the book off to the printing press. It was a tiny 10 page book, filled with recipes and cartoon characters spewing

Irish sayings. It was just enough to whet the appetite.

I got quotations from several printers for business cards and labels and toyed with creating a more professional look for my business. I imagined myself to be the dancer in the logo, as this new enterprise was taking shape. I could not wait to present my new products at the Dun Laoghaire farmers market that August. It felt so exciting to give samples and explain that the products were made using my own recipes and the finest and freshest ingredients, with no additives or preservatives. I rehearsed and perfected my sales pitch. Eventually, I phased out all the imported sauces and chutneys.

We tried some new tropical jams like pineapple and mango. However, making these using fresh ingredients proved to be too difficult and too expensive. So I shelved those products and focused on developing more sauces. In October, I added tamarind chutney and Jamaican jerk marinade to the range. Tamarind chutney had always been one of my favourites as a child growing up in Trinidad. We would eat it as a dip with phulorie (a fried dough), or as a sauce on saheena and fried fish. It was going to be a tough sell to the Irish, but forever the optimist, I decided sampling, sampling and more sampling would be the answer. The sales pitch had to be more creative and it had to relate to what people already knew. I created a recipe for a Trinidadian style curry sauce. This was the type we would cook for rotis and curried vegetables. This sauce was called Caribbean Curry Sauce. The new sauces were packaged in a 280ml bottle with a medium sized neck, ideal for pouring.

At the time I was launching my products in the shadow of a well advertised UK product. This new Jamaican Bar B Q sauce, called Reggae Reggae Sauce, was promoted on the UK Dragon's Den. People constantly compared my products with this sauce. It was a steep climb in many ways. As summer disappeared, people told me they could not eat tropical food in the winter. This was also a strange concept, since I never associated eating with the weather. It was an additional obstacle to overcome. There was no easy way to change people's thoughts or behaviour in a short time. Very few people believed a woman living in Ireland could produce sauces from her own experience and resources. I had to be working for someone else. This was a common misconception which I had to disprove continuously.

I used any opportunity I could find to promote my new products. No event was too big or too small. Since I was now producing my own sauces, I qualified for a subsidised spot in the annual SHOP Ireland Expo. This event featured food products and support services for the industry. Innovative food products from around the country were showcased to buyers from retail and catering.

I entered four of my new products in the competition for the Product of the Show Award. If I were successful with even one product, it would give me advertising very early in the game. My stand was basic, with a table and shelf creating the look of a small gourmet food store. I did not have the funding that some of the other seasoned producers had at their disposal, but it felt good to be participating in the Enterprise Board's group of companies. My Rasta Pasta sauce won a Certificate of Commendation in the Product of the Show Award category. I was surely very lucky to be considered with this brand new product. The sauce was mild and had the rich tropical flavour of green mango. This was typically used as a vegetable by Hindus in the Caribbean. The unique flavour, blended with tomato sauce and Italian spices, had won the favour of the judges.

I was soon able to build a fan base in the markets and fancy food shops for my Rasta Sauce. However, the product was too expensive to mass produce for supermarkets. The ingredients were so expensive, especially fresh mango. I also went overboard with packaging, designing custom made ribbon and paper caps which needed individual placement over the screw on bottle caps. The product was destined for limited sales in limited gourmet food shops and markets.

In the meantime, I was unable to pay Lynne all the funds spent on producing my bottled sauces as soon as they were made, which left her with a huge cash flow problem. A large company may have been able to absorb the costs, but for a small producer, this was suicide. We had to part and I had to find alternatives for production. I searched around Waterford city for a commercial kitchen I could use for production and came across a catering company owned by an enterprising business woman who ran two service stations in the town. At her catering kitchen, her chef and assistant made sandwiches and ready to eat meals for the service stations, and they also produced food for weddings, first communion parties and other events. I convinced her she could make extra money if I used the kitchen at night with my crew to make sauces. We would be out of everyone's way and would clean up after we were done. We were to leave the facility ready for the morning staff.

I suggested a fee of €150 for the night, no matter how many hours, and this was accepted. I recruited some African girls from the Tramore asylum seekers' centre to help me prepare ingredients and bottle sauces. This massive project of shopping for ingredients, bottles and caps, bringing everything to the commercial kitchen, preparing ingredients, cooking in large pots, and pouring by hand went on for two months.

The most difficult part of the night was packing up at the end, usually after midnight and carting away the goods back to Tramore. Sometimes, we finished after 1am. My staff became irritated and tired of my crazy, driven, and unreasonable demands. I only had one supporter, Dorcas, who consistently helped me. She became a very good and reliable friend. Bottles had to be labelled by hand and I sometimes got Tiffany and one of her classmates to label them at a price of 10 cents a bottle.

As the whole prospect of hand making sauces became unsustainable, I contacted a small bottling firm based in Kilcoole. The owner had offered his bottling services on several occasions and I decided to accept the offer. We reviewed recipes and created an arrangement where this company would produce my four best sellers. The owners were a husband and wife team. The wife, who was a food technologist, took my recipes and scaled them up to the size of their large cooking vat. Enda, the husband, managed operations. He gave me a per unit price for each product and I was present at the first production run to see that their workers had made the products according to my specifications. Christmas was approaching and it was vital to get large quantities of products ready for the Craft Fair at the RDS. This was the big occasion to sell and I wanted to have enough stock on hand for this and other Christmas markets.

I was given a team of Lithuanian workers to manage. Only one spoke broken English. That was a challenge in itself to get them to peel and cut up tropical fruits and vegetables. By the end of the day, I had learned a few Lithuanian phrases and made a proper mess of the whole production room. We had crates of mangoes on one side for the Rasta Pasta sauce, bananas on the other, many crates of coriander, green onions, regular onions to chop and fry for curry sauce etc. This was also the day that the county health inspector decided to pass through the facility for a surprise visit. The owner was not on site at the time. The inspector was horrified to see fresh fruits and vegetables strewn all over the facility and left screaming. She had a litany of woes that needed addressing. Drains had to be put in, the ceiling had to be replaced and the air from the cooking vat had to be vented.

The Broken Key

Agricultural shows were also on my agenda in 2008. I signed up for the Tullamore Show and enlisted the help of Laura, an industrious refugee woman who lived in Tramore. I had got Laura's name and number from one of Sean's friends. She helped me cook for markets, load vans, unload the food, set up the stall and do whatever else needed to be done. Her native language was French, which was a bit of a challenge, since she was unable or unwilling to converse with customers.

I signed up for a stand at for Cork Southwest Music Festival in Skibbereen. This was going to be my first time at a music festival and I was very excited. I made arrangements to rent a generator to run lights and hot plates, since this was a night time event. We planned to peel potatoes, chop mangoes and make everything on site. I was going to sell fresh Rasta Pasta for this event and had special banners made.

We loaded up the van with the tent, sinks, food stock and some boxes of sauces and other dry goods for good measure. It was a feat of great skill to pack so many items into the small van and we still had to leave some space for the generator, which I was to collect in Cork city on the way to Skibbereen. We had to arrive on site at noon, which I could not understand since the music wouldn't start until 5pm. I guessed the organisers wanted all booths to be set up and vans out of the way by the time the party goers arrived. I grabbed the car keys and loaded up the last few items into the van, then slammed the door shut. It was already 9am and it would take three hours to get to 'Skibb'.

I tried to put the key into the ignition. It would not go in. As I looked at the key, I saw that the top had broken off.

The world was spinning. We had spent an hour and a half packing and re-shuffling everything in the van so it could fit properly and the poor little van was buckling with the excess weight. I crawled out of the van exhausted and collapsed on the ground, heaving and sobbing, trying to figure out what to do next. Poor Laura could not console me.

When I was finally able to regain composure, the first thing I did was call Sean. He was an 'ideas man'. He would know what to do. He suggested calling key cutters in Waterford to see what they could do. The only key cutting store open on a Saturday said they would not come out because the key probably had to be ordered from a car dealership. It was an Opel Combo van, and Opel would need the Vehicle Identification Number (VIN) to cut the key. When I bought the van, it had not come with a spare key and I had never considered making one. In hindsight, this was a mistake.

What was I going to do? I had invested a tidy sum of money for the event's rental fee, ingredients and supplies and other necessities. We decided I would rent a van. Because it was a Saturday, it took a great deal of time to call all the car rental offices in Waterford City. Some said they had rented all their vans and scolded me for not having an advance booking. Others were closed for the weekend. Finally, Budget Car Rental in Dublin said they could find a van at their branch in the Waterford Airport. I was to go there immediately to get it. Sean took me to the airport. It was empty. Even though all the doors were open, not a living soul could be seen for miles around.

'Hello! Hello! Anyone from Budget Car Rental here?' I called.

Finally a lad came from a room at the back. He was not expecting anyone, but he had a van available. I had to return it on Sunday because someone had booked the van for

Monday morning. I told him I could manage the return deadline very well, and I was able to drive off with the van. Thank God for Budget Car Rental.

When we got back to Tramore, Laura, Sean and I removed everything from my van and loaded up the rental van. This took another full hour and by 11am, we were able to leave for the event. We still had to stop in Cork city to get a generator and buy gasoline and a container to fuel the generator. When we got to the site in Skibbereen at around 2:00 pm, we were scolded for arriving so late. I was happy to even get there.

The night proved to be a comedy of errors and lessons in what not to do when selling at a music festival. We tried preparing food from scratch.

The crowd could not wait and went elsewhere for a ready meal. The electric burners were pulling too much electricity for the generator. The food cooked very slowly. We ran out of gasoline for the generator. I had to leave the festival, running down the street to find the lone garage open in Skibb late on Saturday night. Lights at my stall were dim because of the poor electricity supply. Laura was tired and grumpy. We had been working since 7:00 am non-stop that morning. It was close to midnight. She retired to the van and sulked.

The saving grace was my friend Aisling whom I had met while trading at markets in Dublin. She and her brother helped me sell then pack up at 1:00 Am. I should have known to prepare food in advance for re-heating on site. I was leaning to do mass catering while at a Festival! This was mad. But I laughed at myself.

We set off for Tramore late. I knew there would be no traffic on the way back. We got back to Tramore at 3am the next morning. Laura was pouting from fatigue and discontent, and I had blurred vision from sheer exhaustion. The next week, I had two keys made to ensure I never again had to go through such drama.

Brand New Van

As Christmas approached, it was once again time to gear up for the Craft Fair at the RDS. I hoped to finish all my production at the factory in the days leading up to the Craft Fair at the RDS and just store boxes of sauces in my storage room at the house. On the last planned production day, and the day before the opening of the Craft Fair, my trusty van broke down on the main street of Kilcoole. It was 5pm, already dark and I didn't know a soul in the town. I had stopped to top up fuel before taking the drive down to Tramore. The van refused to start. The engine was dead. That was really strange. Just two weeks before, I had taken the vehicle for a full service at a garage in Tramore run by two religious brothers. Several people in the petrol station tried to start the vehicle. One truck driver offered to tow me down one of the side streets in an attempt to kick start the battery. One driver had cables and attempted to give me a booster, but to no avail. The engine did not budge. It was great to see people chip in and help a damsel in distress. Irish men were still gallant in that way. Eventually, everyone had to go back to work or home and could no longer help.

I tried calling Sean to tell him my woes, but he was in London and was not answering his mobile phone. In fact, he had not called for days and acted quite mysterious about his business trip to London. It made me suspicious about his motives. I knew his profile was still on online dating sites. I had seen a page open one day when I was visiting his home. I wondered what woman he had planned to meet on his business trip. The thought made me sick to the stomach. He was not available to help and not available to console me during a time of great distress. It was one of the few times I felt extremely alone in Ireland.

I called the factory owner, Enda to rescue me. He had already left the factory for his home in County Dublin and kind soul that he was, volunteered to come back to help. He found some old straps and towed me to a garage near to the factory. We left the vehicle in the yard of the garage so a mechanic could look at it the following day. Enda offered to lend me one of his delivery vans, since I had put out €1,000for a stall at the RDS. We transferred boxes of sauces and many other items from my van into his van, and I started the long drive on the N11 back to Tramore. This was only my second experience driving a sixteen- footer van and I was determined to be extra careful not to scratch and dent this one. I made several detours in County Wexford to fill up the engine. At that hour many petrol stations were already closed for the day. I finally found a late night station with the best price on a road off the N11.

When I got back to Tramore, it was already 11pm. I was working on pure adrenaline. I loaded every possible item I would need for the Craft Fair into the van: tables, decorations, products, the trusty cash pan, customer response sheets, etc. Luckily I had laid everything out in the large corridor of my home the night before, so I was able to work like a machine. I tried to load more than what I needed, since there was no guarantee that the mechanic would be able to repair my van and I would have to return the borrowed van. The launch of my new products at the RDS had certainly started with a bang.

Wednesday, the first day of the Christmas Craft Fair, tended to be very crowded since it was the 10% discount day. Traders had to arrive extra early to be set up by 9am. The show itself ran from 10am to 10pm. How was I going to find the energy for that one after my ordeal the night before? The beauty about being self employed was that tiredness was never part of my vocabulary. I was so excited to be at the show and to show off my products, I forgot that I was even supposed to be tired. I worked and worked, smiling at everyone and chasing off pesky children. Sales were fast and furious that day. I was able to give Enda €600 in cash, with a promise to pay off the balance I owed him by the end of the weekend. He was shocked and said I could have his van for another day if I needed it. Of course I needed it. I didn't even have a plan as to how I was to go back home to Tramore at 10pm that night.

Luckily I had booked Caroline, my friend Daphne's niece, to help me on Thursday and Saturday of the five day show and that gave me the opportunity to find a replacement vehicle. I also had to cook more aloo pies and saheenas. I went to the Opel dealership on the N25 next morning and walked around, looking for a van. I didn't want anything too old and was determined to find something right away. The salesman, Shane, sensed my urgency and was only too willing to oblige. I explained that my Honda van had broken down in Kilcoole on Tuesday night, it was at a garage and I wanted to trade it in for a slightly used van. He asked what kind of condition it was in. I said the body was fine, but I didn't know what was wrong with the engine. I didn't tell Shane that the inside was dirty with debris from markets and events, or that there was a bit of mould on the upholstery. After all, dealers could fix anything if they were motivated. I gave him the name and number for the garage which held my old van and he seemed satisfied with that. He said they could arrange to tow the vehicle from Wicklow back to Waterford. That was fine with me. I could not imagine how much it would cost me to tow the vehicle back to Waterford.

Before I knew it, I was trading in a vehicle which the dealer had not yet seen. In return, I was buying a slightly used, shiny black 2008 van with only 10,000 kilometres on the dial. I thought I was signing papers for a loan when in fact they were papers for a lease with the exorbitant rate of 10.5%. I was so desperate I didn't care. My thoughts were only on getting a van that would not break down for the next few years. Shane made a million telephone calls. They were the kind that smiling car dealers make. Within two hours, the van was mine. This was surreal and the largest acquisition I had ever made in such a short time. I made arrangements to get my borrowed van back to Kilcoole and picked up my new van at the car dealership later on that evening.

Shane promised to give me a spare key, which could not be found that day. He promised to give me a net to prevent goods from flying forward and hitting me in the head from the back. He also promised a carpet to put on the wooden tray in the cargo hold. I had to pester him for three to four weeks to get these items. The promises had somehow escaped his memory after I drove off the lot.

On the last day of the Craft Fair, I was able to load up the remaining goods in my new van. Traders and old friends wondered where I had gotten the extra shiny black van, comparing it to my old beat up white van. The drive was smooth and less noisy. I considered myself fortunate to have such a wonderful new toy.

Sean had miraculously re-appeared after his sojourn in the UK. I asked if he had been run over by a bus, because I hadn't heard a word from him in four days. He said orange juice had fallen on his mobile phone one day. It was strange that the UK hotels and streets hadn't been equipped with telephones or telephone booths. He said he was very busy and had not even called his daughter that weekend.

Strained Relationship

When I moved into my new home, Sean insisted I have a huge house warming party. He was going to invite all his friends and the Mayor of Tramore. I refused to subject myself to such close scrutiny in the small town and he reacted almost violently to my refusal. He said I was stubborn and house proud. I stopped short of staging such an event when I realised the implications. I would be cooking, cleaning, and entertaining people who had little or no knowledge of me. I had met all of his friends on previous trips to Tramore and observed with great horror the way they discussed each other's affairs.

Another of his woes was that I had sold my living room furniture in Dublin and had not bought a new suite. I was waiting to find an antique suite for the living room to match the period home. Since I had not seen anything I liked, I was happy to wait. Tiffany and I used the loft as our sitting room. The television was in the loft and we had two extra single beds and a futon in the loft, decorated with pillows and cushions. It made a very cosy living room. With ceiling windows looking up to the sky or out to the ocean, we would sometimes spend day and night up there. But Sean was incensed by my casual attitude to furniture.

'Where will people sit?' he asked. 'Where will you entertain?'

He was annoyed at the size of my television. It was only 14 inches in width. According to him, the child needed a large flat screen TV and cable channels. I did not watch TV and had no intention of subscribing to cable. We would get a flat screen TV when I had extra cash to throw around.

The final nail in the coffin for him was when I recruited a whole crew of Polish painters to repaint the lower floor and hallways leading to the second floor. Again, I was determined to create a tropical feel in my home. I had two walls in the living room painted yellow and one purple. The kitchen was huge but very dark, with only one small window, so I had it painted a bright yellow. The boring pastels in the hallway were transformed into ice-cream beige and magenta.

'You're changing the whole character of the house.' Sean exclaimed. 'These colours are wrong.'

At that point, I decided to stop calling him or speaking to him. He had done nothing to help physically or financially and was too distressed over my decision making. He needed time to calm down and take a break. I managed to get contacts from him for a plumber and electrician. I asked the electrician to put in telephone points in every room, the kitchen the bedrooms, the loft. The request was puzzling to him. Every home in Ireland had one telephone in the hallway and that was it.

I had a small toilet installed under the antique staircase. It was a work of art, with its special 'behind-the-wall' septic tank. One plumber looked at the job and refused to do it. He claimed the closet was too small and I would not want to put anything in there. He also said he would have to dig to put down sewage pipes and it would be too much work. He then called the following week to find out when he should start digging. I told him it would not be necessary and I had made alternative arrangements. The second plumber put in a tiny toilet and a tiny sink in one corner. I did my own wall paper work and decorating to make the wash closet pretty. It was sitting room only; you could not stand upright in there.

My plumber doubled as a wannabe rock star at night. He and his other 50-something year old friends had a band. They sported long greasy hair and balding heads and played at pubs around Waterford. I went with Sean one night to their performance. They ploughed through many a rock and roll hit. Sometimes they were good, but sometimes they were not. I had to close my eyes to listen; it was painful to watch. The drummer looked like he might collapse from the years of cigarettes and alcohol abuse.

Sean's behaviour became more contrary towards the end of the year. In October, I asked him to meet so we could discuss whether it was worth continuing to be partners. He was seldom available to meet and claimed he had to take care of his teenagers. This was a strange concept since they were seeking more independence and usually went off with friends. He craved their attention. We met one morning at one of his coffee hangouts, where he would sit and watch people and chat with acquaintances while devouring a newspaper. He said he was busy all the time with his kids and the dog. I would just have to accept things as they were and fit in. That should have been my cue to walk away, but my devotion knew no bounds. I thought maybe I would keep myself very busy and see him occasionally.

The Big Match

Sean's friends from boarding school were meeting in Dublin for a big rugby match to be held at Croke Park. Sean insisted that I attend since everyone was bringing the wife. After the game, one of his best friends was hosting everyone for dinner at his house in Stillorgan and he had to have his woman on his arm. He also said that I had to pay €80 for the rugby ticket. I told one of my friends about this and she laughed hysterically.

'You don't even like rugby and you would put out €80 for a ticket? Have you lost your mind?"

Sean had said he would pay for hotel accommodations at the lovely five star Radisson Blu St. Helen's in Stillorgan. It was one of our favourite places to go for a drink when visiting Dublin. My friend said that if he wanted a trophy woman, he should pay for the game, the hotel, everything. After all, I had to work the following day at a food event and get up early, doing it all myself to make a living. She was right. I told him sales were down and if he wanted me to go, he would have to get my ticket. He was annoyed but obliged. The rugby match took place on Saturday 22nd November, 2008, a historic day when Ireland would play against Argentina to seal a place in the Rugby World Cup. We first met the group for drinks before the game at a huge pub in Clontarf and then walked en masse to Croke Park.

On the way, an elderly gentleman called out to me.

'Hello! Welcome to Ireland.'

'Thank you', I said.

'Do you know why the government let all you people into the country?'

'No, tell me why'.

'To strengthen the gene pool! Too much in-breeding.'

I just smiled and walked on. As I looked up, I saw a huge billboard lamenting the high incidence of cystic fibrosis in Ireland. Maybe the gentleman had seen this too and wanted to reassure me that my kind was welcome.

Every peacock in Sean's entourage ruffled his feathers to display his great importance to the others. Observing this preening ritual was very amusing. The game was exciting from beginning to end, with Ireland beating Argentina 17 to 3. We left for dinner in Stillorgan. Taxis here and taxis there, the day was proving to be an expensive trial for poor Sean. Luckily, my van was parked at the hotel and we made a detour there to get it and avoid additional taxi fares.

The dinner went on forever, leaving very little chance for Sean and me to spend any time alone. We crashed and were up early so I could go to the Dun Laoghaire Farmer's Market, and that was the weekend. Sean had well extended any budget he may have planned for and I hoped he had at least impressed one of his buddies in the whole exercise. I found the women in our entourage quite friendly and straightforward in comparison to their husbands. We got along well, which was a welcome relief.

Bittersweet Christmas

Christmas markets and events kept me busy every weekend until the end of the year. I planned to go back to Trinidad on holidays. I had no intention of spending another quiet Christmas in Tramore watching the ex-husband and wife fight over their children for attention and approval. The last weekend before Christmas, I was working at the Cork Christmas market. It was held on Friday, Saturday and Sunday and I drove back and forth every day to set up and dismantle my stand. Sean insisted that I go with him to the Alabama 3 concert at the Grand Hotel in Tramore. *Alabama 3* was a British band that mixed rock, dance, blues, country, and gospel styles. The whole town was buzzing with excitement and everyone had a ticket. I barely even knew their music, as was the case with most bands that everyone was excited about. But since it was really important, I agreed to dress up and go after I got back from Cork city.

I was exhausted, but put on a lovely bustier top and frilly lace skirt with high heeled sandals for the occasion. I had to look my best, even though my feet ached. I asked Sean to drive me to the Grand Hotel. It was two blocks away but it was uphill. He was understandably annoyed but he did it. Then it took a long time to find parking. Still, we got there in good time and it was amazing to see all the Tramore residents out in their numbers. They were dancing too. Generally, people over 35 did not dance until they were absolutely plastered drunk. However, for Alabama 3, all generations came out, and they sang and danced. People knew all the words to the songs. It was fun to watch, until I was almost run over by the dancing ex-wife.

'Hi Lindy. Are you enjoying the music?'

'Yes. It's great', I said and calmly danced in another direction.

Sean was visibly uncomfortable. Later, I heard one of Sean's friends loudly consoling the woman that Lindy had to be at the event too and it must be very hard on her. I told Sean shortly after that I was very tired, which I was. I had to work the next day and had had enough fun for one night. He said he would not be staying overnight. He was responsible for his kids that night. That was fine with me. I was annoyed with the whole town at that point.

The countdown began for my Christmas vacation in Trinidad. Sean asked how I could leave him to have Christmas dinner yet again at the ex-wife's house. I said he was well used to it and probably enjoyed going there. I asked him if we could go out one night and have our own Christmas dinner before I left. He seemed very pre-occupied, and said we would probably do something when I got back. It was the day before I left and he was too busy to stay over. He said he had to feed the dog, gave me a hurried kiss and left. I could not believe his behaviour. I was second, third and even fourth place to all the other important people in his life, including the dog.

11

MOVING ON

The Break Up

When we returned to Tramore after the holidays, I was determined that I was going to tell Sean to get lost. I promptly called him to come over for dinner the next evening. I spent hours preparing a meal for a king. I prepared roast duck and a host of other delicious dishes. Since school had not started yet, Tiffany's friend Joyce came over to spend time with her. They ran upstairs and downstairs, playing for hours while I prepared the meal and fixed the table for dinner. Sean arrived promptly at 6pm.

I brought cream of broccoli soup to the table.

'Where's the bread,' Sean asked.

I had no bread and wondered, with six other dishes on the table, if bread was absolutely necessary or was he just being difficult.

'How can I eat soup without bread?' he said.

'Joyce, do you like duck?' I asked.

'I don't mind.'

Tiffany had always hated duck.

'The poor little ducky,' she would say when she was small. 'Mommy, how could you eat duck? That's terrible'.

Thankfully, I had salmon too, so everyone had something to eat. After dinner, the girls went off to play. Sean and I chatted for a few minutes and he said he had to leave because of an early start in the morning. How cold and calculating he was. I knew something was wrong. His face and body language showed disinterest and a general boredom.

The following weekend, I set up a small table at the farmer's market on Priest's Road in Tramore. A few other die-hard traders came to sell and I Laid out my sauces and other goodies. It was January and the winds were fierce and strong. Passers-by bought a few items, then the wind whisked away one of my tables. It went pelting down the street, with sauce samples and crackers following. The day was a disaster. The winds howled all that night and the fence separating my garden from my neighbour's fell over. Sean never called to see if we were alive. I knew that if he was so unconcerned about our welfare, things were really bad.

Later that week, I got the definitive telephone call.

'Lindy, I guess it's finished between us,' he said.

'I guess it is.'

I tried to sound as nonchalant as possible. Was that it? Was that the way to end a four year relationship? I wept in silence. I had loved and cherished this man for so long. We had given each other so much time and attention.

A few days later, he asked to come to the house. I said it was fine, and waited anxiously, not knowing what I would say. I had walked around in a daze for days not knowing what to do with myself. I was tired of crying and wondered what I was really crying for. He had been distant from the first day I moved to his town. He blamed me for his daughter's apparent lack of interest in coming to his house. He also said I had to fit into his schedule. I wanted a man who would make me his number one.

We sat on the bench in front of my house and Sean wept openly. He did not know what had gone wrong. He said he was the problem, not me. He blamed it on his mother not raising him with love and affection. For me the deed was done. I would never beg to get back with him. He had decided to break up and that was final. We hugged farewell and promised to keep in touch.

Art Therapy

I felt isolated in this small town. It was his town. Many of my acquaintances were his friends. I missed him so much I would pass by his house just to get a glimpse of him. At least I had my own home and was not embroiled in another move. But, I needed to find activities to help ease the pain and isolation. I was already a member of the Toastmasters public speaking club. They were a friendly group, but they only met once or twice a month. Tramore had a number of groups of artists so I decided to plunge into the world of art. I was referred to a Venezuelan artist who accepted students at his home in Waterford city. One day, I went into Cahill's store on Main Street, Tramore and bought canvases, brushes and oil paints to equip myself for my new hobby.

I went with some apprehension to my first art class. The artist, Eduardo had said to bring a scrap book and pencils for sketching. Eduardo was Venezuelan, but had spent most of his life studying art and working in Italy. He had recently moved to Waterford. He was stocky, with a jovial face, rosy cheeks, olive skin, and green eyes. He smoked cigars and strong cigarettes and punctuated every hour with a smoke outside. He was delighted to hear that I was from Trinidad. We also discovered that I had visited his home town of Carupano many years before. I immediately knew I had met a kindred soul.

Eduardo gave me two objects to sketch; first a bowl of

oranges, then a plant. He seemed pleased with my efforts.

'You have good eye', he said, and pinched my right cheek.

This was the first of many pinches on the cheek. I was so delighted to be told I had an eye for art. I told Eduardo I had no interest in sketching objects. I wanted to learn how to paint portraits in oils.

'Portraits are the most difficult', he protested.

'Well that's what I want to paint!'

And so I embarked on my first portrait; a Trinidadian beauty queen called Wendy Fitzwilliams, former Ms Universe 1998. Eduardo coached me in the blending of colours and the use of a semi dry brush to slowly work the colour into the canvas. I followed this new hobby with a passion. It helped me to forget my personal trauma. Every time I felt a pang of loneliness for Sean, I painted. I could not wait to show off my portrait to friends far and wide on Facebook. As the weeks progressed, I painted a group of three market ladies, a fat lady and her skinny boyfriend on a bench, and a portrait of my friend's son on the day of his baptism. The paint was barely dry on the canvas before I started a new work. For the most part the painting needed more detail. Eduardo had great patience with me. If I told him I was done with a painting, he would just say:

'Ok, sign your name and put the date.'

Another instructor might have been annoyed with the lack of detail, but Eduardo didn't seem to mind. He wanted me to enjoy what I was doing. I used Caribbean magazines for inspiration and bright colours to lift the canvas and lift my spirits. That winter was very cold and with little trading. A recession was in full swing. Painting had become my refuge. Before I knew it, I was able to churn out a variety of portraits and oil paintings of people in various situations.

I decided to stop selling to shops in 2009, because it was too difficult to retrieve money from them. I was to only sell at markets and food shows getting cash on delivery. I longed for summer festivals to start so I could earn more money. Unfortunately, I had to stop going to art classes because I was not making enough money to support the hobby. So I told Eduardo I was leaving, but would probably come back after the summer break.

Tiffany's Blues

Tiffany noticed that Sean had not been coming around. She asked what had happened to him. I had to tell her that we broke up. She took the break up harder than I did. She was depressed for days and could barely eat. I also noticed her school work was suffering because she was so distracted. The most logical explanation I could determine was her feeling of losing a second father figure. No matter how distracted or distant Sean's behaviour towards her had been, he was still a father figure in her little world. With no father in the picture, she felt abandoned. She constantly asked why Sean would not contact us and what I had done to chase him away. No answer I gave would suffice. Not only did I have to battle with my own feelings of abandonment, I also had to take the blame for chasing the father away.

I decided to take Tiffany to a rock concert in Dublin in an attempt to cheer her up. Pussy Cat Dolls had a show at the newly refurbished O_2 Theatre on the Quays in Dublin. I was curious to see the massive upgrades that had been done to this great venue. We drove up from Waterford early to get a good parking spot and give ourselves enough time to enter the facility. Unfortunately, the organisers made patrons stand outside until 15 minutes before the scheduled starting time. It was very cold that night and we had not prepared for the wind chill factor as winds picked up across the Liffey. We stood in the queue for about an hour and Tiffany got angrier as time wore on. By the time we got to our seats, she had made up her mind not to enjoy the show. When I stood up to dance, she told me to sit down; I was making a fool of myself. Other mums who were also there danced while their teenagers were absorbed in sending text messages about the event to friends. It was a lively show. After driving the distance and paying for two tickets, I was determined to make the most of it. Lady Gaga was the new, unknown artist opening the show. She performed in front of a small screen, gyrating to pre-recorded music. The response to her performance was lukewarm. The Pussy Cat Dolls were the ones the crowd wanted to see.

Finally, they arrived on stage. It was clear that lead singer Nicole dominated the show. The other girls were little more than accompaniment. We stayed until the end and then we drove home. Tiffany had school the next day. She moaned about going to a concert in the middle of the week and how tired she would be. Much to her annoyance, I played loud rock music all the way home.

Crazy Farmer's Night Out

To beat the winter blues, I decided to go back onto the dating scene. I dreaded having to pick through the frogs again to find Prince Charming. But if I sat around moping and feeling sorry for myself, I would remain unhappy for a long time. So I shook off all the self doubt and fear, and went online to find a speed dating event. It had worked in Dublin; it might possibly work in the sunny South East. However, I had my doubts. To me, Waterford was very conservative and in many ways stuck in a 1980's time warp. I decided to set my sights on Kilkenny. Viewed as a party town, up and coming, and full of artsy people, Kilkenny held potential. I registered for an event there to see what lively people I could meet. The event was at the River Court Hotel, on the banks of the Nore River across from Kilkenny Castle.

I always got lost in Kilkenny. I would always look out for Kilkenny Castle to get my bearings. However, since the event was at night, I could not see a castle. I just drove around until I hit High Street and then, using my homing pigeon techniques, I was able to find the entrance for parking at the hotel. After daydreaming for a few seconds about romantic walks on the banks of the river, I went in to register for the event.

When I walked in, the organisers were right at the door to greet me. They looked like a husband and wife team who had been in the matchmaking business for decades. He looked like Elvis and she matched the look. They were well prepared, with name tags, pens, paper etc. I scanned the characters around the room to see if there were any interesting prospects. Not wanting to seem too anxious, I ran to the ladies' room to freshen up. When I returned, I sat and chatted with a few of the ladies while we waited for others to arrive. A group of six women walked in together. I didn't know anyone. How could they have so much moral support?

Then the official proceedings started. My first prospect was a tall lanky fellow with large eyes and short cropped black hair. He said he lived in Waterford and played Gaelic football. I tried to look interested, but I was not. Did anyone at the event even live in Kilkenny? The next three prospects were all farmers. A stocky, grey haired man spoke about rising at 5am to tend to the animals. He was recently widowed with three big sons. I had visions of myself barefoot, with a scarf tied around my head, cooking in the kitchen for Paddy and the boys and shuddered. The next farmer was from Tipperary. He was quite good looking, with a scar on his nose and very pushy.

'I like you. Let's get together some time. Where are you from? How old are you?'

I evaded the interrogation with vague answers.

'Let's not waste time. We've only five minutes,' he said. 'I does be a very impawrtant man in Tipperary Town. Everyone tells me good mornin' when I walk in de town'.

I nicknamed him Crazy Farmer and for a brief moment, I imagined selecting yes for this character. However, my better judgement prevailed. I would have to review the others on offer.

I met a grain farmer, a dairy farmer, a horse breeder and then finally a farmer who seemed to have travelled a bit and even guessed my country of birth. He got a big 'Yes' on my score card. How refreshing, I thought.

During the break, all the ladies rushed to the powder room to chat and compare notes. We laughed and giggled. I wondered if all the speed dating candidates in Kilkenny would be farmers. Fortunately, I met an accountant from Cork and a banker from Tipperary. They were also friends with Crazy Farmer. I gave them both a 'Yes', simply for not being farmers, and left the event swiftly after the last score cards were submitted.

The next day I went eagerly online to see the matches and found that the candidates I had chosen had also selected me. We exchanged a few email messages and I arranged to meet the well travelled farmer at the Tower Hotel, Waterford city's most central and convenient hotel with parking. In fact, I met several other candidates at the Tower hotel and became worried that I would be recognised as a woman who met strange men for drinks, even if in my case it was a ginger ale or cranberry juice.

My accountant match gave my telephone number to Crazy Farmer since the man was very keen to meet me. He said he wanted to take me out to the finest restaurant and was disappointed I had not selected him. I said it was ok for us to get together, so we arranged to meet at Sabai Thai restaurant at the Mall in Waterford. I had forgotten what he looked like and hoped that our plan to meet in the bar at the front of the restaurant would help me recognise him. Luckily, there was one man and two ladies sitting at the bar when I got there. Crazy Farmer was a fairly good looking man, well dressed in an expensive striped shirt, short black hair and a scar on his nose. The scar I remembered. He was texting furiously to someone and even as we got our table, he continued to be pre-occupied with his texting.

This fine dining Thai restaurant had a wealth of choices in seafood, vegetarian, and meat dishes; enough to confuse even the most skilled Thai food connoisseur. Crazy Farmer, who obviously had no experience in ordering Thai food, went for chicken chow mein. I found an interesting fish dish and settled in my chair. Crazy Farmer dipped in and out of conversation and text messaging. It must have been a case of attention deficit disorder, I thought. After the meal, I said goodbye.

'Maybe we could meet another time.'

'But I came all the way from Tipperary to see you,' he protested.

Whoever he was texting got more attention than I did, I thought. I rushed to my van for a swift escape. Then he started texting me, about what a nice night he had had and when we could meet again. In the following days, I received text poems, phone calls, and requests to meet again. It was funny to receive the same poem the following week, with another woman's name inserted in it. I decided to immediately send the poem back to Crazy Farmer and insert his name in the lovely poem just for a laugh. Even though he didn't appreciate it, it certainly was good 'craic'.

I broke down after dozens more telephone calls and texts and decided to meet Crazy Farmer again for a date. This time, we actually met in a small restaurant in Tramore. This was against my better judgement, since I did not want to bump into Sean. However, Crazy Farmer insisted on it. The restaurant was a five-minute walk from my house. Since I did not want him to know where I lived, I gave directions and then jumped into my van to drive two blocks over. I had to find parking near the restaurant. The restaurant was empty except for one other couple. I had met the owner the year before in the pub with all Sean's other acquaintances; she had had a well-advertised break-up with her own partner. She studied my date closely and asked numerous questions. No doubt this was in an effort to carry news back to whoever would listen to her in the pub the following week.

Crazy Farmer was at his texting best, similar to our previous date and I wondered if I should walk out the restaurant for air and never return. But the seafood meal was delicious and he produced his credit card to pay. Our hostess studied the name on the card with huge fascination. When we left the restaurant, I could see her from my rear view mirror, rushing out the door. She looked up and down the street to see if she could identify Crazy Farmer's car. This was a new level of nosiness, even for Tramore.

Crazy Farmer insisted we go to the pub. I protested, but he would not hear of it. He wanted to prolong the night. We went to The Vic, a regular haunt of Sean and his buddies. Sean's friends sat in the same corner where they always sat. Of course Crazy Farmer had to stand in between Paul and Tony to order his whiskey, while I tried not to be noticed at the table across the way.

'Come over here', he motioned.

As I approached the bar, Paul and Tony's eyes lit up. What could I say?

'Hi guys. How's it going?'

They would have so much to tell Sean as soon when they left the pub that night.

Crazy Farmer swallowed two shots of whiskey, professed that he did not usually drink much and ordered a third. I nursed my cranberry juice and wondered when I could make a quick get away home. He then decided we should go down to the waterfront. I was glad to get away from prying eyes. I jumped into my van and told him to follow me in his car. I was not about to get into the car of a whiskey drinking, crazy farmer.

At the waterfront, we parked side by side and he motioned for me to get into his car. As I sat next to him, I tried to dodge a slobbery kiss.

'I'm a rich farmer,' he said. 'I own horses and have a big farm house in Tipperary.

Do you see the kind of car I'm driving?'

I had to admit I had not noticed his car. I seldom looked at the makes of cars. Observing the colour was my limit. He indicated it was a Mercedes Benz.

'Hmmm,' I said.

He announced that he had booked a room at the Majestic Hotel and I should join him for the night. He promised to be very good. I was horrified that this socially inept man had no clue about charming a lady. I calmly said good night, ran to my van and drove swiftly home.

Crazy Farmer was not deterred and continued texting and calling for many months afterwards. The contact became less frequent with time, but we stayed in touch. He may have hoped for a change of heart.

Festival Fun

From spring right through the summer months and then into fall I participated in countless festivals and markets, which took me around the country, but primarily in Cork and Waterford. I was to learn my way around the south of Ireland very well in 2009, travelling almost 100,000km in my new Taste of the Caribbean van.

One of the highlights of spring was the Waterford Food Festival held in Dungarvan. Since I was a bona fide resident of Waterford County, I was entitled to take part in this weekend event, which celebrated food in all its glory. The Sunday was the main day of this festival, with people from every village around Waterford, as well as neighbouring Co. Cork in attendance. That year, the sun was splitting the rocks. Crowds of people came and they wanted to spend. Dorcas helped me and we could not keep up. People wanted sauces, they wanted hot food, they wanted buns, and they wanted attention and conversation. It was an action packed afternoon. Waterford County Council sponsored the whole event for traders and it was certainly the best in terms of income for everyone that April. At 6:00 pm, everyone left promptly and we had to race to pack up or be run over by the cleaning crews. They worked swiftly to transform the main square in Dungarvan back into a working parking lot once more. When I presented Tiffany my "accountant" with the pile of cash that evening she could not stop counting.

'Look at the reward hard work brings,' I told her.

Another popular Festival was Bloom in the Park. It was a trendy Garden Show which took place every June Bank Holiday week end. I managed to get a place in the Bord Bia sponsored producer's market because I was an Irish food producer. The event ran from Thursday to Sunday, rain or shine in Phoenix Park, one of Ireland's largest city parks. Dubliners and others came out in their finest to shop! They bought plants, food, and everything they could get their hands on. The drive back and forth from Waterford to Dublin every day was tiresome. I did not dare splurge on hotel accommodation, since many events were disappointing and unpredictable that year. I also rose at 4:00 am every morning to cook a fresh stock of saheena and aloo pies which were always a favourite snack with my Dublin fans. They remembered me from the Farmer's Markets. Some customers told me they would stock up on pies, freeze them and bring them out gradually to enjoy. It felt great to have such loyal customers.

Between festivals, I participated in the Waterford city farmers' market at Ardkeen shopping centre on alternate Sunday afternoons and the Dungarvan farmers' market in the Square every Thursday morning. On quiet Saturday mornings, I would go up to the church parking lot in Tramore, sell a few wares, and chat with the locals.

That summer, I became very familiar with event organisers in Cork city and other towns in County Cork, as I made my way to as many events as possible. Traders like the Murphy brothers, who sold pork sausage, became my new family. They were the friendliest brothers I had ever met. They would always look out for me. I even met their mother, who let me park in front of her house when I went away on my two week vacation.

'Hi Jinny. How's it goin'?' the brothers chimed, in their wonderful sing song Cork city accent.

Anna Maria from Chile sold the most unusual costume jewellery. A French couple sold jars and jars of French preserves. Cathal and his wife sold Fair Trade clothing and bric a brac from far away countries. Another couple sold hand crafted silver jewellery. The Sprout Man, Patrick, sold sprouted peas, beans, and grain, with each little bag commanding a generous price. The sprouts and beans made you fart for hours afterwards, but it was a small price to pay for feeling healthy. The Crepe Man sold sweet and savoury crepes with delicious fillings. His stand drew an audience; people loved the theatre of crepe preparation. They would stop and look, just for the sake of looking.

A Greek God sold lamb burgers from a Bar B Q grill and another group sold organic grilled vegetables on skewers. Hector, a Spanish clown who fancied me, made action figures, flowers, and a host of other goodies using skinny balloons. He even made a balloon version of Lindy for my birthday that year, matching the colours of my T-shirt, trousers and hair clip to perfection. He put a balloon-shaped eye on my table cloth when I asked him to keep an eye on my stand. Hector made a host of jokes with passers-by. Traders came and went, but the core of regulars remained.

Some of the customers also became family. I collected email addresses and always alerted them when I was coming to town. That summer, I took part in the Cork Book Festival, the Mad Pride Festival, the World Street Performance Championships, and Cork Jazz Festival. I also traded at the Midleton Food Festival, which turned out to be a hectic Saturday, with fun loving 'foodies' who wanted to try everything as they passed through Main Street in Midleton.

My Trinidad rotis proved a huge success. Irish customers insisted on having a fork to eat the rotis and were puzzled as to why I didn't put rice in the wrap. Having been programmed by fast food restaurants that you put curry sauce on rice, my customers could not fathom other ways of eating curry. If they insisted on rice, I gave it to them. As if my Cork adventures were not enough, I got wind of the All Ireland Farmers Market, an annual event in Enniscorthy, County Wexford. I promptly signed up to take part. There was a competition for the best decorated stall. My helper and I spent the best part of an hour setting up and putting flags all round the top of the gazebo, so we could be visible a mile away. We spent Saturday in Enniscorthy and Sunday in Dunmore East, Waterford for a brand new food festival called "Food, Fun, and Fish". This event targeted Waterford food producers and gave us a chance to show our wares. We lined the docks and jetties in Dunmore East with our stalls. There were so many food stalls that I wondered how we could possibly make money. However, the sun was blazing that Sunday and people came not only from the affluent Dunmore East neighbourhood, but from Tramore, Waterford city and beyond for the event. It was a great financial success for just a few hours in the afternoon.

We were forever watchful for the Waterford City food inspectors. On this occasion, I was over prepared with my hand wash station, hot boiling water and more equipment for heating and testing food than I needed. I looked and looked that Sunday, but they did not show up, much to the delight of all those serving hot food.

At the Kinsale Food Festival, I joined Patrick Champot and the French European traders to sell Caribbean food. That market had become less French than in previous years, and anyone with a reasonable product gained entry. I was approached by a little Chinese teenager, accompanied by a string of Irish girlfriends.

'My name is Crystal and these are my peeps,' she said in the strongest Jamaican accent. 'Ya have any ackee?"

What a surprise in the little town of Kinsale to meet a

Jamaican Chinese girl. We chatted for a while as her Irish 'peeps' listened in amusement. She told me her family had moved to Kinsale some years before and opened a big Chinese restaurant. Later that day, her mother came to give me a big hug. She was so happy to meet another Caribbean person in Kinsale.

I had another surprise that day when an Irish looking red head man approached and said hello. His accent was very familiar, very Trinidadian!

`Hey. What are you doing here?' I asked.

He said his father was Irish and had moved to Trinidad many years before. He had grown up in Trinidad but recently moved back to Ireland. I had heard similar tales from Dublin customers. It felt great to bond with fellow Caribbean souls in this artsy little town of West Cork, with its pretty cafes and boats in the harbour.

I decided to head back to the Cork Southwest Music Festival again in 2009. This time I was armed with curry to feed the nation. The event went on for hours and finally ended at 1:00 am. Revellers who hadn't been hungry early that evening decided it was time to eat and prolong the night. Dorcas and I were faced with a long queue of hungry people.

'We want roti! We want roti,' they chanted.

We had stopped cooking up fresh food at 11:00 pm and had planned to sell what was left. The unforeseen clamour was quite a surprise. We put the stingiest amount of chicken and potatoes in the wrap to make it go as far as possible. Then we started selling curry sauce in a wrap. Finally, even the sauce came to an end and we had to close up. If only we had known, we would have prepared more food. But we had learned our lesson for the next year. We packed up, our eyes blurred with tiredness. As we attempted to leave, we discovered we were stuck in mud. It had rain so much the previous days that the field was water-logged. We had to wait for a tractor to pull us out and tow us to the nearest exit. With the best intensions, Dorcas could not keep her eyes open. I resorted to playing the loudest Techno and House music I could possibly find on the airwaves. By a miracle of God we finally reached Tramore.

The Electric Picnic, a mammoth music festival held at the end of summer was a serious distraction for all music minded and event minded folks. Since I could not afford the exorbitant fees of a full hot food stand, I again applied for the Farmer's Market in the Country Village. The imaginary Village at the festival was a wonderful mix of artificial building fronts, with Disc Jockeys pounding out music. There was the Village bingo hall, the all night bar, the Sheriff's office, the post office, and an inflatable church performing live weddings throughout the day. The best part was that the priest was the DJ. I went in and jumped around in the church a few times. Anyone could be a guest at a wedding. The cast wore yellow and pink dresses and it was evident that any man could also dress as a bridesmaid. Weddings were booked solid all day, for all manner of brides and grooms.

Rain did not stop revellers from dancing in the mud and tramping through the mud in search of food. We stood ankle deep in mud and sold food all day. The health inspectors were a jovial pair of young girls who did not seem to notice the mud. They told us to carry on. However, the traders were very upset with management for not providing flooring in the tent when rain had been predicted the week before. Their best offering was to dump a large mountain of hay next to the market tent for us to put on the floor around us. I found myself scrambling for hay with a whole circus of people from neighbouring tents. The scene was as strange as the prize.

There was no sign posting to alert people that a market was in the tent. So one of the traders decided to print signs at home after the first day, and fasten them to the front of the tent. The sprout man, who had paid extra money for plumbing and electricity, was very disappointed at the weekend's proceeds. He changed the FARMERS MARKET sign to read FARTERS ARK. That drew in the visitors.

As my participation in festivals increased, I enlisted the help of a Waterford catering service to make hundreds of aloo pies and saheena for me. Teaching the Irish chef, a bald, straight-talking guy called Niall, how to make Indo-Trinidadian dishes, proved quite challenging.

'What's the recipe?' he asked.

'There is none. I just cook by instinct.'

'You must have a recipe. Jaysus. How dah feck am I s'posed tah help widout ah recipe?'

I made up a recipe and poor Niall got the aloo pies as close as possible to my samples. They looked different because he made smooth dough in a machine, as opposed to my rustic, hand kneaded dough. And the filling lacked certain flavours, which I really could not fine tune, since I tended to add a bit of this and a bit of that.

With Niall's help, I was ready for the Festival of World Cultures in Dun Laoghaire, Dublin. This Festival was the monster of all festivals, with a reported 100,000 in attendance. It had grown from a small three day event to a huge, widely publicised event, with international performers, craft fairs, and of course food villages of all kinds. I took a stand on the main street along the waterfront to catch passing trade and avail of the lower fees. The Festival fees had risen steadily every year, from €400 for three days in 2006 to a whopping €1,000 for a hot food stand in 2009. I had no intention of working just to pay the County Council. I opted for the groceries stand which closed early, had no electricity, and had to be removed every night. What a tiring ordeal it was and even with a helper, the work proved unbearably tough. The last day, Sunday evening, was usually the most tiring. We had to remove every scrap of rubbish or be fined for littering, then face the long drive home.

Agricultural Aggro

Agricultural shows were also on my agenda in 2009. I signed up for the Tinahely Show in Wexford and the Tullamore Show in County Offaly, with Laura helping me. We got lost again going to Tinahely. When we found the grounds, we were finally able to set up in a row of tents which included cookware, blankets, toys, and other bric a brac. People kept coming despite the rain and mud. The fashion that week was for the most beautiful rain gear: Macintosh boots, rain coats and matching umbrellas.

We were in the middle of serving our curry meals when a small group of organisers approached us, very annoyed.

'You never declared you were serving hot food,' they said.

'What? Is there a problem?'

'Hot food is in another area. You'll have to pay more money.'

'Well, no problem. How much do you want?'

They walked away and had a small conference. They then returned with a demand of €50 extra. The problem was solved, but they were not pleased,

The Tullamore Show was another misadventure. As I

prepared my goods for sale, the rain poured and poured. I was about to cross the bridge in Waterford city for the first day's trading when I heard on the news that the Tullamore show was being cancelled because of flooding. I wept like a baby. It had taken so many hours to drive back and forth, and I had already prepared hundred of euros worth of buns and pies to sell at one of Ireland's largest farm shows. The next day I drove back to Offaly and collected my goods, again risking being stuck in the mud. Then I drove to Dun Laoghaire market in Dublin to salvage what I could in sales of cooked food, but that too was a washout.

But there were moments of light relief in the middle of all the strain. I sometimes traded next to a husband and wife team from Dunmore East who sold bread and olives. The woman did the baking and her husband manned the stall at markets One day I asked the husband why they did not put prices on their products at markets. He said it was because of the "Ass Hole Tax".

'What is that?' I asked, fighting to control my laughter.

He explained with a twinkle in the eye that if a customer was being difficult and fussy, the Ass Hole tax was applied to cover the costs of the aggravation endured. It was the funniest strategy I had heard in years and certainly a most effective way to relieve stress.

Onwards and Upwards

I had often heard about the Ploughing Championships, Ireland's biggest agricultural show. That year, I signed up for the event. It proved to be another mud bath, full of curious farmers passing by for a look. A Tramore friend helped me on the first day of the event, but she was overwhelmed and tired and wasn't able to sell anything. I calmly told her I would be able to manage on my own for the rest of the show.

I went to the Cork Jazz Festival at the end of October and then came November, the dead month when nothing happened. Farmers' markets became dull and quiet as people hid from the November winds and rain until Christmas. I was fortunate to get a big catering opportunity with our Toastmasters club. We were hosting a competition with other groups and someone suggested that instead of ordering soggy sandwiches, I could be paid to cater for the event. I put forth the finest offering of homemade meat balls, salads, fish fritters and dips. It was declared the most elaborate and delicious food at a Toastmasters event. I received a lot of advertising for my sauces and catering skills. I was later asked to cater for the Toastmasters Christmas Party. I could not attend since I was selling at the Christmas Fair in Cork, but the food went down well.

Party Time

In the middle of all the festivals, markets and events, I decided to stage a big birthday bash for myself. I invited my favourite people: Dublin market friends, many of my Toastmasters friends, and others. I had also invited Sean's best friend, Colm and his wife Helgar. Of course word got back to Sean that I was having a birthday party. Then word got back to me that Sean was at his friend's house sulking because he had not been invited. So I did the diplomatic thing, called him up and invited him to the party. Through the rumour mill, word got back to me that he was annoyed at the last minute invitation and did not want to come. He said he had 'let' me come to his 50th birthday party two years before. His ego was really a difficult thing to manage.

I prepared many appetisers, main dishes, salads, and desserts. We ate chicken curry, Bar-B-Q pork chops, and shrimp in tomato sauce, broccoli coleslaw, Spanish rice, chickpeas curry, Greek salad, and a host of other dishes. I had to borrow two stoneware dishes from Helgar for serving. Then I went out and bought extra glasses, plates, and stainless steel cutlery. My guests would not be using anything disposable. Tiffany made a birthday cake for me and my neighbours also brought a lovely cake. It was a feast for 100, when in fact thirty people were there.

We played lively Hip Life and High Life music that I had acquired on a recent trip to Ghana. It was fun to dance all night. Some guests danced, but others were too shy. They just observed and clapped. Of course it rained, so I had a huge gazebo in the courtyard for smokers. The living room made an ideal space for the limbo dancing competition. Everyone had to attempt to dance the limbo. Irish or not, the limbo was a must at my parties. As the guests drank more, the limbo got very lively. Even Colm dipped under the limbo stick head first. I took numerous pictures and posted them on Facebook the next day. No doubt Sean was able to search through all the photos to see what transpired. To the Tramore Toastmasters group, I was chef supreme. One of the members, Liam, wondered aloud how soon I would be having another birthday so he could come over to eat!

Picking uthp the Visitors

My mother, Gloria, was turning 77 and her friend Kim was a few years her junior. Gloria and Kim had been teachers at the same secondary school in Port-of-Spain, Trinidad. They had remained friends well after retirement. Kim, from what I remembered, was very soft spoken with a twinkle in her eye. She cracked jokes sometimes, but always out of earshot when I was growing up. Kim was still very active and physically fit. The years had not been as kind to my mother after retirement. Her body was succumbing to arthritis in the knees and hands, but the worst affliction was the onset of Alzheimer's disease. Gloria was losing her confidence and memory and recognised the fact that she could no longer travel alone. She had loved to travel frequently in her young years, jetting to the United States, England, or countries around the Caribbean. The whole year had passed without a trip and I thought it would be fitting for her to visit me for Christmas with Kim, since I didn't plan to travel. Financially, 2009 had been mediocre and with the recession continuing, I thought it best just to relax and stay put for the holidays.

Needing some funds for the holidays, I worked a three day weekend at the Cork Christmas market on Grand Parade. The usual customers came around, as well as locals passing by for samples out of habit. Even though we were not frozen outdoors like the year before, we were certainly feeling the brunt of the recession. I had to set up outside the main tent that year and had the added challenge of removing the whole gazebo and contents at the end of each night. This was difficult indeed, not only to bear the cold, but to remain cheerful all day, chat with customers and convince them that Caribbean style sauces made unique stocking stuffers. It was a strange idea when uncharacteristic snow was looming on the Irish horizon.

I had baked Caribbean Christmas cakes. These rum cakes, as some called them, were a big hit. When they were tied with red ribbon, cakes of all sizes made wonderful gifts. I made cakes in the shape of small loaves, some with fruits and blackened with molasses and browning. I also made rum cakes without fruit. Cork customers called them buns.

'Oh look at the little buns,' they said. 'Is there enough rum in them to get drunk?'

'You would have to eat about five or six. I put one shot of rum in each cake!'

This was a source of amusement to all the passers-by.

Since that weekend was a bit slow, I decided to only work two days the following weekend when Mammy arrived. I could then spend the rest of the time preparing for Christmas.

I flew to London Gatwick airport to meet Kim and Gloria and came back with them to Dublin. This meant renting a car in Waterford, driving to Dublin airport, leaving the car in long term parking, getting on an early jet out to Gatwick and taking the Gatwick shuttle in between terminals. I met them just as they left baggage claim and took them on the shuttle back to the other Gatwick terminal so we could get our flight back to Dublin. After checking in, I tried without success to get them to eat lunch. It was going to be a long journey flying to Dublin. This was followed by at least two and a half hours' drive to Waterford.

'We had something to eat on the plane', they protested.

'Yes, but that was hours ago!'

Mammy was extremely disoriented and nervous. She spilled all her tea on the table in the restaurant, and was already talking about going back to her house in Trinidad. It was going to be a very, very long day for me. We finally boarded the flight to Dublin and by the time we arrived, the two were at their wits end with fatigue. As we drove to Waterford, Mammy got more and more agitated. The roads were long and winding through every town. I knew every bend, but for the unsuspecting traveller, it was grass, forests, trees, bush and endless bush.

'You are taking me into the forest to kill me,' Mammy protested. 'Where are we going? Put me out now so I can take a taxi home!'

There was no stopping her, and Kim sat quietly, not knowing what to do. Mercifully, we got home in good time and we were able to get Mammy settled in Tiffany's room.

'Where am I?' she asked. 'How did I get here?'

I had to explain about three or four times how they flew to London, via Barbados, then from London to Dublin, then drove from Dublin to Tramore.

'Tra – More – Ray', Mammy kept saying. It was truly funny.

I unloaded the luggage, took back the rental car and retrieved my two-seater van from the parking lot of the rental car company. It was a solid 12 hours of travel for me.

Leo

In November, I met a new guy who drove all the way from Kildare County to visit me. We met, of course at the Tower hotel in Waterford City and had a fine chat. Leo, a retired army man, was running his own security firm with some business partners. He said he had been separated for years, and seemed like an interesting person. He had lived abroad, and had even witnessed battles. He was six feet tall and fit as a fiddle, with thinning fair hair, large bulging blue eyes and a bushy, blond moustache. I tried to read his intentions but failed. He seemed genuine but I had a nagging feeling that something was wrong with him, and hesitated to let him know where I lived or even to get into his large black Mercedes Benz,

He stopped at nothing to impress by taking me to Waterford's finest restaurants. He really liked his food and had dabbled with cooking lessons. He offered to help me set up at markets and food shows and soon started following me to events. I did not know whether to be flattered or annoyed, but let him help when he wanted to. The truth was that I was happy to have a strong helper when I was packing up after a 10 or 12 hour work day.

Leo and I had planned an evening out before Christmas on

December 23rd. When all the visitors were settled at home, I went off on my date. He said I should bring a swim suit and it was a surprise. I loved surprises and wondered what was in store. We started out of Waterford city, crossing the bridge and heading east. Finally, we rounded a bend and went up a small hill to the Brandon House Hotel near New Ross, Co. Wexford. The wooden building looked like a space ship next to a traditional red brick hotel with grand architecture. The view from the patio was picturesque, overlooking fields.

Leo had booked a massage for me at Solas Croi, the newly refurbished spa at the Brandon House Hotel. We were early and were allowed to use the Jacuzzi and steam rooms. It could have been romantic, except that I was not in love. The idea of being out on a date at a spa was certainly a first for me and was very relaxing and enjoyable. We hugged and enjoyed the steamy bubbles in the Jacuzzi. When it was time for my massage, a capable Polish girl massaged my neck and back. I complained about back pains after heavy duty work at events. She gave good advice about exercises I could do each day to alleviate the back strain.

My massage left me relaxed and happy. The girl worked on my neck and back, arms and legs. All the major pains seemed to go away, if only for a while. I then went to dress up in my fanciest outfit, because we were going out to dinner. It was a cancan style lace skirt and a bustier top. Several attempts to zip up the bustier proved futile and eventually the zipper burst. I had no choice but to wear a plain black top that had ended up in the bag by accident. I put on ravishing make up and stepped out.

Knowing that I adored Thai food, Leo had made a reservation at Sabai Thai Restaurant, on The Mall in Waterford. I was so hungry after the long session at the spa. I could hardly wait for the meal. The choices were extensive at this restaurant: soups, salads, main dishes. They used the right mix of lemon grass, peanut sauce, coconut and other authentic Thai ingredients.

By 11:00 pm, I was totally fatigued and wanted to go straight home.

'I have guests at home,' I explained. 'I will have to go back soon to check on things. You know, make sure everything is fine.'

'Do you really have to go home?'

'Yes, I've neglected them long enough'.

Leo delivered me to my front door. I could feel the tension and annoyance oozing from his whole body. After putting in all this time and money, all I wanted to do was go home. It was enjoyable, but I didn't feel the same love and attraction I had felt for Sean. When we arrived at my door, I gave Leo a Christmas card which I had stored in my bag that afternoon. To which he responded by writing up a little card in front of me and handing it over. I felt a bit shocked at his offering, given the amount of money he had spent on lavish nights out.

Christmas in Tramore

I started cooking the Christmas meal a full day in advance, to prepare a wonderful feast for our visitors. Since my mother and Kim had to spend their vacation in an old stone house, where the damp came in no matter how much the house was heated, the least I could do was make them hearty meals.

I prepared roast turkey, ham leg, pork chops, roast lamb, macaroni and cheese pie, rice dishes and various salads. We also ate traditional dark Christmas cake with rum and fruits, ice cream, fruit salad, and any other dish I could throw in for good measure. It was a meal for an extended family of 15, when there were just four of us. Needless to say, we had food for days after Christmas. On Christmas Day, we rose early and had a light breakfast. Kim was clamouring to go to the Catholic Church for Christmas mass. I could not deny them Christmas mass but only had a two-seater van, so I asked Sean the night before if he would mind taking us to Church. I knew his routine well. I did the polite thing and invited him to my home for Christmas dinner, indicating that he had an alternative to Christmas at his ex-wife's if he wished.

About 10 minutes before Sean arrived to take us to church, I went to check on my mother who was dressing feverishly in her room. She was dressed in a beautiful, sleeveless blue and white dress with a light cotton shawl and silver sandals, with a silver handbag to match. The only problem was that it was 1°C outside and the wind was howling, making it feel like -5°C. In her mind, she was probably in the Caribbean on Christmas Day.

'Mammy, please, let's change everything and put on some warm clothes,' I begged.

'But then people at church won't see my dress.'

'They really don't need to see your dress. It's too cold outside.'

It took some convincing for her to wear extra garments. In the meantime, Sean had arrived. He was clearly annoyed he had to drive me and my clan around on Christmas morning. I did not want to delay him an extra minute. We piled in and went to the Protestant church in Tramore, the one with the shorter steeple. Nobody was in sight for miles, not even on the roadway, but a sign indicated mass at 10 am. We then went on to the Catholic Church, which was starting its second mass of the morning. Anyone who was anyone was at Christmas mass. The church goers slumped into a trance as the priest gave his sermon. I spent my time studying all the faces, trying to see which ones I recognised and which ones were unfamiliar. With so much to take in, the sermon and the whole ceremony went along swiftly. I tried to listen to the priest on a few occasions, but he seemed to be talking to himself and the message was unclear to me. It was no small wonder that so many looked lost.

Suddenly there was a flurry of activity. People stirred, got ready to receive the sacrament, and left. Sean collected us and we were swiftly deposited at the front gate. He shrugged off my Christmas hug and said goodbye.

The Christmas menu was a hit with Kim and my mother. But Tiffany noted my exhaustion and blurted out to them: 'You are having a Christmas holiday, but not my mammy!'

After spending two days indoors, we had to get out so I could keep my sanity. We rented a car and I took the girls to see the most recent 3-D movie. My mother and Kim shouted at the screen wearing their 3-D glasses, much to Tiffany's amusement. They really enjoyed the action film. The following day I decided to take them to Cork city for a quick visit. With the short daylight hours, I wanted to leave early in the morning, but it never happened. So we set out close to midday.

'I want to shop at Marks and Spencers,' Mammy proclaimed. 'I want to buy dresses. I have lots of money.'

I knew she had money and had been burning to spend it on something for days. However, I had no energy for a shopping trip, since she could not walk very fast or very far.

As we drove to Cork, I pointed to various interesting places along the way. I had done the drive so many times I felt I could do it my eyes closed. At Swan Lake near Midleton, the fog made the lake barely visible. As I pointed out the area, I noticed that Mammy was wearing her 3-D glasses from the movie the night before. She could not see anything clearly. Kim had no glasses at all and had probably left them at home. So my sightseeing ritual was only for myself.

The following day, we went on an outing to Dublin. December 29th was Mammy's birthday and I wanted to show her the bright lights of Dublin city. It was a cold, dark day, making the drive very dull. When we finally parked the car at St Stephen's Green shopping centre, we had a light lunch. I had planned to walk around Grafton Street and show them a few sights in the city. That plan was short-lived, as my mother complained about the cold within half a block and refused to walk any further. We calmly retrieved the rental car and went off to visit a friend in Finglas, where we had a home cooked dinner, then took the drive back to Tramore. It was not a happy birthday. My nerves were strained to the limit.

New Year's Eve

Leo resurfaced after Christmas and we planned to go out for New Year's Eve. It had been a dream of mine to go out with a nice guy to a dinner dance on New Year's Eve, ringing in the year with bells, whistles and screams of "Happy New Year". This was going to be my one night off, for a change of scenery and fun. Leo had made reservations at Clontarf Castle in Dublin, where we would go to the New Year's Eve party, then stay overnight. I zipped into Waterford city to look for a lovely dress for the evening. I snapped up a beautiful silver mini from an independent boutique. I hated shopping and was happy to find something so quickly. Then I went into Debenhams and found a pair of beaded stilettos and a cylindrical silver handbag that matched the dress.

Kim and Gloria showered me with advice on what I should wear.

'You must wear stockings. You can't have your legs out!'

'That dress is too short. You should have chosen something else.'

'You can't wear a g-string,' said Mammy. 'That's so common and low class for a lady. I'll lend you one of my knickers.'

'Mammy, yours may be a bit too big for me.' I said. 'I'll use what I have.'

Tiffany couldn't stop laughing. It amused her to see the two grannies react in chorus at my preparation for the outing.

I left Kim in charge of the home, with extra food in the refrigerator and ideas for what meals they could prepare. Kim wanted to go for a walk around the small town. I told her this was fine since she was very fit and wanted some exercise. Free at last, Leo and I drove happily out of town. We were very excited about the coming night of fun. It was to be a large dinner/dance with hats and whistles, and an opportunity to stay overnight at Clontarf Castle. I asked a friend who lived in Clontarf to join us for drinks with her partner and she said they might come later on. With the M9 motorway now open, the journey to Dublin was a lot shorter. Reports of a pending heavy snowfall filled the airwaves, but not much had fallen by that time. We would be safely tucked away at night in Clontarf Castle with nothing to worry about when the storm hit. We were on the M9, just passing the Kilcullen exit in County Kildare, when I got a call from my neighbour in Tramore. Kim had fallen in front of the house. She could not walk, and they had called for the ambulance.

12

THE DRAGON'S DEN EXPERIENCE

The Application

In 2009, the popular British programme Dragon's Den was franchised out to Irish television. The programme offered entrepreneurs an opportunity to pitch their businesses to five multimillionaires who were themselves entrepreneurs. If a Dragon liked the business, he would invest money in it. The participant had to prepare a short, insightful business pitch and business plan to impress the Dragons and win some funding. The whole idea appeared very attractive. Several of my customers at the Dun Laoghaire market egged me on to enter the competition. There was always a buzz about the programme when the advertisements came on television. My customers had seen the success of Reggae Reggae sauce and felt that since I had a range of sauces, I had a chance.

'You'd be great on TV,' they said. 'Look how well you explain your business to us'.

Idle chatter was very easy at a market. Presenting figures and business plans to hard-headed business people was a very different matter.

I got an email message one day from the Dublin City Enterprise Board encouraging entrepreneurs to enter the Irish Dragon's Den. The organisers were accepting applications in October and we were not to miss out on the opportunity. As I searched for information on the RTE website, the advert for the Dragon's Den application popped up on my computer screen. I figured the universe was trying to tell me something. I had to apply and see what happened.

I filled in the forms, put together some photos of my

products and assembled a list of all my successes to date in running my business. I felt sure the buzz I had created around my business over the past three years was enough to justify appearing on the programme. Yet when I had gathered all the information I needed, I hesitated. What if I made a fool of myself on national television? I had a million reasons not to send in the application.

I took a walk around the house and then made myself lunch. After an hour's procrastination, I came back to the computer screen to do my business accounts. The application was still there, tantalising me. I closed my eyes and hit the send button. The next day, I got an email message from a filming company who wanted to arrange a time for an interview. The magic had started. Email messages went back and forth and I was able to set up a morning appointment to meet with the production team and present my business.

The Interview

I left Tramore at 5:00 am on a grey morning and made my way nervously to the production company's office in Ranelagh, Dublin. I was too early so I had to sit in my car for almost an hour waiting for the offices to open at 9am. This gave me a good opportunity to practise a sales pitch and review my material. I had brought samples of my products for people to taste. If nothing else, the amazing flavours should have been enough to win them over.

The ladies who greeted me were warm and friendly. We went through details about my business; how long ago I had started and what I had achieved to date. I gave them my samples. They loved the Bad Boy Pepper Sauce for its hot tangy taste. They also loved a new sweet chilli sauce I had recently developed. We spoke about the number of sauces I would present on the programme, the way I would present them and the work I would have to do in preparation for the programme.

I had to show originality and memorise all my figures. As a last step, I had to send them my accounts and projections for at least three years so their accountant could sift through the figures. They did not want anyone appearing on the programme without adequate preparation. The Dragons were going to ask exactly what the money was needed for and what my projected sales figures would be. I reassured them they would have the figures sent by email. On the drive back home, I wondered what I was actually going to send them. I had always done my own book keeping. But however, I did not know how to do sales projections. I was always good at mathematics, so that skill was going to have to push along my creativity.

I looked at the previous year's income and the volume of new products sold to date. I compared market and event sales to wholesale activities and decided the funding had to be used to create enough stock to drive increased wholesale activity. I wanted my products to be in every major supermarket in every major town. I pulled the figure of 200 supermarkets out of the air and I worked with that for the next year's projections. The following year, the sales would double, especially if I were to take on the UK market. I was determined to conquer the UK in my mind. More than anything else, I wanted a Dragon to guide me through the sales and distribution process. I sent in my figures to my contact at the production company and the following week, my application was accepted.

I had to sign numerous documents to participate in the programme. A confidentiality agreement said I would not reveal what happened on the programme before the transmission date. Another document stated that the production company was only responsible for filming and producing the show. Any agreement I signed with the Dragons would be my own affair, not theirs. After all, the show was purely for the public's entertainment. I was happy to sign the papers. Even though I had been attending a full circuit of markets and events nationwide, there was still a large audience that had never seen or heard of my products. I could reach them through TV.

Preparing for the Show

The real work started after my acceptance to the programme. I could not sleep, as I went through an active list of everything I had to do to prepare. Not being able to tell people I was appearing on the programme was an added stress. But I decided to tell my business mentor at a Waterford business incubation centre. She put me in contact with a past Dragon's Den winner. She said this woman could coach me if she had time and could certainly listen to my business pitch for the show.

The production company was very thorough in checking my progress. I had to send a photo, showing how I would display my samples. I sent photos of some stainless steel bowls I used for the markets. They were horrified. They sent back photos of some white ceramic dishes I should purchase. I was told that they would show up better on television. After a full week of staring at figures and projections on my computer day and night, I was having serious difficulty knowing exactly what answers I would give to the myriad of questions I might be asked. I watched a number of Dragons Den episodes online to get ideas.

I decided to break my code of silence and contact a good friend in Tramore, Eamon, who was also part of the Toastmasters club at the time. I knew he was an entrepreneur and had learned that his business received huge funds from 'business angels' in the past. I was sure he would be able to help me with the preparation and that he would keep my secret. I called Eamon one evening to arrange a meeting and told him my story. He was delighted to be of help and very excited by the prospect of my appearing on the show. I dressed casually but with a little flair to go to Eamon's house. He was a very good looking man in my opinion. I knew he was widowed, but could not get a clear idea from anyone in our group if he was dating any woman at the time. I knew he had a teenage daughter close to Tiffany's age and a young son. I secretly craved his attention, but did not dare do anything to indicate my interest. I thought if he was interested, he would have approached me.

When I arrived at his house, his daughter served me a huge piece of chocolate cake, and then disappeared to do her homework. I showed him all the figures I had gathered thus far and told him that I was worried I wouldn't be able to do myself justice on national television.

He stopped me in my tracks. He pointed out that I had given great speeches at our Toastmasters club in the past. I could give a fabulous one minute business pitch on TV. It was not a problem. I only had to practice. We went through exactly what I would say. He then went through the figures and gave me homework to do before I returned with more figures that we could use to produce reasonable projections. As Eamon spoke about the figures, I became mesmerised by his lips and for a short moment fantasised about our first kiss. I had to pinch myself out of the stupor and pay attention to get the full benefit of our meeting.

I worked feverishly for the following two weeks to complete my preparation. It was definitely a very difficult task, requiring concentration to pull as much information together as possible. I then tried to memorise the figures: the income, the profit margins, the year-on-year returns.

I reviewed production costs for all the Taste of the Caribbean sauces, from Banana Ketchup to Bad Boy Pepper Sauce. I compared my current production costs to the production costs I would incur if I scaled up my processes. I calculated historical sales since the introduction of the product lines. Then I developed a sales plan for 2010. This helped to determine what investment I would need from the Dragons to scale up the business. The whole process took longer than I had expected. I got Eamon, as well as my brother who was an accountant, to review the figures and steer me in the right direction. My story had to be plausible or the Dragons wouldn't buy into it.

As far as spending the investment was concerned, I had to itemise each cent, for ingredients and supplies, production costs, and marketing the business. I knew how to apply for grants from the government and had been successful in the past. But I still had gaps in my knowledge as to how to market my business more effectively and how to sell to the big supermarkets. I hoped the Dragons Den experience was going to take my business to the next level.

I went to Eamon's house again to further polish the business pitch. He asked the questions he knew the investors would ask, and helped me polish my answers. It was excellent practise. I practised my answers again with my business mentor at the incubation centre. I also visited the former Dragon's Den winner to ask for her input. I took various outfits to show her. I knew I had to deliver the full package. A memorable outfit, as well as sound knowledge of my business were important. She had been able to do this when she had entered the show. I had a sober suit as well as a multicoloured jacket and skirt. We decided that since I was from the Caribbean, the multicoloured outfit would be better. I practised my sales pitch with her and got some more ideas of what to add in and what to leave out. We then went through some questions and answers based on her experience. Now it was up to God. I just had to follow all the advice I had received.

Filming Day

The filming took place in a large pub on the outskirts of Marlay Park in Dublin. Since I did not want to be too tired after a long drive from Waterford, I asked Tiffany's former babysitter Rana if I could stay overnight at her place in Dublin. I did not tell her what I was going to do the next day. I just said I had a meeting. I asked Rana and her daughter for opinions on my outfits. They both decided I should go as the colourful Lindy they knew. The matter was settled. I rose early and left for Marlay Park. I did not dare wait for Dublin traffic to start. I arrived at 6:30am and could see signs of activity inside the venue already. It was too cold to stay in my van so I had to go in. One of the organisers asked me to sit on the left side of the pub. That was where all the participants would sit. Filming would be done upstairs. The filming was supposed to start early because they wanted to film quite a number of candidates in one day and it could take at least one hour for each candidate. I imagined the furious editing work that had to be done afterwards to produce a 10-minute segment.

I found a warm, comfortable bench, scoped out the ladies room and the pub menu and awaited my fate. The participants started trickling in with family members and friends. How lonely I felt that morning. Everyone else had people fussing over them. I could not bring Tiffany. She was in secondary school and I did not want her to lose a day at school because of my mad meanderings. There were two makeup artists on the other side of the room. I went to chat with them out of pure boredom and asked questions about some of the participants they had seen on the other days.

Even though a wide variety of entrepreneurs presented their ideas that day, when it came to editing, nobody knew in what order the candidates would appear and in which episodes. I had spot number five so I planned to change into my outfit only when the third candidate was being filmed. I did not want to appear too wrinkled after sitting around for hours. When it was close to the time, I put on my red jacket with multicolour splashes and gold puff paint and the matching short skirt. I wore a red vest underneath. The production company had warned against wearing anything too shiny. I wore gold jewellery, gold hoop earrings that my mother had given me, and a gold chain with a lucky elephant gold pendant that belonged to Tiffany.

The only other person I could chat with was the speech coach, who went from one candidate to the next, helping them rehearse their pitches. She had a kind face, looked me in the eye and asked me to deliver my pitch. She advised me to slow down; otherwise my sales pitch would not sound right. I had approximately two minutes; there was no need to rush. I also had to remember to breathe. I certainly had a lot to remember that morning. She was pleased with my performance and said I would do very well.

My stomach was in knots. It was fast approaching midday and my snacks had run out. The production company promised lunch, but I didn't know whether it would be served after my filming or before. I soon found out the Dragons were tired and filming had to stop for lunch. What a disaster it was for me. I was operating on empty energy since it had been impossible to get a comfortable night's sleep. My friend's home had been heated like a summer's day in the tropics the night before. I had been way too nervous to sleep anyway. I had to watch every contestant go in and come out. Time passed painfully slowly.

The Dragons ate their lunch in an area away from the contestants and we ate our lunch on our side of the bar. I was asked to finish my lunch quickly since they wanted to film me walking up and down the steps before my actual interview. I had to walk up the steps slowly three times in my red high heeled pumps, carrying the little white ceramic dish with three bowls of sauce and another bowl with plain crisps for tasting. The filming crew had organised a small table for my products but would not show the big business banner I had brought because my telephone number was on it. They then filmed me walking down the steps. I had to practise placing my little tray of sauces on the table in the middle of the room.

I was finally allowed to see the Den while the Dragons were at lunch. It was a large stark room with hard wood floors, exposed brick walls and windows which were covered with black drapes for the filming. In front of me stood five empty black armchairs in which the Dragons would sit. There was a table with an open briefcase displaying cash. This was to create the illusion of the candidate walking away with a lot of cash. It certainly looked real on TV. I had to return to the makeup crew for a final application of powder and await my fate.

Finally I was asked to ascend the stairs for the start of filming. I walked up slowly, placed my samples on the table and faced the Dragons. I felt weightless. Thank God I had not eaten much. I was so nervous I could feel every inch of my body tremble. I felt so alone. The filming crew would not be sympathetic if I were to decide to
turn back. Their job was to film the event. The producer had tried to put me at ease in advance, but now she was preoccupied with asking the camera man to start and stop. My heart fluttered and my hands shook, but I put on my bravest face and a warm smile. Five Dragons sat before me; four men and a woman. All I saw was the shine on the bald heads of three of the gentlemen and smiles of shock on their faces. The Dragons were blown away by my multi-coloured dress and red shoes.

'You look hot like your sauces!' one of them said, as soon as he saw me.

'Thank you. My dress comes all the way from Trinidad and

Tobago.'

We were off to a flying start. The fierce Dragons were dressed in the finest suits. They wore discreet makeup and looked like wealth and success incarnate. One Dragon had overcome the physical disability of partial blindness to make his fortune in the property market. Another Dragon had a chain of coffee shops and came from a successful career in the food service industry. The female Dragon came from the UK and had made her fortune in internet travel bookings when this industry first took root. Another mogul had made his fortune by continuing his father's chain of men's clothing stores. The final one specialised in marketing companies. It was unnerving to stand before them in the middle of the room, with only a few film crew staff operating from the side of the room. I had to draw every ounce of courage from within to get me through the experience. I tried to forget myself and focus only on delivering my pitch.

'The business and the figures, the business and the figures', I chanted to myself.

The questions and answers went on for at least an hour and a half. It was no wonder the morning's proceedings were delayed. The crew had to stop to powder the Dragons' noses while I stood there, greasy and exposed.

I became more nervous after the first Dragon pulled out of the bidding. He said he loved me and my enthusiasm for my business, but he felt it was too risky to invest. The second Dragon said she was not interested. She was infamous for not investing in businesses, so I was not surprised. I was then left with three possible Dragons to bid on the business. I was asking for €40,000 for a 20% stake in the business. Two Dragons bid for 50% of the business at €40k. The third Dragon offered €40k for 45% of the business. I had no idea what to do. The film crew looked away. I asked for a few minutes to make a decision.

It would have been helpful to call a friend and get advice. But I did not have access to a phone. I stood at the back of the room, hitting the sides of my head as I tried to make a decision. When I turned around, there was a camera in my face. I hoped the head hitting would be edited from the final version. I must have truly looked mad.

When I returned to the floor with my decision, the cameras started rolling again. My logic was that two heads were better than one as mentors. I gave my final answer, accepting the combined bids of the property mogul and the clothing mogul. I declined the third Dragon's offer. What would my friends say about my decision when the show aired the following February?

We all shook hands and the filming ended on a happy note. I was photographed for a website article by Bank of Ireland, the official programme sponsor. I was asked dozens of questions, but was too exhausted to recall what I answered. Then I met briefly with one Dragon to get contact information and set up an appointment. Finally, I made my weary way back to Tramore. Tiffany was thrilled at the news of my success on the programme. But she was sworn to secrecy. The Dragon's Den experience had been surreal. I could not believe it was done. I pictured flashing lights and beautiful bottles of Caribbean sauces on every supermarket shelf in Ireland.

The Handshake

I had to return the following week to film the handshake with the host of the programme. I was supposed to dress exactly as I had appeared the week before. This was quite a challenge, especially to achieve the same hairstyle with my unpredictable hair. The host had to stand on a box to meet my height. With expert editing, no one would ever know. He delivered a wrap up statement and I said two sentences to summarise my experience on the Dragons Den.

This was the end of filming of my Dragon's Den adventure. Tiffany's gold elephant pendant had broken and lost his trunk in the tussle with all the changes of clothes. She was not pleased.

Christmas Meeting

I had a morning appointment with the Dragons the day after I brought Kim and my mother home from the airport. I decided to give myself a break from driving and take the train to Dublin. I left Kim in charge at the house. I also showed her how to navigate around the kitchen. I left early to catch the train to Dublin. I had hoped everything would be fine as the visitors settled down. Luckily, parking was free at the Waterford train station. I was able to squeeze into a spot not too far from the main entrance. I used the journey to collect my thoughts and get paperwork together for the meeting ahead. Having to refocus on business ideas, objectives and the future of the company was not an easy task.

As the train flew through Co. Kildare, my mobile phone started ringing. It was a call from the house. It was Kim, extremely flustered and worried. My mother was trying to run away and had attempted to open the front door many times to take a taxi back to her house. She kept threatening to push Kim over. I felt helpless on the train. There was no turning back. I had to ask Kim to put Mammy on the phone so I could speak to her and reassure her. After about five minutes of talking, she calmed down a little and I promised to return home as early as possible.

When the train arrived at Heuston Station, I tried to find my way to the Four Seasons Hotel in Ballsbridge. Not being able to see a ready bus, I hailed a taxi. Even though I had been really watching my pennies, I felt I had to make a good first impression and wanted to get there on time. I forgot that Irish time was not necessarily American time, and things were usually flexible. It was the first meeting with the Dragons after the filming in November. I was not sure what to expect but remained hopeful. When I arrived, one Dragon was there, sipping tea and saying hello to every second person who passed. The Dragon was a tall man, balding, with a long nose and ears that pricked up. He looked as if he had been born in a suit. This conversation was certainly going to be interesting, I thought.

'She's going to make me rich with these Caribbean sauces!' he said to passers-by.

They all smiled and feigned acknowledgement. They did not know what he was talking about, but smiled nevertheless. He was rich and famous, with businesses all over the country. He could say what he liked to these people. The episode had not come on air yet, and obviously no one knew about the sauces.

Fifteen minutes later, my other mentor showed up and we chatted about the weather, the traffic, Christmas holidays, the programme, and maybe for twenty seconds about the sauces. Their conclusion was that nothing could be done until after Christmas.

Good Lord, I thought. I had left a confused and disoriented mother and her frightened friend at home. Still exhausted from the previous day's adventure at the airport, I had travelled three hours for a 15 minute meeting. There was no expensive lunch, gifts or celebration. One Dragon had to go off to attend to important business. He was getting 'shitloads' of money from someone who owed him.

The other asked if I wanted to speak further at his office, since he had business to attend to over there. I thought maybe that would give me more opportunity to speak to him about my goal of getting his food distribution business to take my product to stores. I went along. He had a Bentley sports car and the butlers of the hotel proudly brought the car around to the doorway. It was my first trip in a Bentley sports car. I told him my mother was visiting and she had progressive Alzheimer's disease. He revealed that his mother was also afflicted with this condition.

I was shocked to see his little office upstairs one of his stores. The place was being refurbished, but I had really expected something grander for a millionaire who owned a few Bentleys. A gigantic, old style Bentley was parked at one end of the little car park. The most splendid part of the office was a large boardroom table on which a collection of exquisite pottery stood. This was a product from another potential investment from the programme. We chatted a little and I got a few names and contacts, then it was time to go back to the train station.

'I'll call you a taxi', he said.

I could pretend to be a Dragon, but I was not taking taxis around the city. I then went through the contents of my wallet, holding my breath. Thank God, I had about €25. It was enough to pay the taxi. I let the driver know I was not new in the city, so he would not charge me the tourist rate. Mercifully, I reached the train station before my scheduled departure. I wondered what surprise was waiting for me at home.

Three hours later, when I returned, everyone was calm. I fixed dinner. Kim and Mammy protested that they weren't hungry, but when I placed the food in front of them, they ate ravenously. It was sad to watch the mental deterioration of someone who had been so grand and forthright in her peak. She had really become a child again.

The Showing

The production crew called me with the good news. It was decided that my segment would open the series of the Dragons Den on February 25th, 2010. It was quite a task to keep the whole thing a secret for so many months. I started telling a few friends, to ensure they would be at home in front of the television to actually see the episode. The day before the programme went on air, I emailed everyone on my list so they would know about it.

I was called to Dublin for a press conference on the morning of the Dragon's Den airing. A few participants had been selected for the press conference, held at the famous Shelbourne Hotel on St. Stephen's Green. Several suites were rented out by the sponsor, Bank of Ireland. We had many refreshments and drinks. Since my programme was opening the whole series, the excitement was incredible. We had make up done and re-touched. Photographers took pictures. The Bank of Ireland sponsors took pictures. Then we sat down to watch the first episode. It was hard to look at myself on the screen. I giggled nervously as I watched the final edited version. It contained all the highlights, with humour and entertainment, business questions, fashion statements, drama and anything else that would amuse an audience. It was skilfully edited. Everyone was pleased with the product. We posed repeatedly for the cameras and had our noses powdered several times by the makeup artist. I felt on top of the world and very wealthy that morning. We all left happy, with promises to keep in touch and meet again.

After posing for every photographer to be sure I would get media mileage, I hurried to Leo's house for our own celebration. I had received a DVD from the TV production company, so I was able to show him the programme before it aired. He was very gracious, presenting me with a large bunch of flowers and a splendid home cooked meal to celebrate. Then I made my way back to Waterford to watch the programme with Tiffany. We screamed and celebrated. Friends and well wishers called for a long time afterwards to say how much they had enjoyed the programme.

http://www.youtube.com/watch?v=hgztCScWxxs

13

GOODBYE BAD BOY

A Snowy Beginning

As soon as my neighbour had broken the news about Kim's accident, I rang the house. Mammy said Kim went off walking on her own and should have stayed at home like the rest of them. The paramedics had taken Kim out of the house on a stretcher. Mammy wondered where the ambulance staff were taking her friend.

Since we were almost in Dublin, Leo and I decided to go on, with the intention to return early next morning. I felt so guilty having a poor old woman, a visitor, come to my home and meet such disaster. I felt guilty too because I was not on site to take care of her. Was I being a bad mother? I felt three times guilty for leaving three "children" unattended and wondered how I could ever enjoy my night away.

I called a Tramore friend who agreed to accompany Kim to the emergency department at Waterford Regional Hospital. Tiffany said she was making pasta for granny and everything was under control.

By the time we checked in, we were exhausted after the news and long drive and took a nap, waking up just in time for the dinner and dance. Dressing up in our finest, we went to the ball room to join the other guests. After years of neglect, Clontarf Castle had been renovated to its current splendour as a four star hotel. We enjoyed looking at the old suits of armour in the hallway where remains of the ancient castle stand right in the middle of the lobby.

We sat at a large round table with five other couples. By chance, two other mixed couples were seated at our table.

This was a unique coincidence. The room was decorated with balloons and each couple received party favours, including a crown and a hat that said 'Happy New Year 2010'. We chatted with everyone and when the dance music started, we took to the floor. Leo was not much of a dancer, but he tried to imitate my enthusiasm as I bounced around.

At midnight, everyone hugged and greeted each other shouting Happy New Year. It was a wonderful atmosphere, even though I kept thinking about the absent ones – Tiffany looking after granny, and Kim alone at the hospital in a strange country. I would have to go back as soon as I could. We looked outside and it was snowing heavily, more than ever before. The city was not equipped to clear snow from the streets. We were lucky to be indoors that night. At 1am, I asked Leo if he wanted to dance one last dance and he looked relieved. He was tired and we had to rise early next morning to drive back.

We had breakfast in the beautiful, sky lit atrium which served a buffet breakfast starting at 7:00 am. Why were so many other people awake? I thought we were the only crazy ones who would be attempting to hit the road early. It seemed like some had never gone to bed. Not having much of an appetite, I picked at the meal. I was anxious to leave; the warnings on the news were clear.

We decided to take the N11 along the coast instead of attempting Carlow and Kildare County. Surely road conditions would be better, we thought. But the roads were particularly bad in Dun Laoghaire-Rathdown County area, where the snow remained several centimetres deep as we drove through. The car's wheels were spinning in some places. Only one lane was functional most of the way. We had to drive at a snail's pace not to fly off the road. Only a few other brave fools were out, but I was determined to get back to Waterford to oversee the situation.

We did not stop, but it still took three and a half hours on the motorway to reach Waterford, with some near misses and skids along the way. As we neared the city, I called the hospital to find out what was happening with Kim. A friendly voice informed me that she had just gotten out of surgery and her hip was replaced. I could not go in to see her until visiting hours later that afternoon. The whole world had certainly turned topsy turvy on my one night out.

Leo left me and went straight back to Dublin. I got home to find a mountain of dishes and Tiffany and Granny chatting quite happily. After clearing up the mess and cooking a meal, I made my way to the hospital. I always became nervous and anxious at hospitals, but I had to go and visit poor Kim. How afraid she must have been in this strange hospital in a strange country. She was resting comfortably and had been given pain killers. There were three other patients in her room and two were quite chatty and entertaining. I hoped that chatting with roommates would make her stay a little brighter.

I tried to visit each day to follow her progress to recovery. In the meantime, I called Kim's daughter in Trinidad to come to Ireland for the journey back home with her. Kim was not allowed to travel for another three weeks. She had to spend some time with a physiotherapist. It was funny the way this hospital could accept a patient not knowing about insurance coverage. They did not ask about insurance until days after completing a major surgical procedure. Luckily my mother, in one of her good and sane moments, had thought to purchase travel insurance before the journey. And it was a God send under the circumstances.

The hospital was ready to discharge Kim and I could not take care of her. I was trying to get the business started again after the Christmas break. I asked if she could stay at the hospital to recover. They complained many times about a healthy person taking up a bed when they had emergency situations requiring beds. I asked them to indicate when she would be well enough to travel. Only then she should be released.

Since Kim could not use her ticket to return to Trinidad, I made arrangements to book her on another flight. In the meantime, my mother had to go back to Trinidad. Winter was no good for her and I had to start working again. I then had to face the dilemma of how to let her travel on her own? My brother and I decided to do a relay of sorts. I would ensure she boarded the plane to Barbados at Gatwick airport. He would fly to Barbados to meet her when she changed planes. As I handed her over in a wheel chair in London, I kept asking the attendant to make sure she got on the plane and did not walk around. She kept pretending to give me a dig, making all the attendants giggle. She declared she was not a child and did not need assistance. As I flew back to Ireland, I had visions of my mother walking around Gatwick airport and not boarding that plane. I could not sleep until I knew she was safe and my brother had met her. I tried calling him numerous times, but of course he could not answer his mobile phone because he was flying.

Finally, next day, I got news that all was well and Mammy was back at home. But the trip was not without its drama. She was found wandering out of the airport in Barbados because she thought she had arrived home. What an ordeal it had been for all of us, and it was such a relief to know she was safely back at home.

Now it was time to see Kim safely back to Trinidad. Her daughter Kezianne was to fly to Dublin and I gave her directions for getting the JJ Kavanagh airport shuttle all the way to Tramore. On the morning she arrived, I had been doing errands for a while and poor Kezianne arrived in Tramore at 12:00 pm instead of the later 1:00 pm arrival time that I had anticipated. Her mobile phone had no signal in Ireland. She could not get a young store clerk at a road side convenience store to lend her a mobile phone to call me. The girl, without understanding or compassion, just told her to buy credit. So she moved on to another convenience store, run by a young Nigerian girl who was more sympathetic. They called me and I rushed back from my errands to find her in tears. It was really heartbreaking because I knew how long her journey had been. But we got settled, had something to eat, then went to visit Kim at the hospital. It was a good reunion.

I asked Leo how we would get Kim from the hospital to Dublin Airport. He volunteered to be the chauffeur, then he mysteriously stopped calling and disappeared. I decided to rent a car and do the driving myself. When we reached the airport, we were able to get a wheel-chair at the entrance to the airport departure lounge. I left my passengers to check in and swiftly drove back to Waterford. Kim and Kezianne were flying to London to rest for a few days with relatives before taking the long flight back to Trinidad. It was a bitter sweet departure from Ireland, after a vacation gone all wrong…

Scaling Up

The business was demanding my attention more than ever. I tried to find new stores and new ways to get product into the market to capitalize on the upcoming Dragon's Den appearance in February. An entrepreneur who had received funding in the 2009 Dragon's Den episode gave me the contact number for his distributor. This man, Cathal was based in Donegal. I decided to combine a trip to visit potential small stores in Galway city with a meeting with Cathal. He drove down from Donegal and met me just outside Galway on the M6. After missing each other, we were finally able to recognise each other's vans and stop at a road side café. Cathal was a big talker. He promised the world. He praised himself for all the good work he was doing distributing his food products and other people's products. He praised himself for handling my colleague's post Dragon's Den distribution, saying that he was the key to my colleague's success. He talked for almost two hours, revealing who was a scoundrel and who was a rat. When we finally came around to talking about my products, I asked if he wanted to have some samples to try.

He said that if I took him on as a sole distributor he would work magic. My products would be all over the country. His commission for his staff to stand around in small stores while trying to sell was astronomical. By his calculations, he could probably get me into big supermarket chains, but I would have to reduce the per unit price. I would have to pay store distribution costs, his distribution costs, advertising costs, marketing costs, and other costs. The way I saw it, when everyone's commissions and costs were paid, I could well be left with five cents per bottle.

'High volume sales my dear. High volume sales,' Cathal promised. 'I guarantee they will be beating a path to your door! And I will be managing everything!'

Cathal could barely control himself. He could smell and feel the euros raining down on his head. He would pay me one price for the products, whether they were in supermarket distribution or not. It was a rosy arrangement for him. He insisted that I NEEDED him. That was a strange conclusion. Had I not been in business since 2006? He patted himself on the back for being in the right place at the right time to make my business happen. For the whole meeting, Cathal never once tasted my products and did not ask anything about them. This was a frightening prospect for one who was supposed to be doing promotion and sales. I should have known to walk away at that point.

I was to go away and make thousands of bottles of product in preparation for the big promotion. Since I had been selling products at festivals and markets by myself for at least two years, I knew which products had done better than the others. We chose four products to sell in the early promotional stage of this supermarket blitz: Bad Boy pepper sauce, Caribbean Curry, Jamaican Jerk marinade, and Jamaican Jerk Sauce. I took all my savings and started buying ingredients, pallets of bottles, and caps. Thousands of labels were printed – 10,000 pepper sauce, 5,000 jerk sauce, and 5,000 Caribbean curry. I called a supplier of the hot scotch bonnet peppers in London one day in early January. The week I wanted a full pallet of peppers, there was a shortage. Instead of £10, they were £14 a box.

'Send me a full pallet,' I told them.

'That will be £2,000, mam.'

'I'll take it. Just put it on my card.'

I must have spent €10,000 in one day, all from my savings. The Dragons had not yet agreed on my product line, labels, or even a contract, and I had no intention of waiting on them. Time was of the essence.

I contacted Enda in Kilcoole Industrial Estate to use his plant for mass production. I wanted to mass produce quickly. He was fine with this. I was to bring my own ingredients and supplies. I had to pay his staff and pay a fee for use of the plant. So away we went. I also paid to have product stored in his adjoining warehouse. Production had started back up in Kilcoole after a break of some months. The Lithuanian staff could barely speak English. However, I had a knack for communicating with everyone. By the end of the first day, I was getting product made everyone cooperated. Work was work to seasonal and part time staff. These people worked well for minimum wage. I sent Cathal four pallets of products to Donegal, using a trucking company at my own expense. Then we waited with bated breath for the media blitz.

Leo Returned

As if by a miracle or divine intervention, Leo reappeared. He wanted to meet to apologise. Against a good friend's advice, I decided to meet him to hear what he had to say. We agreed to meet at the Silver Sands bar in Tramore for lunch. He apologised profusely for his absence and promised to be good and faithful in the future. He had to sort out family matters, but everything was fine. I made no promises, but kept talking about my trip back to Trinidad for Carnival celebrations in February. In a gesture of kindness, or probably wanting to keep me keen, he said he had to go to the bank machine. He returned with an envelope and said I was not to open it.

'Just a little something for your trip', he said.

I didn't open it. I placed the envelope in my bag and returned home. I was pre-occupied with chores, but then remembered the envelope after an hour. I gingerly opened it to view the contents. Leo had given me a generous sum of spending money. This was a unique gesture. I guessed he wanted to be sure I would come back to him after the trip. I left for Trinidad the next day, not only to enjoy Carnival but to visit my parents. Little did I know I would be making the same journey again within a matter of weeks.

The Dragon's Den Revealed

The next challenge was to have a website ready in time for the media blitz that The Dragon's Den would bring. I needed an e-commerce site, where viewers seeing the programme could order products on line right away. I wanted a site which I could manage on my own, changing images, prices and advertising at will. I went to a Waterford marketing firm for assistance with this project. I spoke about my deadline and the Dragon's Den television appearance. Everyone was excited since they had worked on a similar project the year before with another Dragon's Den winner. All I had to do was pay €3,500 and it would be ready. I looked around for funding. With not a cent coming from the Dragons and time running out, I had to help myself.

I found out that the Waterford County Enterprise Board would give partial funding to entrepreneurs who set up an ecommerce website. I immediately set up an appointment and drove to Dungarvan to meet the woman in charge. I had to pay out the money first then wait for my refund. I would get back 50% of expenses eventually. I had to do it straight away or the company would not make the website active. That was their policy. The young internet guru who was to help me build the website went to a template which was probably used for many a customer and entered my information and images onto it. I had to be very careful in providing every picture and every word, because, as I discovered, the fees did not include imagination or script writing. He wanted to feature the Caribbean stereotype of coconut trees. I had to insist pictures of the actual sauces be used. Eventually we were able to fine tune the website and everything was ready the day before the Dragon's Den show. The site was supposed to go live that day. I left their office after putting €3,500 on my credit card. The accounts clerk reminded me that I would have to pay a 2% fee plus VAT for using a credit card. They usually accepted cash or certified cheque. She subsequently followed up every other day for the 2% fee.

I went online the night Dragon's Den aired to check to see how many hits were on the new website. Lo and behold, the website would not load. I typed the new web address repeatedly and kept looking. Only the old website showed up. Where was my website on such a critical night? I was raging. How could the little upstart make such a mistake? I sent a scathing email immediately, asking for him to make the website live as soon as he entered the office next morning. I then tried to calm down, as email messages of congratulations kept pouring in.

The next day, my website went live with the flimsy excuse that the Internet guru had not connected the old website to load immediately to the new one.

Since Cathal predicted a flood of orders, I held my breath and waited for the telephone calls. He sent me a cheque for €2,000 as an advance for all the sales we were going to get. All I had to do then was pay myself back an additional €15,000 taken from my savings. Negotiations with the Dragons who had chosen to invest in me continued. They did not like my logo and the products had to change to be more acceptable. They called in an expert to change my brand and product image. One of them suggested an image of a lazy boy in a hammock relaxing under two palm trees. At that point, the stereotype of the lazy Caribbean life was extremely annoying. If I had to change everything to fit the elusive customer, including the types of products made, then I would lose my identity and all control of my business.

The turning point came during an appointment with the Dragons, when one of them ordered me not to come next time without my sales figures. His comment struck the wrong nerve. Did I not own this business? Had I not put every cent of my own savings to make it work so far? I decided to walk away from the deal. I had always been proud and tenacious. Nobody was allowed to talk down to me. And furthermore, a 50% share of a business was too much, with two business partners against one. I had not signed any documents so I called and emailed both Dragons, indicating that I no longer wanted a business partnership with them. The shock that a small sole trader would walk away from the big Dragons was beyond comprehension for one Dragon in particular. But sink or swim, right or wrong, I was prepared to do it on my own.

I set up appointments with buyers for large retailers, but could not afford to sell at the low prices they expected. I also could not afford the marketing and promotion fees they charged. It was a bitter pill to swallow. It was not easy to play with the big guns. I had to return to chasing small accounts around the country and selling at events. They were becoming less profitable as the recession wore on. The dwindling disposable income of the average consumer drove them back to meat and potatoes.

I managed to get into a promotion with one large retailer who was starting to showcase small Irish food manufacturers or 'artisan producers' as we were called. We were able to set up and sell our products in stores doing tastings, in return for 20% of the sales price at the till. It was a good deal compared to going through distributors, so I availed of this monthly opportunity. We received payment about 15 days after each event. Some of the other traders had family and friends to work for them, so they could sell in more than one store at a time. During my stints selling at events, I had met only two girls who were able to sell as well as I did. Unfortunately, they were both busy at the time. So I was forced to do the solo routine around the country: one month in Howth, the next month in Blackrock, and another one in Swords. The benefits of this programme were enormous. When people came to farmer's markets in the park, many were just browsing. When they came to the supermarkets, they came to buy food. Some took a bottle of sauce to be polite and simply put it down at another location in the store. We were trained to do a quick 'whip around' the store to find abandoned products in nooks and crannies. It was always a challenge to determine which enthusiastic buyer would have dropped the product and run.

Leo's Final Disappearance

Leo continued his efforts to impress me for a few weeks with splendid dinners and evenings out. We went for dinner at Faithlegg House Hotel, a former grand old residence in Waterford County. We dined on roast pheasant and other fine fare. I was suitably impressed, but forever on guard for erratic behaviour. Later in the month, I was going to one of the first street festivals of the year, the St. Patrick's Day Parade in Cork City. A large street market was set up on Grand Parade for the event. Leo promised to help me sell at my stand for the entire day. He said I did not have to hire anyone; he would do it all. I hired a helper to prepare the food for the event the day before, leaving enough time to go out to dinner that evening.

Leo was staying at the Tower Hotel. He frequently stayed at this hotel when he drove down from Dublin to visit me. I did not want him to come to my home, since I had promised myself never to introduce my daughter to any new suitors unless they were tried, tested, and truly committed. There would never again be any cause for break up agony for my child.

After our dinner, we went back to the Tower Hotel for a night cap. As we passed the receptionists, they looked at us. We went up to his hotel room and within five minutes, there was a loud bang on the door.

'Get out! Get out!' cried a male voice.

I shuddered. What could this be about? Leo went to the door

to investigate. It was the young man from the front desk.

'We've been watching you! You always bring a woman to your room. You paid for a room for one! Get out!'

Leo slammed the door shut and I sat on the bed quivering. I couldn't stay a minute longer in that room. I certainly did not want to wait any longer in case they called the Gardai to force us out. In such a small town as Waterford, I could possibly be recognised and I did not want my business to be tarnished by what people might assume me to be.

Leo gave me his car keys and asked me to walk out calmly and sit in his car while he got his things together. I held my head up high and stepped carefully out of the room, down the staircase, past the glares of the front desk attendants, through the corridor leading to the back of the hotel. Then I crossed the car park and headed straight to Leo's car. I felt so numb and so distressed. My mind went around in circles until Leo delivered me home.

The next morning I rose very early. Leo parked his car near my house. We continued in my van to Cork City. Working on Grand Parade meant unloading early. We set up the bottles of sauces for demonstration. I had also prepared meals to sell so we had to set up chaffing trays with fuel, a hand wash stand equipped with soap and water, an area for reheating food and chilled storage. It was a large undertaking, but I had become used to doing it over the past four years. However, I was not sure if Leo knew what he had volunteered for. He smiled nervously, greeted customers and acted the part very well. He explained the virtues of Caribbean sauces and prepared rotis with great skill after a few tries. I thought he was a good worker for someone who was usually in a suit, driving a Mercedes Benz. The other traders passed to say hello and take a good look at this strange man I had brought to work with me. They were used to seeing me work alone or with one of the

African girls.

When the parade passed, the hungry crowd rushed to all the food stands and we made a steady stream of rotis in one hour. Once the crowd dwindled to a trickle of passing trade, it was time to pack up. My helper was very good at cleaning, clearing and organising the stand. He made suggestions for improvements and products that would work well at future events in the summer.

We drove back to Tramore, exhausted. Since Tiffany was visiting a friend's house that day, I invited Leo into my house for the first time since we had started dating. He wanted to have a cup of tea before driving back to Dublin. He appeared visibly shocked at the size of the house. His big blue eyes bulged as he walked around, looking at my antique styled furniture.

'You don't own this, do you? You must be renting,' he said.

I said that I had a mortgage and I was not renting. He walked around the ground floor, looked out the back door to see what he could see. He used the bathroom upstairs and took another look around. I was not sure what was going through his mind, but my home was certainly three times the size of his tiny house in Kilcullen, County Kildare. I decided not to show him the spectacular sunroom. I didn't want to trigger any jealousy.

The next weekend, I was back at a supermarket in Blackrock doing product tasting and sales. Leo showed up unexpectedly as I was packing up for the day.

'Let's go for dinner,' he suggested.

'Alright, but I don't want to delay too long. It's a long drive.'

We ate a seafood dinner at a pub near Seapoint Avenue in

Monkstown. We chatted for a while over a tasty meal and it was time to leave. He hugged me good bye and I started my homeward journey. On the way down, I got a call from his number. It must have been in his pocket. I said hello several times, but there was no answer. I could hear screaming and a heated argument with what sounded like a woman.

That was the last I ever saw of him.

My attraction for him was weak, so there was no missing and longing, just a nagging question: Why? I drowned myself in my work and Leo was soon a distant memory.

Death in the Family

I continued to do the monthly retail store demonstrations, as the retailer had promised possible contracts for the best selling products. Every time I contacted their buyer, he said he did not think they would sell Caribbean sauces. Needless to say, I saw UK brands of Caribbean sauces slowly creeping onto their shelves, while I had been knocking on their door for two years. The UK products were cheaper and mass produced. I could never compete on price. The irony was that this supermarket announced to the public continuously that they supported local industry.

It was while I was working at one of these artisan demonstrations in Lucan that I got a text message from my brother saying my father had collapsed and taken ill in Trinidad. He had to be hospitalised. He had been fighting cancer for years: first prostate cancer, then colon cancer. I went to the parking lot and called Dad on his mobile phone. Luckily he had his phone with him at his bedside. His speech was slurred and muffled. I asked him to stop scaring us with all the collapsing and hospital visits. He tried to muster a laugh but could not. He was obviously in a great deal of pain. I felt a nervous twinge as I realised that the end was near for him. When I had seen him in February, he had been extremely frail and could barely walk. I went back to work with a heavy heart.

I told one of the other product demonstrators about my father's situation and packed up early for the day. There was no way I could concentrate when I felt so helpless. I was thousands of miles away and could do nothing for my dad. Later that night, I got the call to say that my father had passed away.

I was shocked at how fast this happened without even having the opportunity to speak to him again. Who would listen to the stories of my travels? Who would give advice about difficult situations? Who would cook that special meal for us when we went back to Trinidad to visit? Tiffany would have no grandpa in Trinidad to visit again. What a sad and lonely night it was. I made arrangements for Tiffany and I to fly back home for the funeral and called several friends to tell them of his passing. I called Sean, looking for some comfort. He was the only person in Tramore who had met my Dad during his visit to Trinidad. He knew him and enjoyed his company.

Sean asked me to come to his home for a chat. I drove over there not knowing what to expect. He brought out wine and drank it by himself. He should have known I was not fond of alcohol. He hugged me and asked how I felt about my father's death. He seemed sympathetic. But then he started discussing what went wrong with our relationship. He could not believe I had moved on so quickly after our break-up. He had heard that I was dating. I was annoyed he would use this opportunity to scold me about my love life.

He spoke about not wanting to be alone when he got older. His children hardly visited him in those days. I couldn't believe he was using the occasion of my father's passing to look for pity. He expected me to give him a therapy session.

I had no patience for this type of behaviour during my time of grief. I calmly said goodbye and left.

The visit to Trinidad was bittersweet, a celebration of my father's life and a chance to reunite with cousins who had flown in from the United States for the funeral. We scattered my father's ashes at the ancestral home of the James' in St. Cecelia, Tobago. He would have liked that.

14

ESCAPE FROM ÉIRE

Tiffany's Brush with Death

Tiffany took her grandpa's death very badly. It was one more situation in a long list of bad news in her recent life. She had been experiencing a period of severe depression and feeling unwanted. Her best friend Joyce from secondary school had turned against her suddenly and without warning. She started taunting and teasing Tiffany. Tiffany was unable to ignore the teasing. She lost her appetite and slept badly. Her grades began to plummet. Joyce was able to enlist the help of another friend to deliberately exclude Tiffany from group activities. They kicked over her school bag and tripped her in the sports grounds and insulted her in various ways. My attempts to explain Tiffany's spiralling depression to the school counsellor and principal proved futile. Nothing was done.

As Easter approached, Joyce stepped up the bullying. She instructed Tiffany which expensive Easter egg I was to buy for her. I told Tiffany if I was going to buy anything, I would choose what I wanted to buy. I even had to intervene in a telephone conversation, when Joyce demanded money from Tiffany. Joyce screamed at me, saying she was having a conversation with her friend and I had no right to interrupt. I put her in her place and hung up. Needless to say, Tiffany felt the full backlash of her rage in school the following day. She declared she would see to it that Tiffany never had another friend in school again.

Tiffany began complaining about hearing voices. These voices insulted her and told her bad things about herself all the time. They always shouted at her. I dismissed this as a passing phase and told her the voices were not real and she should focus on her work. Unfortunately, her schoolwork continued to deteriorate rapidly, even in favourite subjects like Home Economics. She failed Maths, English and other subjects. I sent her away to the United States for the summer so she could get a break from Waterford and enjoy some good times with her aunt. When she returned to Waterford she seemed unhappier than when she left.

'Why do you want to live here?' You are not happy here,' she accused. 'You don't have any friends. Your life is miserable. I hate you!'

It went on and on for weeks. It was very difficult to focus seriously on work. Friends advised that all teenage girls went through this phase and it would end one day. After the summer holidays, I asked the principal to move Tiffany to a different class, since she was terrified to go to school. One morning, when I went to the school to visit the principal, the bullies passed through the main lobby to get a good look at me. The school staff seemed unskilled in handling any child who was out of the ordinary. If you could not fend for yourself and fight, you were doomed.

I felt I had no one with whom to discuss Tiffany's behaviour. Some of my family members blamed me for Tiffany's depression. I was an absent parent, because I had to work and travel all the time.

'You are never home', they said. 'You must spend more time at home'.

But I figured that if Tiffany was prone to depression, staying home and lavishing gifts on her would not work. It was not possible to force her into group activities to meet new friends. She was convinced the only way to join an activity was to join with friends; otherwise no one would speak to her. This was a concept I could never understand. I generally went to organised activities by myself and spoke to whoever would speak to me when I got there. But my philosophy and ideas could not make a dent in her way of thinking. With the change of class room, Tiffany met some new students who seemed friendly. But she still had to sit next to Joyce in a few classes because teachers assigned the seating.

Tiffany's behaviour continued on its erratic course. She was still hearing voices. One night, when I returned from a Toastmasters meeting, I saw her standing on a window sill, laughing out loud. This was at 9:30 pm. The next day I left early for a meeting at the Bord Bia office in Dublin. I assumed everything was fine at home. Tiffany would pack her lunch and go to school at the correct time as usual.

As I drove back to Waterford that evening, I called the house and there was no answer. I thought nothing of this. Tiffany might have been ignoring my calls for some reason. I arrived home at 8:00 pm and called her name. There was no answer. I ran upstairs. She was not in her room, not in the bathroom, not in the attic, not in my room. I started to panic. Where could she be? She always came straight home from school. She was not in any school clubs, so there was no reason to stay out late. I checked the telephone for messages and found my own message from earlier that day. Then there was the strangest message from her school.

'Mrs James, your daughter Tiffany was absent from school after lunch,' it said.

I played the message a few times. How could this be? Tiffany was always very obedient, never missed a class and never thought of misbehaving. I called one of her classmates, who said she had not seen Tiffany in class after lunch. Then I called my friend, Michelle, who had the telephone number for another classmate, Meaghan. Meaghan had also noticed that Tiffany was absent from school in the afternoon. Where could she be? I sat down, pondering what to do next and who to turn to, trying not to panic. The only logical thing to do was to search for her.

I called Michelle and Andy and asked them what I should do. They said to ask Meaghan to think where Tiffany could have gone and see if she would help look for her. By this time, it was after 9:00 pm. The wind began to howl and a rain storm started. It was not the kind of weather in which to search for a lost soul. But we had to do it. I called the Tramore Garda station to file a report and they sent an officer to the house immediately. He took a full description of Tiffany and I gave him some photographs. She still had her school bag and would have been wearing her uniform. As word got around, someone said they had spotted her crying on Lower Branch road in the afternoon. But that had been many hours ago. I sat wringing my hands, as the pain welled up inside. My child was lost somewhere in a rainstorm, cold and alone. She thought the whole world was against her. I tried not to panic, as friends and neighbours combed the beach and deserted areas looking for her: They even looked in the gardens of Botanic House next door.

I called Sean and his friend Colm, and Colm's wife Helga came to stay with me for moral support. Sean was not able to offer consolation in this situation. He thought Tiffany had killed herself. This made me mad. By 11:00pm, with dwindling hope and no clues, my neighbour who was a Garda decided to call out the search and rescue helicopters. It was too dark for anyone on the ground to see with the raging storm in progress. The helicopter scanned the beach, the back strand, the sand dunes, and the rocks all along Tramore Bay, using infra-red lights to pick up any signs of life. Finally, after midnight, word came back that she had been spotted on top one of the sand dunes, a few kilometres from the end of the long beach.

It was only at that moment that I was able to cry. I let out a deep wail of relief and of joy, as all the pent up emotions of the past few hours were released. My baby had been found. She was still alive, and that was all that mattered. We drove down to the beach. The paramedics, guided by the helicopter lights, were able to go on foot to pull Tiffany off the sand dunes and put her into a thermal blanket. They then took her on a stretcher to the waiting ambulance on the beach, and drove back along the beach to the main road. The paramedics said her body temperature had dipped to a critical level and she could not have survived much longer. The exposure to such low temperatures that stormy night was lethal.

When I finally got into the ambulance, I saw Tiffany, pale in colour and drenched to the bone from the rain. She had a mildly guilty expression on her face. I held her to me, sobbed and kissed her cheeks over and over again.

'Why Tiffany? Why? Why did you run away? Why did you come out here? "I thought I had lost you.'

Her only answer was that she didn't know what all the fuss was about. She was trying to get away from the voices. They were so loud she could not concentrate in school. So she had to go to a quiet place. She had planned to come home later but had no idea what time it was. We went immediately to the emergency department and Helgar stayed with me. It took at least three hours to get attention. We had brought a change of clothing for her and eventually, we got an appointment to see a psychiatrist. There was no psychiatric ward for children at the Waterford hospital and she could not be left unsupervised in the adult psychiatric ward. We had to go back home.

I was afraid to let Tiffany out of my sight. I was afraid she would run away from the house again. I spent the rest of the night in a paranoid state, listening for opening doors and movement. As daylight came, calls of concern flooded in.

Friends tried to console me about the ordeal and asked if Tiffany was ok. The school principal came to visit. Michelle and my neighbour came to ask what help we needed. I had a prescription to fill for some medication to calm Tiffany and a friend went to the pharmacy to get the medicine for me. In the evening, Tiffany's classmates came with a large get well card signed by all the students. She did not like the card but accepted it graciously.

Recovery

I could not keep Tiffany in bed all day without something to look forward to. Her appointment with the doctor was the following week so I had to find ways to occupy her. I could not work. I cancelled my slot in the Midleton Festival that weekend and got Dorcas to work at the booth for me at the Waterford Festival. Some good friends in Waterford were sympathetic with our situation. Their thirteen year old daughter had also had a bout of serious depression. They invited us to dinner.

We eagerly awaited the appointment with the doctor. He was very kind and gentle as he spoke to Tiffany. He prescribed medication but cautioned that Tiffany would need extensive observation to find the best method of treatment for her. He had heard that a spot had recently opened up at a teenage psychiatric clinic in Cork city and advised me to take it as soon as possible. Before I knew it, I said yes and then wondered how I could send my child to such a place. We visited and found the staff to be very gentle and caring. The facility was like a home, with only six teenagers. I imagined Tiffany would get good care and attention. They received nutritious meals and patient privacy was well protected.

We returned with Tiffany's clothes. I was assured Tiffany would be able to do some school work each day with the other children. She would be given medication to ease the depression and its symptoms. This was a facility run by the health board. We were very fortunate to be able to avail of their help. The improvement was remarkable, but it took four weeks for significant change to take place so she could come home.

I had all Tiffany's belongings removed from her locker at school. She was never going back to that school again. I didn't blame them for her depression, but they weren't equipped to deal with her problems. I learned about a tutor at home programme sponsored by the school board and applied to have a teacher come to the house to do work with Tiffany. A substitute teacher from the school was recommended for the role. She came a few days a week to review work, getting guidance from the teachers at school.

It was early November and I needed to decide what my next decision for Tiffany's education would be. I heard about a boarding school in Cork run by the Church of Ireland. They had helped a number of local children who had suffered from depression. I made an appointment to see the principal and we drove to Cork. The fees were high, but not as high as private schools in Dublin, and the place came recommended by psychologists. The principal was very young. Both Tiffany and I could not believe he was in charge of this very old college. We were taken around the building to see the classrooms and dormitories. Everything seemed ancient and I wondered how Tiffany would survive there. I asked the principal point blank how he would handle an incident of bullying. This was my great fear. If Tiffany were bullied at boarding school, she had no escape. But with small class sizes and a sympathetic staff, the school was able to maintain a comfortable environment. I asked if they had diversity at the school and was told that they had students from West Cork, Cork City, Midleton, and even Waterford. That made me smile. I submitted the application forms and did not hear another word.

Decision to Leave

I had applied to several schools in Dublin but none had space for Tiffany. The Tramore school kept asking when she was returning to school, as she was due to sit the Junior Certificate exam the following June. I did not know if Tiffany would get into a school in any other town. I decided to look abroad. We were Canadian citizens. Tiffany had been born in Montreal. If you lived in a specific neighbourhood in Canada, the school was obliged to accept your children. I did not want an uncertain future, so I made my decision. We would move back to Canada and start a new life.

I had to work swiftly. I had to sell the house, sell or abandon the business, look for a job in Canada, and find a place to live. I had to get a moving company to pack and move all my belongings across the Atlantic. I made many lists of things to do and timelines of when they should be completed. There was little time to waste; Christmas was approaching.

I tried selling off stock through some new distributors based in Kilkenny and Cork. I also tried collecting money owed to me. That was the most difficult thing to do. Cathal the Donegal distributor and his wife tried selling me back some of the pallets of product they had greedily snapped up in January. They could not sell the products. Since I had already put out cash to make more products, it made no sense to take back their out of date stocks.

Cathal's wife called me a few times, screaming and hollering,

'We helped you get started. We were there for you at the beginning! Take back this product now! You owe us big time!'

She threatened me that if our paths crossed I would be sorry.

I did not take threats like this lightly. People had been known to carry out insane threats without thinking.

Another distributor was annoyed that he had to pay me for product he had held for over 90 days. He skilfully avoided my phone calls and texts. I asked my accountant to call from his mobile phone and arrange to collect the money owed, as well as the unsold stock. It had become a nightmare.

I tried selling the mountain of ingredients and packaging I had stored in a paid facility in Waterford. I had pallets of bottles, caps, and 70kg of turmeric. The bottle distributor had more stock than they could handle and refused to take back my four pallets of bottles. I gave away most of the ingredients and sold off what I could at less than a quarter of the price. When I asked the processor in Kilcoole if he wanted pallets of bottles, he accepted them readily, but he never paid the full balance, since he knew I was leaving the country. There was not enough time to run after small sums of money with so much work to be done. I listed most electronic appliances and market equipment online for a quick sale. The calls started coming in. Slowly but surely, I was able to get rid of storage cabinets, chest freezers, hot plates, tables, stands, and gazebos. One couple decided they could help me sell off items at flea markets. They filled their van to the roof. It is a mystery still how much they were able to sell. Whatever I could not sell went to various friends in Dublin.

The Green Escape

The thought of losing my carefree lifestyle and independence caused so much pain. I could barely look at myself in the mirror every day. I cried so many times looking out my bedroom window at the Irish Sea and contemplated the future. Tiffany and I tried to remain hopeful that the future would be better. And I had to be brave for her. I had to act as if I knew what I was doing. In fact, I felt like crawling into a corner and hiding. I resolved not to tell anyone. People were too full of fear and would try to transfer their fear to me.

We did not tell many people about our move because we did not want them to talk us out of it. We told a few friends in Dublin: Mary, Rana, Babba, Daphne, Andrea, and Susie. In Tramore, only Dorcas, my ever present helper, knew our dilemma. I had come to rely on her heavily. She was to guard my secret at all costs. People who knew about the move were excited for us and wished they could come too. My family was excited to have us move closer to Trinidad and the United States.

I was moving without having a job in hand. This was a risky prospect for anyone. I had limited savings available for the move. I was not sure how long this money would last. Selling the house proved to be a lost cause. My real estate agent reasoned because Christmas was a quiet time, she would not be looking for buyers.

I was unable to sell my business because it would mean selling recipes and goodwill. In times of recession, goodwill was a scarce commodity. A great deal of unfinished business was going to be left behind. But, I had to move swiftly before I changed my mind. My emotions see-sawed back and forth. There was fear, then hope, then worry, then despair, then hope again. How was I going to do this alone? We were invited to stay at an old friend's house in Canada while we got settled. I hadn't been in touch with that family for many years so I was not sure what to expect. We had no big farewell parties and no gatherings before we left. There were no long goodbyes, no rehashing of events past, and no chats with acquaintances over a pint.

The moving company came as scheduled on December 16th to pack my belongings. Two friendly Eastern European men in uniforms came to size up the task.

'First we pack. Then we load,' they said.

'Work away,' I told them.

They worked from early morning until late evening, rolling and packing. They started on the ground floor in the living room and dining room, emptying cabinets and book shelves. They wrapped glasses and dishes. I feverishly packed four suitcases with the necessities for the first month of our arrival in Canada. I had to think of what we would need when we had no access to the belongings in the 40 foot container. I decided to put all our important documents in boxes to send by post to Canada. It was impossible to put our worldly goods in suitcases without being extremely overweight. Only God knew what I would need to get settled. I drove up to the post office and they weighed the two boxes. The price tag was €300. I told them that was a crazy amount for two boxes. They suggested that I put everything into one big box and recommended the dimensions. Luckily, we had many boxes and packing material around the house because of the moving company. I grabbed the most appropriate box, re-arranged my belongings and went back to the post office. This time, the price was €160. That was more like it. Even though it was Christmas time, I felt my box would get there in good time.

The following day, packing continued in the upper rooms of the house, with a third worker from the moving company to finish the job. All the beds and wardrobes were dismantled. The chest of drawers was wrapped whole with contents. Since our kitchen utensils were packed, we had to buy prepared meals and use up the remaining groceries. With two mega trucks parked on the pavement in front my home, surely the town would know I was moving. We told the neighbours we were travelling for Christmas. It was not a complete lie. I still had to sell my washing machine and dryer. We could not take any large appliances across to North America, because the voltage was different. I called around to see if anyone knew anyone who wanted to buy a washing machine and dryer. The mother of Tiffany's Nigerian classmate spent every second day in church. She was a great resource.

Within a few hours, I had a Nigerian couple at my door looking at appliances, negotiating and re-negotiating. The moving staff skipped around them, hauling boxes to the truck. They complained about the price tag of €400 for a washer, drier, and an old refrigerator. This I thought was extra generous. They went away with one appliance in their car and promised to go to the bank machine and return with the money.

Two hours passed and they had not returned. Tiffany laughed at me, the moving company lads laughed at me. Did I know these people? What were their names? Where did they live? I had no clue. Just when I was resigned to feeling stupid and having to leave perfectly functional appliances in the house, the doorbell rang. The couple had come back. Their story was about a malfunctioning bank machine. They had €300 and said they wanted to buy all three appliances.

'I thought you were not coming back'.

'My sistah, we are people of God! Of course we were coming back. My sistah, please accept €300. It is Christmas time and we have to buy presents for our children. You can't take away the money for their presents.'

By that time, I was so tired and distracted. I just told them to go with the remaining appliances. In the end it was better than leaving them in an empty house. We helped them to load their car and they went off with happy smiles.

All the remaining Bad Boy sauces were packed onto two full pallets. They were my creation. I had spent a lot of money making them and I would spend years eating them myself if I had to. The moving company was to load the pallets of boxes into the 40 foot container too. I was paying €9,000 for the shipment, so it was in my best interest to get my money's worth.

I had asked Dorcas to come and help me clean up after everything was removed from the house. I gave her all the remaining food, an old boom box and anything else that she could use right away. We loaded the huge suitcases into the van. Since all the beds were gone, I had made arrangements to spend that night at my German friend Andrea's house in Dublin. We cleaned and mopped and left everything in tip-top shape. After all, the house was still up for rent and for sale. The signs were there and people could still visit. If a buyer were to materialise out of thin air, the house could be shown as it was. The only furniture left in the attic were the old futon and desk from the previous owner. I didn't like them and didn't want them.

When the last floor was mopped and the refrigerator in the kitchen cleaned to perfection, I went to every room in the house to bid it farewell. Tiffany did not join me on this farewell trip. She helped Dorcas pack the rest of our belongings.

We piled into the little van, hugged Dorcas goodbye and then set off for Dublin. The remaining clothes and shoes that simply could not fit anywhere were deposited in the clothing bin at the last petrol station on the way out of Tramore. I could not even look back. It was too painful.

With a huge smile on my face, I told Tiffany, 'Now, off to start a new life. We cannot look back.'

Andrea's house was in Blackrock. Andrea was such a kind soul. Sad to see us leave Ireland, she made us feel as comfortable as possible that night. After a quick hot shower, I could barely keep my eyes open. All I remembered was watching part of the movie Bad Santa, and then drifting off to sleep. We did not have to rise early, since we had no place to go that day. So after a late start and a German breakfast, we made our way through the city taking all the suitcases to my African friend Babba's house. Babba was another faithful friend through thick and thin. She had agreed to house us until our flight two days later. I felt like a homeless creature with my worldly possessions in a few large suitcases. The feeling was a bit degrading.

Next I had to decide what to the do with the faithful van. It was not attractive to any buyer, despite its 2008 license plate. I had racked up more than 100,000 km in less than two years. Added to this was the fact that it was leased. The balance owed made it a challenge to sell to anyone. Crazy Farmer had said I should drive it to Dublin Airport and leave it in the parking lot when I left. He said many Irish leaving the country for good were doing that. I could not. After all, my logo, address and mobile number were clearly printed on the van. A large wrap around border of red, green and gold Rastafarian colours decorated the van. It was hardly a van that could hide unnoticed. Andrea said I could park it near her place the day before I left. She would call the bank to collect it.

After such a hectic few weeks, we decided to spend our last two days in Ireland relaxing and shopping. I took Tiffany and Babba's daughter Izzy out for an evening at the movies in Santry. Then on Saturday night, Babba and 'Lady Sue' came with me for a last night on the town. We decided to go to dinner and then dancing. These girls perhaps never went out to dinner and were not familiar with which restaurants were good in the city. I suggested passing by the restaurants in Little Italy off Ormond Quay. It was drizzling. Babba who had many allergies began to itch because it was drizzling and she had to walk. We had parked a few blocks down from Ormond Quay. She felt she could not walk, so we had to take a taxi. I protested at the ridiculous the idea. But, I was outnumbered, so I stepped into the taxi with them. As we crawled through traffic for two blocks, the meter went up to €6 and the girls asked me to pay since they could not find change. By that time I was fuming.

We went into the Morrison Hotel on Lower Ormond Quay. My friends thought it was too dark to recognise the food. We then went into Bar Italia and waited in a queue to get in. The girls may have well been reading Greek. The dishes were unfamiliar and unappealing to them. Since I did not like pasta, I said I would have a rice dish: seafood risotto cooked with white wine. They also ordered seafood risotto. And so we waited, and waited, and half hour later, the dishes came out. The rice was pale and under cooked. One could count the number of pieces of seafood in the rice, and the flavour was as interesting as cooked oatmeal.

But we made the most of it. The waiter was cute. Unbelievably, there was still a queue when we were leaving. The girls took a taxi and I took the three minute hike to the Arlington Hotel. As I got to the door, they alighted from their taxi.

'Hey, I know you,' I teased them.

The bar was packed and drunken revelry had begun. We danced to whatever the live band played and everyone was happy. Bernie, Susie's Irish friend from Ballymun, joined us and we danced and danced. At midnight, the basement opened for late night dancing and we moved downstairs. Babba finally relaxed and started her crazy dancing on the floor. It was funny the way the Irish lads were keen for a dance with this extra energetic African girl. Her antics on the floor were sometimes embarrassing for me. But there was no stopping her. She was happy and I was out for the night. Her husband was watching the kids and nothing could stop us.

While Susie was chatting up boys half her age, I watched the dancing frenzy. The low ceiling made me feel a bit claustrophobic. By 2:45am, the floor started to clear.

'Do we have to stay until every light is turned on?' I protested.

'Lindy, relax. You're leaving Dublin soon. Just dance.'

But my weary feet could go no more. I just sat and laughed at the drunken crowd and waited until my hostesses decided to leave. I was the designated driver and had to walk four blocks to get the car. The girls asked one of the men they knew to give me a piggy back ride to the car. He was a burly Irish lad and did not seem to mind. He said my friends were drunk and mad. Poor man, I was not fat, but I must have been heavy. He was happy to deposit me and gave me a big hug. On the way home we had to stop for a late night snack from a chipper on O'Connell Street. It was a happy night out and a wonderful farewell to Dublin.

The next day I called for a taxi to the airport, and Tiffany and I started our journey at 9:00 am on December 21st. Even though it had snowed heavily all morning, some flights were still leaving. We checked into our flight on time and went to the departure gate. As we waited, snow continued to fall. We saw some old friends from farmers' markets and told them we were on our way to Toronto. They were spending Christmas in Amsterdam with relatives.

Then suddenly, all flights from Dublin were cancelled on the afternoon of December 21st because of the snowstorm.

Without warning or notice, the Aer Lingus screens went blank and those passengers with Blackberry mobile phones alerted the rest of us when they got email notices of the cancellations. Not an attendant was in sight. We went back to the luggage carousels to collect our luggage. Then we joined the queue of a thousand plus for the Aer Lingus ticketing counter. This was at around 6:00 pm and we needed to find out what to do next. The queue was a mile long; it curved around the full width of the terminal and we were last in line.

We got to the top of the queue around 1:00 am next morning, only to be told we were in the wrong queue. They could not change the ticket because it was purchased through Expedia.com, not Aer Lingus. In addition, one leg of the journey was with Aer Lingus to Amsterdam. The other leg of the journey was with KLM from Amsterdam to Toronto. They could not possibly assist with this. We were told to go to the Aer Lingus standby counter, which was not going to open until 4:00 am. Many passengers took refuge on the floors of the terminal, both upstairs and downstairs. I decided to get in the stand-by queue and wait for the 4:00 am opening. I had been on my feet or sitting on luggage for seven hours. Three more hours would make little difference. We were not alone. Hundreds of others joined the queue. It was a time to chat and exchange horror stories of travelling and missing flights. Many had missed important parties and weddings. And many would probably not get to see family for Christmas if we did not get on a flight.

When the standby desk opened, we were able to get a coupon for the first flight next morning to Amsterdam. However, we were told we would have to go on standby from Amsterdam to Toronto, because we had missed our connecting flight. Arrangements could only be made with KLM in Amsterdam.

The early flights to Amsterdam were all cancelled because the airport authority was unable to clear snow from the runways. This was the problem in a country not used to snow. By late morning, hundreds of people were on standby, if they hadn't left the airport in frustration. We could not get any confirmation or information from any of the staff. I heard through word of mouth that we were to go to the counter and stand there in case passengers were called for flights that had begun to leave. We waited eagerly in the mob on the other side to hear our names.

I was lucky to hear a uniformed person read out the name Jenny Lee without a microphone.

'That's me!' I screamed.

I told Tiffany to watch the smaller hand luggage which had all my jewellery and money. I pushed forward, pulling the large suitcases behind me. There was no space in the mob for a trolley. I pushed my way toward the counter. Some weary travellers helped propel my mini refrigerator suitcases over the heads of other standby passengers. As I pushed towards the counter with our passports in hand, all my energy came back. We finally got our boarding passes and went directly to the security check point.

Finally, we were soaring above the clouds. We were leaving Ireland after almost two days in the Dublin airport. As I looked down at the city, so many memories came back. A flood of tears and emotions overcame me. I would not miss the darkness and the rain. I would not miss the recent talk about recession and how bad the country was. The doom and gloom, and unravelling of scams by Government Ministers and others were too much to stomach. I would miss the casual, Bohemian lifestyle I had enjoyed in the last few years. Working at events and markets around the country had been the most educational experience in my life. I would miss all the interesting people we had met over the years. The banter with friends and acquaintances helped changed the way I viewed the world. Who knew what adventures lay ahead of us in a brand new city, in a brand new life.

Recipe of Farewell to Ireland

Ingredients

8oz Luck

2 cups Love

2 tsp Friendship

2 tbsp Ambition

1 tsp Jealousy

1 tbsp Depression

Bad Boy Pepper sauce to taste

½ cup Anticipation

2 cups Excitement

1 cup Disappointment

3 lb Hard Work

3 tbsp Loss

8oz Hope

1 lb Bravery

Method

Pre-Heat oven to 350°F

Fry Luck in Love in a non-stick pan

Combine Friendship, Ambition, Jealousy, Depression, Anticipation, fried Luck and Love in a big mixing bowl

Escape From Ireland

Add a dash of Bad Boy Pepper Sauce to taste

Stir in 3 lb of Hard Work

Grease a baking tray with disappointment and loss

Bake for six and a half years until light brown

Cool and serve with side dishes of Hope and Bravery

Serving Size: Too many people to mention and everyone we met along the way.

GLOSSARY OF CURRENT IRISH SLANG WORDS AND PHRASES

Aggro - aggravation

Ah sure – verbal equivalent of a shrug.

An Lar – The City Centre,

Ath Cliath – Irish Gaelic for Dublin.

Banjaxed – broken. Used to refer to both machinery and people who are injured. Also exhausted.

Banter – idle chat with lots of jokes.

Bean gorm –Irish Gaelic for black woman,

Bejaysus – Exclamation used when someone witnesses something astonishing.

Biro – a pen.

Black pudding – blood sausage

Blow In – New to an area. The family could be in the third generation and living in the same home for fifty years, but they would still be considered Blow Ins.

Bob's yer uncle – you'll be okay, you'll be sorted.

Carvery – a reasonably priced roast pub lunch, with potatoes and boiled vegetables.

Chancer – someone who tries to get away with swindling other people.

Chancing your arm – trying your luck.

C'mere till I tell you – what you say to show that you've some good gossip to share.

Craic – crack, atmosphere of fun.

Cop on – understand.

Culchie – word used by Dubliners to describe people who live outside the area known as The Pale, Dublin and surrounding counties.

Currach – traditional boat made with wicker and tar, most commonly used by West of Ireland fishermen.

Curry chips – French-fried potatoes (chips) covered in curry sauce.

Cute Kerry hoor – someone who's able to buy and sell you and cut corners if needs be. Co. Kerry is particularly associated with this kind of behaviour.

Deadly – brilliant, very impressive.

Eejit – fool.

Feck – Irish swear word. Can also be used as an adjective, 'feckin,' as in, "where did I put my feckin' keys."

Gas – great fun, funny.

Gob – mouth.

Gobshite – stupid person.

God loves a trier – said about someone who continually tries but fails. .

God love him – an expression of pity for someone's plight.

Go n'eiri an bothair leat – Old Irish saying meaning "May the road rise with you."

Go raibh maith agat (Gurra mohagut) – Irish Gaelic for thank you

Grand – okay, fine.

He's not the full shilling – he's not entirely mentally sound.

Hoover – used to refer to any brand of vacuum cleaner.

I couldn't be arsed – I couldn't be bothered.

In fairness – a phrase used to get people to see things from another perspective. Can be used to soften the blow before a person disagrees with you.

Jackeen – a Dubliner.

Jacks – toilet.

Jumper – a sweater or jersey.

Knackered – exhausted.

Lads – term used to address a group of people. Similar to guys or folks

Langer – A slang word used in Co. Cork, Southern Ireland, for an unpleasant, annoying or stupid person.

Manky/mangy – dirty.

Mighty feed – good meal.

Piss-up – drinking session with the aim of getting drunk.

Rashers – fried bacon.

Roasting – very hot; or a time when someone is criticized publicly as a joke.

Rubber – eraser.

Selection box – a selection of chocolate bars packaged together in an attractive box. Usually given out at Christmas.

Shite – crap, shit.

Shut your gob – shut your mouth.

Slainte (slauncha) – An Irish toast, means health.

Slan/slan abhaile – Irish Gaelic for goodbye, safe home.

Slash – pee.

Slashed – drunk. Other variations include pissed, plastered and langers.

The black stuff – Guinness.

There's both eating and drinking in it – that's a hearty meal.

Tight – stingy, mean with money.

Tinker/traveller – Irish travelling people, who live in caravans on halting sights. Recognised as a separate ethnic group. Tinker is an older word, now rarely used.

Walk of shame – the walk home after a night out, when everyone knows you haven't gone home because you're still wearing your best clothes.

Yer Man/Yer Wan – The man, the woman. Used to refer to people you don't know.

You're Grand – that's okay, don't worry.

ABOUT THE AUTHOR

Jennylynd (Lindy) James was born and raised in Trinidad and Tobago. She studied Food Science at McGill University, Canada where she earned a Ph.D. then worked in this field for over 15 years. Her work in the food industry took her many places including Florida, California, the Republic of Ireland, and Canada. In Ireland, Lindy developed Bad Boy Sauces, her own range of Caribbean style sauces and seasonings. She ran this business for five years with 'artistic flair'. It was in the beautiful seaside village of Tramore, County Waterford she was motivated to do oil painting and sketching. Her tumultuous life experiences and adventures while living in Ireland have been the inspiration to create the memoir 'Escape from Ireland'. Lindy now lives in Bloor West Village, Toronto, Canada where she has embraced self expression in art, music, and writing as a new lifestyle.

http://jennylyndjames.com/books